Literacy Practices in Transition

NEW PERSPECTIVES ON LANGUAGE AND EDUCATION
Series Editor: Professor Viv Edwards, *University of Reading, Reading, Great Britain*
Series Advisor: Professor Allan Luke, *Queensland University of Technology, Brisbane, Australia*

Two decades of research and development in language and literacy education have yielded a broad, multidisciplinary focus. Yet, education systems face constant economic and technological change, with attendant issues of identity and power, community and culture. This series will feature critical and interpretive, disciplinary and multidisciplinary perspectives on teaching and learning, language and literacy in new times.

Full details of all the books in this series and of all our other publications can be found on http://www.multilingual-matters.com, or by writing to Multilingual Matters, St Nicholas House, 31–34 High Street, Bristol BS1 2AW, UK.

Literacy Practices in Transition

Perspectives from the Nordic Countries

Edited by
Anne Pitkänen-Huhta and Lars Holm

MULTILINGUAL MATTERS
Bristol • Buffalo • Toronto

Library of Congress Cataloging in Publication Data
A catalog record for this book is available from the Library of Congress.
Literacy Practices in Transition: Perspectives from the Nordic Countries/Edited by Anne Pitkänen-Huhta and Lars Holm.
New Perspectives on Language and Education: 28
Includes bibliographical references.
1. Literacy--Scandinavia. 2. Education--Scandinavia. 3. Scandinavian students--Europe. 4. Multilingualism--Scandinavia. 5. Scandinavia--Languages. I. Pitkänen-Huhta, Anne. II. Holm, Lars.
LC156.S34L58 2012
302.2'2440948–dc232012036456

British Library Cataloguing in Publication Data
A catalogue entry for this book is available from the British Library.

ISBN-13: 978-1-84769-840-7 (hbk)
ISBN-13: 978-1-84769-839-1 (pbk)

Multilingual Matters
UK: St Nicholas House, 31–34 High Street, Bristol BS1 2AW, UK.
USA: UTP, 2250 Military Road, Tonawanda, NY 14150, USA.
Canada: UTP, 5201 Dufferin Street, North York, Ontario M3H 5T8, Canada.

Copyright © 2012 Anne Pitkänen-Huhta, Lars Holm and the authors of individual chapters.

All rights reserved. No part of this work may be reproduced in any form or by any means without permission in writing from the publisher.

The policy of Multilingual Matters/Channel View Publications is to use papers that are natural, renewable and recyclable products, made from wood grown in sustainable forests. In the manufacturing process of our books, and to further support our policy, preference is given to printers that have FSC and PEFC Chain of Custody certification. The FSC and/or PEFC logos will appear on those books where full certification has been granted to the printer concerned.

Typeset by DiTech Process Solutions.

Contents

Contributors	vii
Preface	xi
Literacy Practices in Transition: Setting the Scene *Lars Holm and Anne Pitkänen-Huhta*	1

Part 1: Literacy and Identities in Transition   **25**

1 Narratives on Literacies: Adult Migrants' Identity Construction in Interaction   27
  Anne Golden and Elizabeth Lanza

2 Literacy in Negotiating, Constructing and Manifesting Identities: The Case of Migrant Unaccompanied Asylum-Seeking Children in Sweden   54
  Åsa Wedin

3 Privileging Identity Positions and Multimodal Communication in Textual Practices: *Intersectionality* and the *(Re)Negotiation of Boundaries*   75
  Sangeeta Bagga-Gupta

Part 2: Local Practices in Transition   **101**

4 Multilingual Classrooms as Sites of Negotiations of Language and Literacy   103
  Line Møller Daugaard and Helle Pia Laursen

5   Skills as Performances: Literacy Practices of Finnish
    Sixth-Graders   119
    Mia Halonen

6   Multimodality in the Science Classroom   140
    Monica Axelsson and Kristina Danielsson

7   Discourses of Literacy on an International Master's
    Programme: Examining Students' Academic Writing Norms   165
    Laura McCambridge and Anne Pitkänen-Huhta

Part 3: Policies and Practices in Transition   **187**

8   Localizing Supranational Concepts of Literacy in Adult
    Second Language Teaching   189
    Lars Holm and Sari Pöyhönen

9   Teacher Reflections Under Changing Conditions for
    Literacy Learning in Multicultural Schools in Oslo   209
    Anne Marit Vesteraas Danbolt and Lise Iversen Kulbrandstad

10 Bilingual Teachers: Making a Difference?   228
    Rita Hvistendahl

Afterword
On the Move: Transitions in Literacy Research   244
David Barton

Contributors

Monica Axelsson is an Associate Professor in Language Education at Stockholm University. She holds a PhD in bilingualism with special focus on Swedish as a second language, and her main interests include multilingualism, subject literacy and second language learning. In these fields, she has many published works to her credit.

Sangeeta Bagga-Gupta is a full Professor at Örebro University, Sweden. Her trans-disciplinary research encompasses traditionally separate fields like literacies, mono-multilingualism, multimodality, learning and identities (ethnicity, gender, functional disabilities, especially deaf). Using multi-scale ethnography, she studies everyday life, policy and socio-historical dimensions inside and outside institutional environments, primarily from anthropological, sociocultural and postcolonial approaches. She is interested in the policies and social practices related to *marginalization* and *equity* in different regional sites focusing on support systems (such as schools, health care and non-profit organizations). She is a board member of the Swedish Research Council and heads the multidisciplinary National Research School Literacies, Multilingualism and Cultural Practices in Present Day Society.

David Barton is Professor of Language and Literacy in the Department of Linguistics at Lancaster University and Director of the Lancaster Literacy Research Centre. His main publications, with others, have been concerned with: rethinking the nature of literacy; carrying out detailed studies of everyday literacies; and exploring the relations of literacy and learning. His most recent book is *Language online: investigating digital texts and practices* (Routledge, 2013, with Carmen Lee).

Anne Marit Vesteraas Danbolt is an Associate Professor of Norwegian and Head of Department of Humanities at the Faculty of Teacher Education at Hedmark University College. Her research areas include literacy and second language learning, and she has taken part in several projects collaborating with primary school teachers. Together with Professor Lise Iversen Kulbrandstad, she has published the books *Tekstsamtaler* (Talking about Texts, 2005) and *Klasseromskulturer for språklæring* (Classroom Cultures for Language Learning, 2008). In addition, she has coordinated a Norwegian funded Master's Program in Literacy and Learning at the University of Namibia and the University of Zambia.

Kristina Danielsson is an Associate Professor in Language Education at Stockholm University. She holds a PhD in Scandinavian languages and her main research interests are subject literacy and multimodality. She has a number of publications to her credit in these fields.

Line Møller Daugaard is a Senior Lecturer and Head of Centre for the Study of Language and Literacy in VIA University College, Denmark. Her research interests are in linguistic practices in the language classroom. She is also working as a research assistant in the longitudinal research project, 'Signs of Language' (2008–2014), and in an ongoing PhD project, she explores minority language teaching in Danish primary schools.

Anne Golden is a Professor of Norwegian as a Second Language at the Department of Linguistics and Scandinavian Studies, University of Oslo, Norway. Her main field of research is literacy in a second language, with a focus on vocabulary issues. She has published on second language acquisition, language in textbooks with a focus on metaphorical expressions, Norwegian grammar from a second language perspective, the use of learner corpora in research and identity in migrant narratives, as well as on the history of second language research and second language writing in Norway. She is one of the editors of *NORDAND*, the Nordic journal of second language research.

Mia Halonen earned a PhD in and is an Adjunct Professor of Finnish Linguistics in the University of Helsinki. At present, she works as a researcher in the Centre for Applied Language Studies, University of Jyväskylä. Her area of expertise is linguistic constructions of interactional practices which she has studied both in informal and formal spoken interactions and in writing practices in schools and social media. She has focused especially on practices by which participants 'perform and do themselves' and published on these issues from various angles.

Lars Holm is an Associate Professor and holds a PhD in literacy and globalization. His general research interests are in language and literacy in multilingual and postcolonial educational settings. He has lately carried out research in language testing concepts and practices in educational contexts, and he is working as an external researcher in the research project 'Signs of Language' (2008–2014), examining the literacy testing practices in multilingual classrooms.

Rita Hvistendahl is a Professor of the Teaching of Norwegian and Acting Head of the Department of Teacher Education and School Research, University of Oslo, Norway. She has been an Adjunct Professor of Literacy at Umeå University, Sweden.

Contributors ix

Lise Iversen Kulbrandstad is a Professor of Norwegian at the Faculty of Teacher Education, Hedmark University College, Norway. Her main research interests are literacy, second language learners, school development and teacher education. She has published several books and articles, among them *Lesing på et andrespråk* (Reading in a Second Language, 1998), *Lesing i utvikling* (Reading Development, 2003) and has co-authored with Anne Marit V. Danbolt both *Tekstsamtaler* (Talking about Texts, 2005) and *Klasseromskulturer for språklæring* (Classroom Cultures for Language Learning,2008). Kulbrandstad is one of the founders and editors of *NORDAND*, the Nordic journal of second language research, 2006–2010.

Elizabeth Lanza is a Professor of Linguistics at the Department of Linguistics and Scandinavian Studies, University of Oslo, Norway. Her main field of research is multilingualism, and her work is sociolinguistically oriented. She has published on identity in migrant narratives; language socialization of bilingual children, language ideology, linguistic landscape and research methodology. She is on the Editorial Board of *Bilingualism: Language and Cognition* (Cambridge University Press), *Multilingual Margins* (University of the Western Cape, South Africa), and *IMPACT: Studies in Language and Society* (Benjamins). She is the leader of the interdisciplinary research project 'Language, Culture and Identity in Migrant Narratives' funded by the Research Council of Norway.

Helle Pia Laursen is an Associate Professor in the Department of Education at Aarhus University, Denmark. Her research interests are in language and literacy in multilingual settings. She is working as a Project Director for the longitudinal research project 'Signs of Language' (2008–2014), which explores children's interpretation and creation of signs in multilingual classrooms. She is one of the editors of *NORDAND*, the Nordic journal of second language research.

Laura McCambridge is a lecturer in English Language at the University of Jyväskylä. She is completing her PhD on the norms of English academic discourse in *lingua-franca* contexts. Her research focuses particularly on students' writing practices on an International Master's Degree Programme at a Finnish University.

Anne Pitkänen-Huhta received her academic training at the universities of Jyväskylä, Finland and Lancaster, UK. She received her PhD in English from the University of Jyväskylä in 2003. She works as a Professor of English, Language Learning and Teaching, Department of Languages, University of Jyväskylä. She is also the Head of the Department of Languages. Her research focuses on multilingual literacy and discourse practices, especially of young people, and foreign language learning in formal and informal contexts. Her research employs ethnographic and discourse analytic methods.

Sari Pöyhönen works as a Senior Researcher (Language Education Policies) at the Centre for Applied Language Studies (CALS), University of Jyväskylä, Finland. Her research and writing deal with notions on language education and integration policies, and linguistic and ethnic minorities. Her doctoral dissertation in applied linguistics (2003) was an ethnographic study on Finnish language teachers' professional identity at the peak of the transition period of Russian education and teaching. At present, she is involved in two projects focusing on migrant education and language education policies, called Participative Integration in Finland (2010–2013) and Transforming Professional Integration (2011–2014), funded by the Academy of Finland.

Åsa Wedin is an Associate Professor in Education at Örebro Iniversitet and in Swedish as a second language at Dalarna University. She holds a PhD in Linguistics and her main research interests include multilingualism and literacy. She has published a few books for teacher education in these fields.

Preface

The authors of this volume were brought together by a series of exploratory workshops, funded by The Joint Committee for Nordic Research Councils in the Humanities and Social Sciences (NOS-HS) in 2009–2010. The aim of the series of workshops was to bring together Nordic researchers working on different aspects of literacy, multilingualism and the changing living and learning environments, and thus to initiate and promote critical research on literacy practices in the Nordic countries. The focal questions examined in the workshops were related to the processes of change in the literacy practices in Nordic countries, to the construction of identities and membership in and through literacy practices and to the role of education in responding to societal changes. The group of researchers included 20 scholars from four Nordic countries: Denmark, Finland, Norway and Sweden. The group came together for the first time in December 2009 in Jyväskylä, Finland, in the first days of winter with temperatures below −20 °C. Most people did not know each other beforehand and our backgrounds differed quite substantially, but after two days of intensive discussions, it became clear that our work was connected and this connection was *literacy in transition*. Three more workshops were organized in Stockholm, Copenhagen and Oslo, and the foundations of the book were refined together.

This volume stems from the tradition of (New) Literacy Studies, which to us means examining literacy as a social practice rooted in the histories and cultures of societies and communities and in the personal trajectories and experiences of individuals. New Literacy Studies as an approach to studying literacy has always been sensitive to the changing contextual nature of literacy practices and thus researchers have been keen to open new gates and explore new territories where literacy has a role. Even the very beginning of literacy studies was rather radical, as it rose as an opposition to prevalent views of literacy as an autonomous and transferrable cognitive skill. Thus, literacy studies has been constantly spreading to new directions. This said, one can ask why this volume, why now? What *new* does this volume bring to the area of literacy studies, what *new* avenues does it explore and which *new* directions does it point to? As literacy practices are always contextual, there is bound to be something in the current societal context that calls for literacy researchers to stop for a moment and see where we are now and where we should be going.

Current Nordic societies are characterized by discourses of 'knowledge economy', 'learning society' and 'life-long learning', and this has raised education into a very high position on the general political agenda. Parallel to and embedded in this process are the constant and quick changes in the sociolinguistic and communicative landscape. In this volume, we seek to examine the nexus of the more and more complex sociolinguistic landscape and the increasing societal demands to education, and the consequences these have on literacy practices. Thus, our aim is to broaden the scope of literacy studies by showing how, on the one hand, the global flows connect to local literacy practices in specific settings and, on the other hand, how individuals make sense of, enact, contest and transform the culturally, historically and socially based literacy practices they encounter in their constantly mobile and changing life spheres.

We have chosen to use the word transition in the title of the book and this has several reasons. First, as a dictionary entry *transition* means 'the process in which something changes from one state to another' (*Collins Cobuild English Language Dictionary*) or 'the process or a period of changing from one state or condition to another' (*OED*). What we wish to highlight with *literacy in transition* is the importance of taking a close look at the processes in which we find ourselves in, the processes which are fast, unpredictable and messy. Second, in linguistics *transition words or expressions* are words that signal how ideas are meant to relate to each other and they thus create cohesion in text or speech. In literature, *transitions* are similar elements that signal changes. With these linguistic and literary meanings of transition we wish to emphasize the integral relationship between processes of globalization and literacy, both for individuals and communities and both for practices and policies. Yet another meaning transition appears in is in the movement called *transition network*, which at the outset seems completely unrelated to literacy. An outcome of this movement is the establishment of transition towns in different parts of the world, which have taken local small-scale initiatives to tackle global challenges. The network 'supports community-led responses to climate change' and the initiatives 'are actively and cooperatively creating happier, fairer and stronger communities, places that work for the people living in them...' (http://www.transitionnetwork.org/). With this meaning of transition we wish to highlight the centrality of examining literacy at the intersection of the global and the local and in that way empower the local actors to take initiative and challenge the global forces.

We wish to thank the NOS-HS for funding our project and the whole group of people taking part in the series of workshops and engaging in lively and insightful discussion on and around literacy: Monica Axelsson, Sangeeta Bagga-Gupta, Kristina Danielsson, Line Møller Daugaard, Qarin Franker, Anne

Golden, Mia Halonen, Rita Hvistendahl, Lise Iversen Kulbrandstad, Helle Pia Laursen, Ulla Lundqvist, Minna-Riitta Luukka, Laura McCambridge, Kirsten Palm, Sari Pöyhönen, Elina Tapio, Kari Tenfjord and Åsa Wedin. We also want to thank professor Sari Pietikäinen for her insightful comments on an earlier version of the introductory chapter.

Anne Pitkänen-Huhta and Lars Holm
Jyväskylä and Copenhagen
June 2012

Literacy Practices in Transition: Setting the Scene

Lars Holm and Anne Pitkänen-Huhta

This book is about language, literacy and education. It is about mobility, change and complexity and the repercussions these have for people, practices and policies. Contemporary society is characterized by constant, fast and unpredictable mobility of people, goods, ideas and values. Literacy is often at the heart of the profound changes we are experiencing: when people and societies are on the move and in flux, literacy is inevitably an issue because it is something that is taught and learned, that is adopted, transformed and appropriated and that is used to categorize and classify people. Moreover, when people think about literacy, they automatically seem to link it with education – directly or indirectly. Changes in society have also led to the growing influence of supranational agencies such as the EU, the European Commission and the PISA consortium, which in different ways have relegated the regulatory power and authority of nation states by an up-scaling of certain educational concepts and perspectives (Collins *et al.*, 2009). Literacy is indeed in transition in our postmodern societies and since adequate literacy skills are considered a basic prerequisite for full participation in society, it is important to examine literacy practices in education. Recently, there have been calls for closer examination of the complexities of literacy practices in present-day societies in order to help understand the connection between global flows and local contexts (e.g. Brandt & Clinton, 2002; Baynham, 2004; Warriner, 2009).

Against this backdrop, this volume sets out to explore the intersections between transnational processes of mobility and the local, situated character of literacy in and around education. The close, detailed empirical analyses aim to unravel how these connections show in and have an effect on individuals, practices and policies. The chapters in this volume draw on literacy studies, (critical) applied linguistics and post-structuralist ideas of language and literacy as socially constructed. The detailed studies and descriptions of what is going on in and around literacy in education brought together in this book can hopefully be used not only as a springboard for further theoretical and methodological reflections but also as a point of departure for the developing discourses of literacy in education in a time of constant and rapid change.

The Setting

The contexts that are described in the chapters in this volume are situated in what are called the Nordic countries. These countries are Denmark, Finland, Iceland, Norway and Sweden. Together, they form not only a geographical location but also a space that is historically and culturally connected and that has a certain shared public image as a region of welfare states. In official documentation and public perception, the Nordic countries are democracies where everyone has equal access to education and participation in society, they are technologically highly developed and they have a long history in literacy teaching, with fairly stable high standards of literacy skills. Literacy has throughout history been valued in these societies and has been considered important in providing access to education and citizenship. Moreover, the Nordic countries have long been multilingual and multicultural communities, as there are a large number of minority languages, especially in the northern and eastern regions. However, as any modern society, the Nordic countries are affected by global and translocal flows that inevitably have repercussions for individuals and communities. As a consequence of mobility and techologization in society, new kinds of multilingualism and multiculturalism have risen which call for re-conceptualizations of language and literacy.

Examining literacy practices opens one window into the consequences of these flows. Increasing cultural and social heterogeneity inevitably changes and diversifies the literacy practices at both the societal and the individual levels. At the same time, specific types of literacy and literacy practices become privileged and are then considered essential in education; in order to fulfil general political and educational expectations, one has to understand what kind of literacy practices are valued and how to show competencies in order to gain affirmation and recognition (Hall, 2002). Curricula, textbooks, tests and classroom practices have a role in specifying what will count as literacy and what kind of literacy practices are valued or marginalized in society (Luke, 1997a). Literacy is therefore never ideologically neutral: every use of text is shaped in and by its social context, which means that even the most established and institutionalized concepts of literacy can be traced back to social and cultural conventions, needs, and values (Gee, 2000). For educators and researchers, it seems crucial to investigate the boundaries of different literacies and literacy practices as contested concepts in order to get an understanding of learners' identity work and of the power relations related to the increasing societal super-diversity around literacy (see Blommaert, 2010).

Theoretically, this volume has three starting points, each of which will be elaborated on in the sections below. First, we subscribe to a social view of literacy, which entails a close examination of literacies in relation to individuals, practices and policies and their connection to societal changes in general. Second, the volume draws on recent theorizations of mobility and globalization and seeks to open discussion on how the global and local meet in literacy practices in and around education. By foregrounding issues and theorizations on language and globalization and discussing their repercussions for current literacy practices, we hope to broaden the scope of literacy studies to the intersection between locality and globality. Third, the authors take a post-structuralist critical and interpretive stance to examining identities, practices and policies, and in accordance with the ideals of critical applied linguistics seek to reveal relations of power between local practices and wider social orders. Even though we look at literacy in a specific geographical context, namely that of the Nordic countries, the issues raised are not specific to that context only. Instead, this particular context – or rather space – reaches beyond the boundaries of nation states and becomes any context in the current globalizing world.

In the following sections, we will first discuss the why and how of studying literacy in transition. Then, we will place our empirical examinations in the tradition of literacy studies, that is studying literacy as a social practice, by giving an overview of the field relevant to the argument in this volume. Next, our understanding of what is 'critical' in studying literacy in education is explicated, after which we will discuss the methodological underpinnings of the chapters. Finally, an outline of the chapters is presented.

Researching Literacy Practices in Transition

In this volume, we have set out to examine literacy practices in transition. Why is it that literacy and literacy practices are in transition? The answer to that question is that since practices are always contextual and rooted in the cultures, histories and discourses of societies and communities, they are tied to the changes these societies and communities undergo. The current changes have been explained by phenomena and concepts such as postmodernism, post-structuralism, the collapse of the nation states and globalization. In this section, we will examine some of the complexities that put literacy practices in a state of transition.

The extensive body of research on literacy as a social practice has considerably enhanced our understanding of the situated and variable nature of literacy as a social practice. The emphasis has thus far been strongly on local practices, which has been a natural consequence of the need to oppose the prevalent autonomous views of literacy as a cognitive skill. Research has shown that literacy is never neutral, and the often intense public and political debates about literacy reveal that a high emotional and ideological value is attached to literacy. Literacy clearly plays a central role in relation to many of our society's major concerns. It is, however, significant that in political discourse literacy mostly appears as a 'neutral' – or autonomous (Street, 1984) – phenomenon, thus demonstrating that a 'normalization' of a specific conceptualization of literacy with a specific ontology and specific values and beliefs is an essential part of the dominant political discourse around literacy. This political discourse might lead to an understanding of literacy as a transparent term and not as a contested concept. In local practices, however, these 'global' norms are challenged and dislocated, and it is therefore very important for literacy researchers to take a closer look at how political conceptualizations of literacy relate to and are re-conceptualized, (re-)interpreted and localized in literacy activities, which take place in new kinds of spaces, and thus to create dialogue between the global and the local.

The current changes in society, including globalization and the ensuing technological developments, have greatly increased the complexity of social activities. Globalization is not only an economic phenomenon, concerned with *global markets or common markets beyond the nation states*, but it is also, and above all, a social and cultural phenomenon that influences the everyday lives of most people one way or another (McKay & Bokhorst-Heng, 2008). Globalization is seen as both a positive and a negative phenomenon: for some, it is a force that makes the world smaller and unites people across nations, whereas for others it appears as something that causes a loss of cultural and linguistic diversity and leads to divides between different groups of people, rather than eradicating differences (McKay & Bokhorst-Heng, 2008: 1). Scholte (2000: 3) characterizes contemporary globalization as deterritorialization, as it points towards changing social spaces and complex interrelations between global and local spaces. This has generated an unpredictable global/local hybridity with new and complex forms of literacy practices (Blommaert, 2010).

The changes challenge and transform language, literacy and education in many ways and thereby also challenge literacy research, both ontologically and epistemologically; in other words, there is a need to reconsider both the objects of study and the methods we use to gain knowledge of literacy practices in contemporary societies. Recently, there have been calls both for more research on transnational literacies and literacies affected by the global flows that are characteristic of societies today and for more research focusing on the connections and interplay between the local and the global (Baynham, 2004; Brandt & Clinton, 2002; Warriner, 2009). The movement of people can no longer be described in terms of emigration, immigration or assimilation: the term 'super-diversity' has been used to refer to the constant unpredictable movement of people and the emergence of unstable and diverse communities (Vertovec, 2007; Blommaert, 2010). Blommaert (2010: 5) talks about a sociolinguistics of mobility, where the focus is on not 'language-in-place', but 'language-in-motion'. People move across spaces and their linguistic resources move with them, taking new shape in new places. This has inevitable repercussions for literacy research, and calls for new kinds of conceptualizations of language and literacy: literacy has to be examined from the point of view of transition.

The increased complexity of social activities relates, on the one hand, to languages, scripts and modalities, and on the other hand, to space and place. It can no longer be assumed that a literacy event takes place in a certain space, at a certain place and in a certain language, with one specific script and through one modality only. Technological developments in particular have profoundly transformed the ideas of space and modality. Meanings are created not only in writing but also in a complex mixture of visual and auditory modes. Translocal connections between people also affect the way languages are used: languages are mixed and hybrid forms are created to serve the purposes of the users. Thus, the social activities of which literacy is a part have become increasingly messy and fuzzy, and this has consequences for literacy research on several dimensions. What counts as literacy has to be dissected and analysed and new methods of studying literacy are needed. This is exactly what this volume aims to do.

Researching Literacy in Transition as a Social Practice

The chapters in this volume draw on the tradition of studying literacy as a social practice. In the following, we present an overview of the development of research in this area. The social approach to literacy research goes beyond a basically cognitive understanding of literacy, in which literacy is seen as a skill, as something people have learned (or have to learn) and therefore know, and regards literacy as something people do, as an activity and as a social practice (Barton & Tusting, 2005). Accordingly, to study literacy from this perspective means to examine the social activities of which literacy is a part (Barton & Hamilton, 2000) and to take into account the values and attitudes, the histories and cultures and the personal experiences that people draw on when they are engaged with literacy. The basic assumption of literacy as social practice is a shared view in the chapters in this volume.

The social approach to literacy rose in opposition to an overwhelming and seemingly neutral (or autonomous, as Brian Street expresses it (1984)) view of literacy, which was based particularly on psychology, and which made causal connections between the skills of reading and writing and the wealth and prosperity of the Western world. The seminal work by scholars such as Scribner and Cole (1981), Heath (1983) and Street (1984) in the 1980s gave rise to a new approach to literacy, namely literacy as social practice, which reached its peak in the 1990s and early 21st century. Their work was based on anthropology and sociolinguistics, and this could therefore be called the social turn in literacy research, similar to a more recent social turn in research on second language acquisition (see e.g. Block, 2003; Lantolf, 2000; Lantolf & Thorne, 2006), a turn away from the prevalent psychological views of literacy. This turning point in literacy research shifted the focus away from an individual's skills, their development and measurability, to individuals in communities and networks, people's understandings of literacy and the values society places on some forms of literacy; from a generalized skill of reading and writing to multiple literacies. Methodologically, this meant a shift from quantitative and experimental measuring to more sensitive qualitative methods such as ethnography, case studies and discursive approaches.

The earliest body of research included close ethnographies of specific communities in the Western world. The Lancaster group of scholars in particular laid one of the foundations for this strand of literacy research that examined the situated nature of literacies (see e.g. Ivanič, 1997; Barton & Hamilton, 1998; Barton et al., 2000). Another strand of early literacy research expanded the inquiry outside the West and included ethnographies in indigenous communities in the Global South (e.g. Aikman, 1999; Kalman, 1999; Papen, 2007; Prinsloo & Breier, 1996; Street, 2001). Yet another strand reached out to special communities such as prisons (Wilson, 2000) or churches (Tusting, 2000). In the 21st century, the focus has also shifted to multilingual communities, mostly in the UK (Martin-Jones & Jones, 2000) and in indigenous communities such as the Sami in the northernmost part of Scandinavia (Pietikäinen & Pitkänen-Huhta, forthcoming).

More recently, literacy research has expanded into educational contexts, albeit mostly in English speaking contexts or English as a second language contexts. Within the framework of critical literacy, especially in the United States, educational practices have been criticized, challenged and reformed by researchers and practitioners such as Morrell (2008), Ladson-Billings (2009), Rodgers (see e.g. Rodgers et al., 2009) and Gutiérrez (e.g. Gutiérrez et al., 1999; Gutiérrez et al., 2010). But there is also a growing body of research in non-English speaking contexts, including in the Nordic countries. There are studies with young children's early literacy development in Sweden (e.g. Fast, 2007), in multilingual contexts in Demark (Laursen, 2011) and with adolescents in a foreign language context in Finland (Luukka et al., 2008; Pitkänen-Huhta, 2003; Taalas et al., 2008). A considerable body of research has also focused on adult and continuing education, carried out especially by the Lancaster Literacy Research Centre (e.g. Barton et al., 2007; Papen, 2005) and also elsewhere (Holm, 2004; Franker, 2011). Academic literacies from a social perspective have also been studied quite extensively, in the UK context in particular (Lea & Street, 1998; Lillis, 2001) and also elsewhere (see e.g. McCambridge & Pitkänen-Huhta, this volume).

Perspectives on Critical Literacy in Education

In addition to sharing an interest in examining literacy as a social practice, the authors of this volume wish to make connections and contributions to current discussions on education, language education in particular. Our shared view of literacy in education is connected to recent discussions on critical applied linguistics.

There is an extensive and diverse body of research on literacy in education in multilingual and multicultural contexts, with the term 'critical' being commonly used as a signpost to describe and characterize the different research traditions. From a general epistemological perspective, it is possible to identify at least three research strands that differ considerably in their conceptual understanding of the meaning of 'critical' and therefore in what are considered to be central research questions and objectives.

First of all, Paulo Freire (1970) used the term 'critical' to refer to the capacity to use language and literacy as a means for political and economic emancipation. Using Marxist theory, he described a binary dialectic universe of oppression and liberation, and argued that the political and economic emancipation of the peasant and working class in colonial contexts was a central objective of the critical literacy he was advocating (Luke, 2004, 1997b). Freire saw literacy as a means for the reinstatement of voice and agency of the 'oppressed', and argued for participatory education – for a 'pedagogy for the oppressed' that started with people's local conditions and concerns (Pennycook, 2003). In this way, critical literacy was always a political project about fundamental changes in literacy education and in society, and in the interests of marginalized groups and learners. In Freire's understanding of critical literacy, the focus is on the possibility of different 'oppressed' languages and cultures and forms of knowledge being allowed a pedagogical role in literacy. Freire's work has been criticized among other things for its reductive view of the oppressed and oppressors, for having an over-optimistic view of the effects of critical literacy and for being based on the epistemological assumption that there is a knowable body of material and political reality available to dialectical analysis and dialogic education (Luke, 1997b; Pennycook, 2003).

Second, for researchers such as Edelsky (2006), Ladson-Billings (1992) and Gutiérrez et al. (2000), with a base in US educational anthropology, 'critical' relates primarily to providing equal access to literacy. With a point of departure in literacy measures and other indicators of school success, the emphasis is put on the disparity in academic and literacy performance and competence between different groups – for instance, 'students of color' and 'the general White population' (Ladson-Billings, 1992: 312), 'Latino-students' or 'English language learners (Gutiérrez et al., 2000). To overcome and eliminate this disparity and to achieve 'equity in education', a 'culturally relevant approach' to literacy teaching is proposed (Ladson-Billings, 1992). This tradition shares with Freire an engagement with marginalized groups in education, but differs from the Freirean approach by focusing on how to give marginalized groups equal access to the *existing* powerful forms of literacy and language in education through different forms of 'multicultural' or 'intercultural' education. This understanding of 'critical' has been criticized for remaining tied to a liberal democratic politics of equality, with a tendency to disguise important power relations and stratification dynamics in education by naturalizing literacy testing and other knowledge regimes (Holm & Laursen, 2011; Pennycook, 2003: 99).

Third, drawing on post-structuralist educational theories, 'critical' relates to yet another meaning. Martin-Jones (2007: 171), for instance, uses the term 'critical' to characterize research that aims 'to reveal links between local discourse practices…, the everyday talk and interactional routines of classrooms and the wider social and ideological order'. This understanding of 'critical' in education is an interpretive research tradition focusing on the deconstruction and examination of how dominant texts and discourses position and define human subjects in relations of knowledge and power. According to Martin-Jones (2007), this approach arose out of a concern with the ways in which 'educational policies *and* classroom practices contribute to the reproduction of asymmetries of power between groups with different social and linguistic resources' (Martin-Jones, 2007: 171). Differing from the Freirean approach that relates 'critical literacy' to oppression and liberation, or the approach that relates 'critical literacy' to equality in education, this approach relates 'critical literacy' in education to the power relations at work in everyday classroom life. As a consequence, research in this tradition is directed towards the ways in which literacy values and discourses of literacy learning are produced and reproduced in and through the interactional practices of classrooms, towards the complex ways in which classroom participants draw on the linguistic resources available to them and finally towards revealing the consequences of these practices for the construction of different social categories (Martin-Jones, 2007).

The researchers in this volume are indebted to this critical, interpretive research tradition. However, looking at the more and more complex sociolinguistic landscape around us makes it relevant and timely to try to take our research a step further, from post-structuralism to post-linguistics, to use Pennycook's (2003) term. Pennycook has been concerned with how to relate post-structuralism to detailed text analysis. Our concern is of another order and is related to how in our research we could respond to the increasing diversity and rapid changes in society regarding literacy practices. It is this interest in the theoretical and methodological challenges of researching literacy in transition that brought the authors of this volume together and led to the theorization and conceptualization of a new sociolinguistic landscape put forward by researchers such as Vertovec (2006, 2007) and Blommaert (2010). This volume contributes to the qualitative, ethnographic and situated body of literacy research since all the studies in the volume examine specific glocal contexts of literacy use. At the same time, it also contributes to the growing body of literacy research related to education but with a special focus on the interconnections between the global and the local. By taking an interpretive critical perspective on literacy practices, the empirical studies reported here are able to focus on change and transition, and on the new interfaces these create for literacy practices.

Methodological Challenges in Examining Literacy Practices in Transition

In an attempt to meet the challenges put forward by the complexities described above and their repercussions for literacy practices, the chapters in this volume use diverse methodologies. To capture the finely graded transitions in literacy practices, multiple methods have to be used and existing methodologies challenged and reinterpreted. Sometimes, it is relevant to look at the narratives individuals provide, sometimes the discourses of literacy need unravelling, or the policy documents on literacy need to be analysed, or action research is needed to initiate change and engage local actors. The underlying common core is formed, on the one hand, by the concepts of practices and events, but even these concepts are challenged and reinterpreted in the analyses. On the other hand, all the chapters share an interest in ethnography and case studies and thereby seek to discover and understand the nuanced practices and discourses in glocal practices.

The concept of practice forms the basis of literacy research in the social framework and it has therefore been discussed extensively, and to some extent with different definitions. There are basically two sides to literacy practices: one is the concrete human activity related to literacy and the other is the values and attitudes people place on literacy. Street (1984, 1995, 2000, 2001) combines these two under the same concept *practice*, whereas other researchers (e.g. Barton & Hamilton, 1998) use the term *literacy event* to separate the observable activities from the abstract constellation of practices. Street (1995: 162) defines literacy practice as 'a broad concept, pitched at a higher level of abstraction and referring to both behaviour and conceptualisations related to the use of reading and/or writing'. Barton and Hamilton (1998: 6) distinguish events from practices and define the latter as 'the general cultural ways of utilizing written language which people draw upon in their lives'. In the chapters in this volume, the concept is used in two ways. In some cases, literacy practices refer to culturally recognizable patterns of behaviour, for instance, for constructing texts, which can be generalized – or inferred – from observing literacy events (Barton & Hamilton, 2000; Street, 1995). In other cases, literacy practices refer to 'observable, collectable and/or documentable specific ethnographic detail of situated literacy events, involving real people, relationships, purposes, actions, places, times, circumstances, feelings, tools, resources' (Baynham & Prinsloo, 2009: 6).

Many of the chapters also refer to the traditional fundamental unit of analysis in the social practice approach to literacy, the literacy event, which has been discussed by researchers (Baynham, 2004; Baynham & Prinsloo, 2009). The interactional point of departure in the practice approach to literacy research is another recognised topic (Brandt & Clinton, 2002). Heath's well-known and groundbreaking work, *Ways with Words* (1983), provided social practice studies of literacy with a common and discrete unit of analysis: the literacy event. However, the bounded and local nature of this unit of analysis has recently been criticized as problematic (Brandt & Clinton, 2002; Collins & Blot, 2003). The notion of an event implies a distinct and distinguishable structured set of local activities, but much literacy activity is certainly not like this. On the contrary, classrooms and other communities are often characterized by a mixture of many different literacy activities in which participants are not in the same time/space coordinates. As Baynham and Prinsloo (2009) argue, in a text-saturated world with travelling and media-connected resources and repertoires it might be extremely difficult to identify events.

A critical discussion of the event as the unit of analysis is more than a methodological challenge. It has epistemological implications for the understanding of fundamental concepts within the social practice approach, in which it is considered axiomatic that literacy practices are inferred by observing literacy events (Barton & Hamilton, 2000; Street, 1984, 1995). Based on the interactional focus in the social practice approach to literacy research, Brandt and Clinton (2002) have criticized New Literacy Studies for disregarding the materiality – the texts – that are inevitably involved in literacy interactions. Going back to Heath's definition of the literacy event as 'any occasion in which a piece of writing is integral to the nature of participants' interaction and their interpretive processes' (Heath, 1983: 392), this disregard does not seem to be logically inherent to the definition of the unit of analysis but more a result of a research tradition that seems to have had its main interest in the interaction around texts rather than in what the texts brought with them into the interaction.

Founded on this argument and drawing on Latour's (2005) Actor–Network Theory (ANT), researchers like Brandt and Clinton (2002), Clarke (2008), Prinsloo (2008) and Lenters (2009) have argued for what might be termed 'a material turn' that installs artefacts as central to literacy research in order to give due weight to the significance which material artefacts bear in the social world (Baynham & Prinsloo, 2009: 10). Central to Latour's theorizing is the understanding that society is comprised of human and non-human actors (or actants) and that research might benefit from tracing the objects that circulate within and between sites of human social interaction 'as "things" which are necessary components of social networks or practices' (Baynham & Prinsloo, 2009: 10).

The ongoing theoretical proliferation and development in the understanding of the object of inquiry is characteristic of the social practice strand of literacy research and reveals at the same time openness to new theoretical perspectives and, due to its ethnographic orientation, a high degree of sensitivity to contemporary societal and global processes of change. This has generated an open-ended research tradition with a rich variety of research questions. This diversity in research interests and analytical tools also means that in this volume no specific standardized use of concepts is given priority. The shift in focus from the local to the translocal has resulted, for example in bringing together and reinterpreting data from earlier local studies in a translocal perspective in several contributions to this volume (e.g. Bagga-Gupta; Holm & Pöyhönen). The openness is also evident in those contributions that examine how material texts are integral to identity construction (Golden & Lanza; Wedin) or how texts are interpreted in educational practice (Kulbrandstad & Vesteraas Danbolt; Hvistendahl). The complexity of defining the literacy event in multilayered classroom settings or in translocal communities is also present in some contributions, which call for re-conceptualizations of the traditionally used objects of inquiry and units of analysis (Daugaard & Laursen; Halonen; Axelsson & Danielsson; McCambridge & Pitkänen-Huhta).

Methodologically, this book could be called multi-sited ethnography if we take ethnography to be not only a method but also a theoretical approach to language and literacy as social and contextual. Not all the chapters are ethnographic in the strictest sense, but all can be characterized as qualitative in-depth case studies, with many applying detailed discourse analytic methods. They all focus on individual cases or specific contexts and practices, but together they provide a multi-site cross section of literacy practices in the present Nordic context. But, as discussed above, this geographical location is not simply that and nothing more. Instead, it is seen as a space which is connected to other spaces in multiple ways: the focal participants are mobile and connected to other real and imaginary spaces, and the discourses, values and policies are not stable and rooted in one location only, but travel across spaces.

Outline of the Volume

The chapters in this volume all share an interest in examining literacy in relation to education in the context of transition. Some central questions that are posed in the chapters are: What images and conceptualizations of literacy and language are created in a local context under global conditions? What discursive resources and ideologies are mobilized? How are they enacted? What conflicts or conflicting identities evolve around the conceptualization of literacy and language? How does literacy as a locally situated social practice connect to globalization and how does this relationship reveal relations of unevenness and power?

Light is thrown on the intersection between societal change and literacy in education from three perspectives in this volume: from the point of view of *individual actors*, *local practices* and *policies*. In other words, literacy practices play a role in people's life trajectories and identity construction, in our interactions with others in local educational practices and in educational concepts and policies and in how practitioners make sense of these. These research perspectives go beyond a research focus on how children (and adults) 'best' learn the institutionally valued literacy. Instead, they represent a broader research perspective on literacy in education based on the assumption that identity, practices and policies are constitutive aspects of the construction of literacy in education. It has to be borne in mind, however, that these perspectives cannot be kept separate, but rather individuals, practices and policies are inherently interconnected and are in constant dialogue. The parts of the volume merely provide different windows on the same phenomenon.

Part 1: Literacy and identity in transition

Part 1 focuses on identities and how they are constructed in, through and around literacy. The detailed empirical analyses will show how literacy is integral to people's identity construction and how this construction often takes place and is made visible and/or invisible in literacy practices and textual (policy) documents. Drawing on post-structuralist perspectives on identity (Hall, 1992; Norton, 2000; Weedon, 1997), the chapters see identities as multiple and dynamic and as a site of struggle. Identity construction (or subjectivity) is understood as discursively constructed and always socially and historically embedded (Norton & McKinney, 2008). This indicates that identity is 'always in process, a site of struggle between competing discourses in which the subject plays an active role' (Norton & McKinney, 2008: 194). This socioculturally inspired understanding contrasts with the more psychological concept of identity as static and uni-dimensional and has led to a much more complex understanding of language and literacy in education. The research interest in identity construction in language and literacy education was initially directed mainly towards language and literacy learners (Norton, 2000; Toohey, 2000) but has been broadened lately and is now also directed towards language and literacy teachers and language and literacy researchers (Barkhuizen, 2011; Norton & Early, 2011). In literacy studies, the seminal work on writer identity by Ivanič (1997) laid the ground for examinations of identity construction in academic literacies (e.g. Lillis, 2001).

In the chapters in this part, identity constructions around literacy are examined in different contexts. In Chapter 1, Golden and Lanza investigate the various ways through which adult migrants in Norway position themselves in narratives and provide ideological stances towards language learning and literacy. The theoretical point of departure is a constructionist understanding in which identities are perceived as negotiated, emergent and performed in interpersonal communication, and therefore narratives are regarded as providing a good way in to the study of identity. The data for this study come from focus group interactions in semi-structured interviews with migrant doctors. The analysis of the narratives reveals how individuals take a stance to the transition to new literacies in a new homeland and thus to their identity construction. The authors argue that focus group narratives have an educational potential by offering students the possibility of negotiating different identities and insights into language and literacy diversity.

Chapter 2, by Wedin, also focuses on a specific group of migrants and examines the role of literacy in the negotiation, construction and manifestation of identities among unaccompanied asylum-seeking children in Sweden. Theoretically, the author is drawing on Canagarajah's (2004) Foucault inspired distinctions between a macro-social level *selfhood* that is mainly imposed or ascribed in relation to institutional roles and ideological subjectivity and a micro-social level *voice* in which the ascribed identities are resisted, negotiated or modified. The data come from a close involvement with three young boys over a 14-month period and consist of participant observation and a wide range of written artefacts. The close analysis of the literacy practices in which the boys participate shows how the boys are constructing voice in the reconstruction of their identities by using the literacies, languages and modalities they find useful.

Bagga-Gupta's research on identity construction in Chapter 3 focuses on how identity positions and language varieties are made visible or invisible in social practices and policy-textual worlds. The study is inspired by poststructuralist intersectionality approaches that recognize borders and boundaries as analytically relevant spaces for research. In order to demonstrate and discuss how intersectionality can be operationalized, data sets from both the North (Sweden) and the South (India) and both non-government organizations and educational institutions are brought together in this chapter. The analysis and discussion of different sets of multimodal data focuses on written communication in everyday life and demonstrates how static boundaries within education make invisible the diverse nature of language learners and how the organization of the learning and instruction of language varieties is a normative position with an inherent reductionism that is at odds with the fluidity that emerges in the analysis of micro-level social practices.

Part 2: Local practices in transition

This part focuses on local practices in and around education, but the locality of practices is also always understood in connection to the global. Being connected to social practices, literacy practices are never just about literacy, as practices involve 'ways of talking, interacting, thinking, valuing, and believing' (Gee, 1996: 41). What is important for the argument in this part is the idea of practices linking patterns of literacy activity to broader social, cultural and historical structures (Street, 2000: 21). Street (2000) further argues that methodologically this means that practices cannot be understood simply by observing literacy events; it is necessary to interview people and link their experiences to theories. This methodological approach to practices arises from the anthropological and ethnographic traditions, which are in principle based on observation and interviewing. People's actions are, however, often unconscious, and direct reflection on one's own practices can reveal only some aspects of practice, as Tusting et al. (2000: 216) point out, while other aspects may not be open to reflection.

In this part, we adopt a discursive view of language and literacy and therefore the approach to studying literacy changes somewhat. By closely examining discourses of, in and around literacy we can gain deeper insights into the attitudes and values embedded in practices and unravel the connections between literacy activities and broader social structures. Blommaert (2008) argues that in ethnographies of literacy the products of literacy – texts – have been artificially separated from practices. We should not separate products from practices but rather see the product as an inevitable and inherent part of practice: '"Practices" always yield "products"... "products" therefore contain traces of practices and can disclose the nature of such practices, and ... products themselves yield practices' (Blommaert, 2008: 13–14). Thus close discourse-analytic examination of these products, that is texts (Blommaert, 2008) and talk (Pitkänen-Huhta, 2003; Jinkerson, 2011), can reveal practices, simply because texts and talk inherently are practices.

The chapters in this part adopt slightly different approaches to local practices, ranging from a focus on specific activities around literacy in particular settings to a focus on the discourses constructed around literacy. Chapter 4, by Daugaard and Laursen, examines a multilingual classroom in Denmark as a site of negotiations of language and literacy. Classrooms have never been homogeneous, in many senses, but in the present era of global flows and new forms of mobility the heterogeneous nature of classrooms is more prominent than ever. In this chapter, the classroom is characterized as a messy marketplace, in which language ideologies and identity options are maintained, contested and negotiated. The close examination of literacy practices in the classroom in focus in this chapter shows what transitional processes take place when people move across spaces and how the sociolinguistic reality of the classroom clashes with the educational conceptualization of 'the bilingual student'. The analysis also shows how multilingual children actively claim – and transform – linguistic space in the classroom.

In Chapter 5, Halonen looks at the literacy practices of Finnish Year 6 pupils from the perspective of performance used in the Goffmanian framework. The focus is on writing at school and on how the students play around with traditional formal standards and the more informal registers of writing in performing a writing task. The point of view is sociocultural and so writing at school is seen as a multilayered and multi-ideological social situation. For the student, the writing task is a performance in which they move along a continuum from being a formal school writer to being an informal everyday writer, and at the same time present some of their multiple identities. The author shows how the students skilfully produce simultaneously in-school and out-of-school practices and present themselves both as good students skilled in conventional literacy practices and as resistant students carrying out a school task but completely diginative in everyday practices. Halonen further shows how skilled the students are in completing the task and at the same time showing their attitudes and positioning themselves in the situation.

The authors of Chapter 6 have adopted a social semiotic multimodal perspective to examine literacy in the science classroom. Here, Axelsson and Danielsson examine the multimodal meaning-making resources used in Year 2 and Years 8/9 science classrooms to see what modes are foregrounded and how the modes are combined in the two different age groups. The science classroom is a particularly multimodal learning environment and learning science involves a lot more than acquiring the linguistic aspect of scientific discourse. The close analysis of science literacy in the two classrooms shows that in the lower level classroom there is relatively limited integration of modes for meaning making, whereas with the older age group meaning making involves a high level of multi-modality and the combination of modes appears to be the rule. It also appears that the ways in which various modes and representations can be used for meaning making is supposed to be learned implicitly.

Finally, in Chapter 7, McCambridge and Pitkänen-Huhta aim to unravel discourses of literacy on an international master's programme by examining the writing norms of academic English. These kinds of English-medium master's programmes have appeared in recent years in different parts of the world and are a prime example of new mobile communities. The chapter adopts a sociolinguistic perspective and aims to understand the norms of English use within these programmes as discourse communities in their own right, and how the norms reflect the social world in which they exist. These emergent transnational communities of mobile academic writers form an interesting arena in which to examine literacy in transition, as the global and local meet in students' discourse on good, normal and correct academic literacy in English. The take on literacy practices here is on discourses around literacy, that is on how people make sense of what they do with literacy. The analysis of student interviews shows that the discourses around literacy fluctuate between globally accepted seemingly universal norms of good English academic writing and the very personalized and creative experiences of writing in contexts other than the academic one.

Part 3: Policies and practices in transition

In this part, the focus shifts from individuals and local practices to policies and related educational practices. As already pointed out, these levels cannot, however, be separated, as individuals, practices and policies are inherently interconnected. Policies are enacted, (re)interpreted and transformed through the interaction of individual actors in local arenas, and this is never just a top-down implementation of a given strategy.

The current changes in literacy and language education policies are a part of a much broader trend and have a clear international dimension. Accountability and the comparability of test results come high on the political agenda in many countries, including the Nordic countries. Literacy is central to this process. The demand for nationally comparable results seems in many countries to have led to a clear tendency to reduce what counts as literacy to measurable and standardizable qualities (Elstad & Sivesind, 2010; Menken, 2008; Nichols & Berliner, 2007). This makes it important to deconstruct the pre-constructed notions of literacy that inform the policy and practice of literacy education. The tenor of the current political discourses around literacy seems basically to reveal two positions. One discourse might be termed the 'demand discourse', and it relates the changing educational demands to new digital technologies and to processes of globalization within a knowledge society (Gebhard, 2004; Street, 2004). The other discourse might be characterized as the 'crisis discourse', and it relates a perceived lack of literacy to unemployability, to the social exclusion of certain groups and thus to a threat to societal coherence and progress (Holm & Laursen, 2011).

In Chapter 8, Holm and Pöyhönen investigate how a conceptualization of literacy in a specific document put forward by a supranational agency, the Council of Europe, is localized within adult second language education in Denmark and Finland. The document is theoretically seen as a shared, mobile authority and artefact. After explicating the central values and assumptions in this concept of literacy, the complex dynamics between national and supranational forces around the conceptualization of literacy is researched by employing a multi-sited research approach (Marcus, 1995). Data come from two research projects in two different arenas: a six-month ethnographic fieldwork-based classroom study in Denmark and a development project in a national political arena on setting goals for education designed to integrate migrants into Finnish society. The authors argue that in this document literacy has been conceptualized as something authoritative and objective that is beyond critical scrutiny; furthermore, the concept does not appear to be a suitable point of departure for educational planning but is more of a political tool that is increasingly being used as a demarcation line for inclusion and exclusion in ever more globalized nation states.

The focus in Chapter 9 is on teacher reflections on literacy learning in schools that have increasing numbers of migrant pupils in Oslo, Norway. The background for this study is formed by the many political initiatives introduced by changing Norwegian governments during the past 10 years to strengthen reading results after what was considered a bad PISA result in 2001. Through an action research project, Danbolt and Kulbrandstad investigate how teachers reacted when politicians suddenly made great changes in the curriculum in order to improve reading results. The analysis demonstrates the great pressure on both school heads and teachers to focus on improving the results in reading tests, one result of which was to teach literacy in level-based groups. However, the analysis also indicates that teachers in the innovation projects were eager to change their teaching practices in ways that could strengthen the literacy learning of all pupils. The authors finally argue that action research can promote reflections on teaching practice and be a useful support for teachers in their daily work with literacy learning under changing circumstances.

Chapter 10 also examines teaching from a teacher perspective, but in this chapter the focus is on bilingual teacher students in Norway. Hvistendahl points out that political interest in bilingual teachers in Norway is related to the idea that the teaching staff should be representative of the population at large, and to the idea that bilingual teachers might function as good role models. It is thus not a need for multilingual competences or multilingual literacies that is central to initiatives to increase the numbers of bilingual teachers in Norway. With a point of departure in Jill Bourne's identification of bilingual teacher roles, Hvistendahl analyses data from a pilot project with eight female teacher students and demonstrates how the teacher students in different ways and with different rates of success try to create space for bilingual literacies in Norwegian schools.

The volume ends in the Afterword, written by Professor David Barton from Lancaster University. David Barton reflects on how the contributions in the volume tackle the idea of literacy in transition over a wide range of areas but with the common thread of literacy as a social practice. He also points out how the volume contributes to literacy studies and, even though situated in the Nordic countries, is relevant to discussion of the subject globally.

When examining the processes of transition from three perspectives, the contributions in this volume show that literacy practices are indeed in transition in our contemporary mobile society. In connection to individuals, the chapters point to individual agency in literacy practices, when people maintain, contest, negotiate and transform the identity positions and categorizations on offer to them. The close empirical analyses show how attention to micro-level phenomena is a powerful tool in uncovering the fluid and situated nature of human identity. In relation to practices, the chapters show how our sociolinguistic landscape is in constant flux and how there is often a clash between various — often global — categorizations, such as the bilingual student, and the social reality in which we live. The chapters also show how skilfully individuals draw on various resources, such as language, modality and genre or register, when navigating in complex social spaces and when taking different stances, positions and orientations as the situation demands. The authors in this volume also show how the global and local meet in discourses and practices, and how people need to negotiate their way in the complex and messy spaces in which they move about and when encountering new emergent practices. As to policies, the analyses show how the concepts and frameworks developed by supranational agencies may function as discursive forces, thereby stipulating what counts as legitimate conceptualizations of language and literacy and consequently appropriate and normal practices. Global pedagogical ideas and literacy practices are too easily and uncritically adopted by policy makers, when in fact they call for professional reflection and informed adaptation to local practices. The result is that practitioners struggle to find a space for new kinds of practices, in the classrooms, for example.

This volume challenges present trends towards the global standardization of language and literacy education. Instead, it promotes the idea of literacy as a multiple, multilingual, multimodal and constantly contestable and negotiable phenomenon, which calls for the development of language and literacy education that is sensitive to the needs and experiences of the individual actors. It calls too for dynamic interaction between research, practising teachers and teacher education to encourage critical reflections on present teaching practices and openness to their development in the future.

References

Aikman, S. (1999) *Intercultural Education and Literacy: An Ethnographic Study of Indegenous Knowledge and Learning in the Peruvian Amazon*. Amsterdam: John Benjamins.

Barkhuizen, G. (2011) Narrative knowledging in TESOL. *TESOL Quarterly* 45 (3), 391–414.

Barton, D. and Hamilton, M. (1998) *Local Literacies: Reading and Writing in One Community*. London: Routledge.

Barton, D. and Hamilton, M. (2000) Literacy practices. In D. Barton, M. Hamilton and R. Ivanič (eds) *Situated Literacies: Reading and Writing in Context* (pp. 7–15). New York: Routledge.

Barton, D., Hamilton, M. and Ivanič, R. (eds) (2000) *Situated Literacies. Reading and Writing in Context*. London: Routledge.

Barton, D. and Tusting, K. (eds) (2005) *Beyond Communities of Practice. Language, Power and Social Context*. Cambridge: Cambridge University Press.

Barton, D., Ivanič, R., Appleby, Y., Hodge, R. and Tusting, K. (2007) *Literacy, Lives and Learning*. London: Routledge.

Baynham, M. (2004). Ethnographies of literacy. Introduction. *Language & Education* 18 (4), 285–290.

Baynham, M. and Prinsloo, M. (eds) (2009) *The Future of Literacy Studies*. Basingstoke: Palgrave MacMillan.

Block, D. (2003) *The Social Turn in Second Language Acquisition*. Edinburgh: Edinburgh University Press.

Blommaert, J. (2008) *Grassroots Literacy: Writing, Identity and Voice in Central Africa*. London: Routledge.
Blommaert, J. (2010) *The Sociolinguistics of Globalization*. Cambridge: Cambridge University Press.
Brandt, D. and Clinton, K. (2002) Limits of the local: expanding perspectives on literacy as a social practice. *Journal of Literacy Research* 34 (3), 337–356.
Canagarajah, A.S. (2004) Multilingual writers and the struggle for voice in academic discourse. In A. Pavlenko and A. Blackledge (eds) *Negotiation of Identities in Multilingual Contexts* (pp. 266–289). Clevedon: Multilingual Matters.
Clarke, J. (2008) Assembling "skills for life": Actor network theory and the New Literacy Studies. In M. Prinsloo and M. Baynham (eds) *Literacies, Local and Global* (pp. 151–172). Amsterdam: John Benjamins.
Collins, J. and Blot, R. (2003) *Literacy and Literacies: Texts, Power and Identity*. Cambridge: Cambridge University Press.
Collins, J., Slembrouck, S. and Baynham, M. (eds) (2009) *Globalization and Language in Contact. Scale, Migration and Communicative Practices*. London: Continuum.
Edelsky, C. (2006) *With Literacy and Justice for All* (3rd edn). Mahwah, New Jersey: Lawrence Erlbaum.
Elstad, E. and Sivesind, K. (eds) (2010) *PISA: sannheten om skolen?* [PISA: The Truth about the School] Oslo: Universitetsforlaget.
Fast, C. (2007) *Sju barn lär sig läsa och skriva. Familjeliv och populärkultur i möte med förskola och skola*. [Seven children learning how to read and write. Family life and popular culture meet preschool and school]. Uppsala: Acta Universitatis Upsaliensis.
Franker, Q. (2011) *Litteracitet och visuella texter: Studier om lärare och kortutbildade deltagare i sfi*. [Literacy and visual texts: A study about teachers and low educated students in Swedish for adult migrants]. Doctoral dissertation, Institutionen för språkdidaktik, Stockholms Universitet, Stockholm.
Freire, P. (1970) *Pedagogy of the Oppressed*. New York: Continuum.
Gebhard, M. (2004) Fast capitalism, school reform and second language literacy practices. *The Modern Language Journal* 88 (2), 245–265.
Gee, J.P. (1996) *Social Linguistics and Literacies: Ideology in Discourses* (2nd edn). London: Routledge/Taylor & Francis.
Gee, J. P. (2000) Discourse and sociocultural studies in reading. In M.L. Kamil, P.B. Mosenthal, P.D. Pearson and R. Barr (eds) *Handbook of Reading Research III* (pp. 195–207). Mahwah, NJ: Lawrence Erlbaum.
Gutiérrez, K., Baquedano-López, P., Alvarez, H. and Chiu, M. (1999) Building a culture of collaboration through hybrid language practices. *Theory Into Practice* 38 (2), 87–92.
Gutiérrez, K., Baquedano-Lopez, P. and Asato, J. (2000) "English for children": The new literacy of the old world order, language policy and educational reform. *Bilingual Research Journal* 24 (1–2), 87–112.
Gutiérrez, K., Zepeda, M. and Castro, D. (2010) Advancing early literacy learning for all children: Implications of the NELP report for dual language learners. *Educational Researcher* 39 (4), 334–339.
Hall, S. (1992) The question of cultural identity. In S. Hall, D. Held and T. McGrew (eds) *Modernity and its Futures* (pp. 274–325). Cambridge: Polity Press.
Hall, K. (2002) Co-constructing subjectivities and knowledge in literacy class: An ethnographic–sociocultural perspective. *Language and Education* 16 (3), 178–194.
Heath, S.B. (1983) *Ways with Words*. New York: Cambridge University Press.

Holm, L. (2004) *Hvilken Vej ind i Hvilken Skriftlighed? Et Studie af Undervisning i Dansk som Andetsprog for Voksne* [Which way into which kind of literacy? A study of adult second language literacy teaching]. København: Danmarks Pædagogiske Universitet.
Holm, L. and Laursen, H.P. (2011) Migrants and literacy crises. *APPLES – Journal of Applied Language Studies* 5 (2), 3–16.
Ivanič, R. (1997) *Writing and Identity: The Discoursal Construction of Identity in Academic Writing*. Amsterdam: John Benjamins.
Jinkerson, A. (2011) Interpreting and managing a monolingual norm in an English-speaking class in Finland: When first and second graders contest the norm. *Apples – Journal of Applied Language Studies* 5 (1), 27–48.
Kalman, J. (1999) *Writing on the Plaza: Mediated Literacy Practices Among Scribes and Clients in Mexico City*. Hampton Press: Cresskill, NJ.
Ladson-Billings, G. (1992) Reading between the lines and beyond the pages: A culturally relevant approach to literacy teaching. *Theory Into Practice* 31 (4), 312–320.
Ladson-Billings, G. (2009) *The Dream-Keepers. Successful Teachers of African-American Children* (2nd edn). San Francisco, CA: John Wiley & Sons, Inc.
Lantolf, J.P. (ed.) (2000) *Sociocultural Theory and Second Language Learning*. Oxford: Oxford University Press.
Lantolf, J.P. and Thorne, S.T. (2006) *Sociocultural Theory and the Genesis of Second Language Development*. Oxford: Oxford University Press.
Latour, B. (2005) *Reassembling the Social: An Introduction to Actor-Network-Theory*. New York: Oxford University Press.
Laursen, H.P. (2011) Lukket inde i et alt for lille alfabet [Trapped in a much too small alphabet] *NORDAND. Nordisk tidsskrift for andrespråksforskning* [*Nordic Journal of Second Language Research*] 6 (2), 35–58.
Lea, M. and Street, B. (1998) Student writing in higher education: An academic literacies approach. *Studies in Higher Education* 23 (2), 157–172.
Lenters, K.A. (2009) Exploring "limits of the local": A case study of literacy-in-action in a contemporary intermediate classroom. Doctoral dissertation, The University of British Columbia, Vancouver.
Lillis, T.M. (2001) *Student Writing: Access, Regulation, Desire*. London and New York: Routledge.
Luke, A. (1997a) Genres of Power: Literacy education and the production of capital. In R. Hasan and G. Williams (eds) *Literacy in Society* (pp. 308–338). London: Longman.
Luke, A. (1997b) Critical approaches to literacy. In V. Edvards and D. Corson (eds) *Literacy: Encyclopedia of Language and Education* (Vol. 2, pp. 143–151). New York: Springer.
Luke, A. (2004) Two takes in on the critical. In B. Norton and K. Toohey (eds). *Critical Pedagogies and Language Learning* (pp. 21–29). Cambridge: Cambridge University Press.
Luukka, M-R., Pöyhönen, S., Huhta, A., Taalas, P., Tarnanen, M. and Keränen, A. (2008) *Maailma Muuttuu – Mitä Tekee Koulu? Äidinkielen ja Vieraan Kielen Tekstikäytänteet Koulussa ja Vapaa-ajalla* [The World Changes – What Does the School Do? Mother Tongue and Foreign Language Literacy Practices at school and in Free Time]. Jyväskylä: Soveltavan Kielentutkimuksen Keskus.
Marcus, G.E. (1995) Ethnography in/of the world system: The emergence of multi-sited ethnography. *Annual Review of Anthropology* 24, 95–117.
Martin-Jones, M. and Jones, K. (eds) (2000) *Multilingual Literacies: Reading and Writing Different Worlds*. Amsterdam: John Benjamins.

Martin-Jones, M. (2007) Bilingualism, education and the regulation of access to language resources. In M. Heller (ed.) *Bilingualism: A Social Approach* (pp. 161–182). Basingstoke: Palgrave.

McKay, S.L. and Bokhorst-Heng, W.D. (2008) *International English in its Sociolinguistic Contexts: Towards Socially Sensitive EIL Pedagogy*. New York: Routledge.

Menken, K. (2008) *English Learners Left Behind: Standardized Testing as Language Policy*. Clevedon: Multilingual Matters.

Morrell, E. (2008) *Critical Literacy and Urban Youth: Pedagogies of Access, Dissent, and Liberation*. New York: Routledge.

Nichols, S.L. and Berliner, D.C. (2007) *Collateral Damage: How High-Stakes Testing Corrupts America's Schools*. Cambridge: Harvard University Press.

Norton, B. (2000). *Identity and Language Learning: Gender, Ethnicity and Educational Change*. Harlow: Pearson Education.

Norton, B. and Early, M. (2011) Researcher identity, narrative inquiry, and language teaching research. *TESOL Quarterly* 45 (3), 415–439.

Norton, B. and McKinney, C. (2008) An identity approach to second language acquisition. In D. Atkinson (ed.) *Alternative Approaches to Second Language Acquisition* (pp. 73–94). London: Routledge.

Papen, U. (2005) *Adult Literacy as Social Practice: More than Skills (New Approaches to Adult Language, Literacy and Numeracy)*. London: Routledge.

Papen, U. (2007) *Literacy and Globalization: Reading and Writing in Times of Social and Cultural Change*. London: Routledge.

Pennycook, A. (2003) *Critical Applied Linguistics: A Critical Introduction*. London: Lawrence Erlbaum.

Pietikäinen, S. and Pitkänen-Huhta, A. (forthcoming) Multimodal literacy practices in the indigenous Sámi classroom: Children navigating in a complex multilingual setting. *International Journal of Language, Identity and Education*.

Pitkänen-Huhta, A. (2003) *Texts and Interaction: Literacy Practices in the EFL Classroom*. Jyväskylä: University of Jyväskylä.

Prinsloo, M. (2008) Literacy and land at the Bay of Natal: Documents and practices across spaces and social economics. *English in Africa* 35 (1), 95–114.

Prinsloo, M. and Breier, M. (eds) (1996) *The Social Uses of Literacy*. Bertsham: Sached Books and John Benjamins Publishing Company.

Rodgers, R., Mosley, M. and Kramer, M.A. (2009) *Designing Socially Just Learning Communities: Critical Literacy Education Across the Lifespan*. New York: Routledge.

Scholte, J.A. (2000) *Globalization: A Critical Introduction*. London: Palgrave.

Scribner, S. and Cole, M. (1981) *The Psychology of Literacy*. Cambridge, MA: Harvard University Press.

Street, B. (1984) *Literacy in Theory and Practice*. Cambridge: Cambridge University Press.

Street, B. (1995) *Social Literacies: Critical Approaches to Literacy in Development, Ethnography and Education*. London: Longman.

Street, B. (2000) Literacy events and literacy practices. Theory and practice in the New Literacy Studies. In M. Martin-Jones and K. Jones (eds) *Multilingual Literacies* (pp. 17–29). Amsterdam: John Benjamins.

Street, B. (ed.) (2001) *Literacy and Development: Ethnographic Perspectives*. London: Routledge.

Street, B. (2004) Academic literacies and the "new orders": Implications for research and practice in student writing in higher education. *Learning and Teaching in the Social Sciences* 1 (1), 9–20.

Taalas, P., Kauppinen, M., Tarnanen, M. and Pöyhönen, S. (2008) Media landscapes in school and in free time – two parallel realities? *Digital Kompetanse – Nordic Journal of Digital Literacy* 3 (4), 240–256.
Toohey, K. (2000) *Learning English at School: Identity, Social Relations and Classroom Practice.* Clevedon: Multilingual Matters.
Tusting, K. (2000) The New Literacy Studies and time: An exploration. In D. Barton, M. Hamilton and R. Ivanič (eds) *Situated Literacies: Reading and Writing in Context* (pp. 35–53). London: Routledge.
Tusting, K., Ivanič, R. and Wilson, A. (2000) New Literacy Studies at the interchange. In D. Barton, M. Hamilton and R. Ivanič (eds) *Situated Literacies: Reading and Writing in Context* (pp. 210–218). London: Routledge.
Vertovec, S. (2006) The emergence of super-diversity in Britain. Centre of Migration, Policy and Society Working Paper No 25, University of Oxford.
Vertovec, S. (2007) Super-diversity and its implications. *Ethnic and Racial Studies* 29(6), 1024–1054.
Warriner, D.S. (2009) Transnational literacies: Examining global flows through the lens of social practice. In M. Baynham and M. Prinsloo (eds) *The Future of Literacy Studies* (pp. 160–180). Basingstoke: Palgrave MacMillan.
Weedon, C. (1987/1997) *Feminist Practice and Poststructuralist Theory* (2nd edn). London: Blackwell.
Wilson, A. (2000) There is no escape from third-space theory: Borderland discourse and the 'in-between' literacies of prisons. In D. Barton, M. Hamilton and R. Ivanič (eds) *Situated Literacies: Reading and Writing in Context* (pp. 54–69). London: Routledge.

Part 1
Literacy and Identity in Transition

Introduction

This part focuses on literacy in transition from the perspective of identities. The chapters in this volume take a postmodernist and post-structuralist view of identity as discursively constructed and undergoing a process of constant emerging and becoming. This indicates that identity is not only a matter of 'who we are' but also concerns 'what we might become' (Man, 2010: 124). This view of identity makes it possible for the authors to analyze a person's speech, writings and doings with and around texts as a marker of identity that relates to specific and competing discourses. Language and literacy practices thus are not only a matter of fulfilling communicative functions but are also acts of identity, which bear social meaning and are produced in the context of diverse relations of power. We perform our selfness – or who we are – through the way we use – and are allowed and requested to use – language and literacy.

The chapters in this part show that when people move – both locally and globally – they encounter new discourse patterns and have to construct and perform new forms of personal and cultural identity in order to come to terms with the new practices and discourses they encounter and to establish some kind of membership in the new community (see also Norton, 2000). The process of identity formation is thus a process that is closely related to, and is transformed and negotiated across, time and space. Examining identity issues in a time of rapid global change is thus a central research challenge for literacy research which draws on post-structuralist and postmodern theories.

Research on issues of identity has lately been extended significantly through narrative research. In Chapter 1 in this part, Golden and Lanza contribute to this body of research in their analysis of adult migrants' narratives on language learning and literacy. Wedin, in Chapter 2, focuses on the role of literacy in the negotiation and construction of identity by unaccompanied asylum-seeking children, and shows – like Golden and Lanza – that migrants have agency and refuse to be constructed and categorized as victims; rather, they use the resources available to them to navigate in a complex setting and to construct and perform identities. Bagga-Gupta's research on identity construction – Chapter 3 in Part 1 – approaches the subject from another perspective, focusing on how identities and languages – or language varieties – are made visible or invisible in social practices and policy-textual worlds across time and space.

References

Man, J.L.C. (2010) Classroom discourse and the construction of learner and teacher identities. In M. Martin-Jones, A.M. de Meija and N.H. Hornberger (eds) *Encyclopedia of Language and Education, Vol. 3: Oral Discourse and Education* (2nd edn, pp. 121–134). New York: Springer.

Norton, B. (2000) *Identity and Language Learning: Gender, Ethnicity and Educational Change.* Harlow: Longman/Pearson Education.

1 Narratives on Literacies: Adult Migrants' Identity Construction in Interaction

Anne Golden and Elizabeth Lanza

Introduction

The ways in which people use and evaluate reading and writing are embedded in conceptions of knowledge and identity (Prinsloo & Baynham, 2008), while narratives provide insight into views of the self and other within a cultural context, and hence identity. The relationship between narrative and identity can be perceived as operating at various levels, as De Fina (2003) points out, including the use of narrative resources identifying the speaker as a member of a specific community, the use of stories through which social roles are negotiable and the use of the negotiation of membership into communities that share common beliefs and values. Among these common beliefs and values are ideological stances toward literacy. In this chapter, we will address the issue of identity construction that occurs in the presentation and positioning of self in social experiences related to literacy and language learning in the narratives of migrants to Norway. As migrants encounter new languages and cultures, they also encounter new dimensions to literacy, either initial literacy or further literacy in a new language. Migrants' narratives inevitably involve ideological stances toward language learning and literacy and are thus fruitful sites for investigating identity construction in interaction.

Literacy is here understood in line with 'New Literacy Studies' as 'situated social practices embedded within relations of culture and power in specific contexts' (Prinsloo & Baynham, 2008: 2). Construing literacy as (a set of) social practices, studies within this perspective emphasize 'what people do with literacy' (Barton & Hamilton, 2000: 9) and thus encompass the negotiations of selves within these different relations. Hence literacy practices involve values, attitudes, ideologies and social relationships – in sum, how people in a particular culture construct literacy and how they talk about literacy and make sense of it. According to Street (1993), literacy practices are not observable units of behaviour since they involve values, attitudes, feelings and social relationships, including people's awareness of literacy, constructions of literacy and discourses of literacy. Literacy *events*, however, involve reading and writing, and the conception of events stresses the situated, contextualized nature of literacy, that is that literacy always exists in a sociocultural context (Barton & Hamilton, 2000; Lewis *et al.*, 2007).

Through the lens of narratives of personal experience in conversational interaction, we will investigate various ways through which adult migrants position themselves and provide ideological stances towards language learning and literacy, and thus construct identities. We will examine the choice of narratives the adult migrants introduce into an interaction and the linguistic resources the individual employs in the performance of the narratives in interaction. Both language learning and literacy are critical in a postmodern text-based society like Norway, and success in these domains empowers individuals, providing them with added social capital. We will explore these issues through an interactional analysis involving highly skilled migrants with different cultural and linguistic backgrounds.

In the discussion that follows, we first present the notion of identity that motivates our study and in particular the issue of identity in narrative. Stance-taking, agency and categorization are important components in identity construction and will be brought up in this regard. Then we present current research on literacy that focuses on identity and narrative. Subsequently, we present the database that ultimately forms the core of our analysis. In conclusion, we discuss the implications of our results for language education of understandings of complex blendings of cultural and linguistic diversity in communities and institutions, and of new cultural identities and practices.

Identity in Narrative

A recurring theme in narrative inquiry, framed within a post-structuralist approach to the study of the self and the other, is the notion of identity, or rather *identities* (Bamberg *et al.*, 2007; Benwell & Stokoe, 2006). The individual can negotiate and construct many identities along various social axes, including ideological stances to literacy (Lanza & Svendsen, 2007). The approach to the study of identities taken in this chapter is a constructionist one in which identities are perceived as negotiated and emergent in interpersonal communication – the study of how identity emerges at various analytical levels and how these resources gain social meaning (cf. Bucholtz & Hall, 2005).

Narratives structure our experience, our knowledge and our thoughts (Brockmeier & Carbaugh, 2001: 1) and provide a window to the study of identity. Emphasizing the constructionist nature of identity, Benwell and Stokoe (2006: 138) underscore the role of narrative in this process, portraying

... identity as performed rather than as prior to language, as dynamic rather than fixed, as culturally and historically located, as constructed in interaction with other people and institutional structures, as continuously remade, and as contradictory and situational.... Thus the practice of narration involves the 'doing' of identity, and because we can tell different stories we can construct different versions of self.

The sociolinguistic literature on narrative has been highly influenced by Labov and Waletsky (1967) and the ensuing reformulations in Labov (1972) with an emphasis on a closed temporal order in discourse and with a focus on the narrative monologue, the so-called 'big stories' or canonical form of narratives. More recent approaches, referred to as a new narrative turn, have taken stock of this approach by examining 'small stories', or non-canonical forms of narratives – narrative fragments or snippets of talk (Georgakopoulou, 2007). A dimensional approach to the study of narrative proposed already by Ochs and Capps (2001) covers the span between the 'big' and the 'small' stories in which a continuum of possibilities is outlined for five different dimensions of narratives: tellership, tellability, embeddedness, linearity and moral stance. The Labovian approach has been anchored at one end of the continuum, for example including 'one active teller, highly tellable account, relatively detached from surrounding talk and activity, linear temporal and causal organization, and certain, constant moral stance' (Ochs & Capps, 2001: 20). More recent approaches to the study of narrative include other possibilities at various points on the continuum and hence allow for a more in-depth study of emergent identity in interaction. Small stories are also called *narratives-in-interaction* (Georgakopoulou, 2006), and this term underpins the idea that these stories are not merely isolated fragments in the interaction but that they are inherent to the activity or performance. Baynham (2011) highlights the importance of taking such small stories into account in interviews in addition to the range of non-canonical narrative types (generic/ iterative, future/hypothetical and negative).

Identity construction in narrative has also been studied through a closer look at the categorization strategies a narrator employs, as 'self-identities are ... often built on the basis of opposition or contrast with others' (De Fina, 2003: 139). In this regard, we may ask what kind of categories are used for self and other description and which ones are the most salient. Moreover, as narratives are often built around actions, we may investigate what kinds of actions and reactions (and implicitly what kinds of values and norms) are associated with those categories. This approach is particularly fruitful for investigating identity construction in relation to language learning and literacy as migrants usually have first-hand experience with these challenges and thus have many stories to tell that involve both literacy events and stories with evaluations of their own and others' success and failure. The focus in our analyses is on how migrant adults talk about, and make sense of, language learning and literacy and hence how they talk about and make sense of themselves and others in particular settings. Autobiographical narratives (cf. Pavlenko, 2007) are indeed important sites for identity construction as they can provide an opportunity to the speaker for negotiating an identity of empowered agency in discourse. Agency is an interesting dimension to the study of identity as it is the 'socioculturally mediated capacity to act' (Ahearn, 2001). Within an immigrant context, agency and power are closely interconnected. Indeed the notion of literacy itself has a power dimension with some literacies more highly evaluated than others. As Purcell-Gates (2007: 3) notes, literacy is 'always constructed and enacted within social and political contexts and subject to the implications of differing power relationships'.

Through personal narratives, individuals take a stance to language learning and literacy. According to Johnstone (2009: 30), 'Stance is generally understood to have to do with the methods, linguistic and other, by which interactants create and signal relationships with the propositions they utter and with the people they interact with'. In the sociolinguistic literature, there are many key themes that fall under the theoretical notion of stance, with the focus being on the process of indexicalization (Jaffe, 2009: 13). In telling stories involving literacy experiences from before adult migrants arrive in a new country as well as in their new country of residence, they construct trajectories of time and space in their stance-taking perspectives towards literacy practices. And hence they actively engage in identity construction both through their choice of narratives on literacies and through their choice of indexical resources in their narratives on literacies. As Pavlenko (2007: 179) notes, 'To acknowledge the performative nature of narratives, microanalysis of form pays close attention to ways in which linguistic and narrative devices are deployed to serve storytellers' interactional goals and to construct particular selves'.

Literacy and Identity

Current research on literacy has also brought identity into the realm of study. As there has been a move from a skill-based view of literacy, or a view of literacy as cognitive processes enacted independent of people's motivations, interests and other social practices (Street, 1984), to 'an interest in foregrounding the actor or agent in literate and social practices' (Moje *et al.*, 2009: 416), the issue of identity has been increasingly brought to the fore. For example, the social turn in literacy theory and research has resulted in studies of identity's relationship to literacy and literacy's relationship to identity, studies that are called *literacy-and-identity studies* by Moje *et al.* (2009). This move has drawn attention to the role of texts and literacy practices as resources for identity construction. As Miller and Kirkland (2010: 91) point out 'These two shifts in literacy studies – the social turn and a focus on identity – allow for a more equitable view on literacy'.

When talking about literacy events involving others, people often use different labels to characterize or evaluate interactants' actions and hence categorize them. 'Identity labels can be used to stereotype, privilege, or marginalize readers and writers' (Moje *et al.*, 2009: 416), and depending on the value of these labels (positive or negative), they may have a profound impact on the individual. The labels and the literacy practices associated with them may play a role both in an individual's self-identification and in how others perceive the individual. As such, these labels are important contributors to the individual's identity constructions. Some literacy-and-identity studies are motivated by attention being paid to people's new textual practices, and particularly to the agency and power that people may demonstrate when they engage in these practices.

People do identity work as they engage in the practices of everyday life. Studying the doing and representing of identities and studying the narration of identities in action (Georgakopoulou, 2007) are both likely to be 'a productive means of documenting how identities shape the take up or performance of literate practices and vice versa, in large because people move from space to space, position to position, discourse community to discourse community, interaction to interaction, and text to text' (Moje *et al.*, 2009: 430). Hence narratives provide an interesting locus for examining identity construction in relation to literacy, as we take into account stance-taking, categorization strategies and inevitably the degree of agency the speaker negotiates in interaction. A focus on narratives on literacies can thus provide us with a window to migrants' identity construction by showing how individuals make sense of, contest and ultimately transform the culturally, historically and socially based literacy practices they encounter in their trajectories across time and space.

Methodology

The data, which form the basis of this study, come from a database of interactions with migrant doctors, consisting of audio-taped semi-structured and open-ended interviews. These data are part of the SKI project: *Språk, Kultur, Identitet/Language, Culture and Identity in Migrant Narratives,* financed by the Research Council of Norway, 2008–2012. The data were collected using focus groups, varying between two to three adult migrants in interaction with one or two interviewers. Focus group interviews are 'carefully planned discussions designed to obtain perceptions on a defined area of interest in a permissive, non-threatening environment' (Krueger, 1994: 6). Marková *et al.* (2007) promote focus groups as a methodological tool, an analytical means for exploring socially shared knowledge. Interestingly enough, as Relaño Pastor (2010: 83) notes, '… narratives have not been addressed in the focus group literature as an interactional object of study, whose sense-making and argumentative character disclose, more than any other discursive activity, participants' opinions and attitudes about several social issues', which is the purpose of this study. The advantage of using focus groups is that this form of conversation is dynamic in that it enables the participants the possibility to react to one another, to be challenged by one another, to compare experiences and values and to be reminded of similar or contrary experiences. It invites to a freer flow of conversation, compared to an interview. As a whole, it provides natural talk in a situation in which the interviewer has the opportunity to back off and be less visible. A small focus group is easier to manage as it gives the participants less competition in talking and hence we may refer to such interviews as focus group conversations.

Participants

The participants in our focus group conversations are doctors who have lived and worked in Norway for several years. They were recruited among the participants at a lecture given by the first author on the issue of Norwegian as a second language, addressed to a group of medical doctors with a migrant background. This study is based on one particular focus group conversation. Sarah and Angela, two African women, are talking to the researcher, Anne. Sarah has lived in Norway and Sweden since she left her home country at the age of 19 in the late 1970s as a refugee. Sarah speaks predominantly Swedish. The Scandinavian languages form a dialect continuum linguistically speaking, and in communication between Norwegians and Swedes, each will speak his/her language often with some accommodation to the other. Angela came to Norway in the mid-1960s as a refugee at the age of 18. Both women moved back to their respective African countries of origin to live with their families in the 1990s and spent between six and eight years working there. Finally, both ended up returning to Norway. They were still working as professionals at that time of the recordings. The conversation took place in the researcher's home.

The narratives

The entire interview in the focus group conversation may be seen as an overarching narrative (Riessman, 1993) or autobiography since the participants tell and co-construct their lives as migrants to Norway. In the focus group, the interviewer used a semi-structured approach and focused on three different periods in the women's lives. The first period was intended to be around the time of migration to Norway, and questions about expectations concerning their future lives and their challenges entering the county were asked. The following period to focus on was to be some years later, when the first challenges were overcome. The final period was the here and now, the present situation, and the participants were asked to reflect on their lives. The topics initiated were mainly about their encounters with a new language and culture, and the questions were related to their memories, reactions and evaluations of the process. They were particularly encouraged to tell stories about particular events. In doing so, the women told and evaluated several narratives from other periods in their lives. The main overarching narrative thus contains many smaller narratives or small stories, some of which are indeed snippets of talk (Georgakopoulou, 2007). As such, the women's narratives vary along the continuum of narrative dimensions outlined by Ochs and Capps (2001): tellership, tellability, embeddedness, linearity and moral stance.

The topics that are elicited in the conversational segments presented in the analyses are about literacy, and language and culture learning, both in regard to the migrant doctors themselves and in regard to their patients. The analytical tools in this study comprise lexical choice, particularly the choice of pronouns and certain verbs and other categorization strategies, the use of constructed dialogue, as well as foregrounding and backstaging of elements, as analysed in the story-world (in the context in which the story is situated) or in the storytelling world (in the context in which the story is told, that is in the focus group conversation).

The literacy events presented in these narratives deal with cultural practices of both reading and writing. The narratives also deal with reflections on the importance of literacy skills for immigrants/refugees in Norway. The focus in our analyses is hence on how migrant adults talk about, make sense of and evaluate, literacy and hence how they talk about, evaluate and make sense of themselves and others in particular settings. In other words, through their narration of literacy events, the African women doctors construct and negotiate their identities in the focus group conversations.

Identity Negotiation in Narrative: *Once a Refugee Always a Refugee*

Among the different identities Angela and Sarah negotiate in interaction – immigrants from the old days, Scandinavians, highly educated doctors, well-integrated women, individuals with no material needs – their identities as refugees are a recurrent motif. Drawing on Goffman's (1981) classical theatrical metaphor, in which there are front stages and backstages, we may say that although their identities as refugees come to the front stage at times in interaction, they nonetheless persistently loom on the backstage at other times. This recurrent identity construction on the front stage does not necessarily bring in accounts of literacy events; however, it forms an important backdrop for the many narratives on particular literacy events.

Sarah and Angela negotiate their identities as refugees in interaction with Anne as they talk about learning Norwegian in general and in particular how some of their patients struggle to learn the language. Both women are very aware of the situation refugees are in nowadays and that being a refugee has indeed become more challenging (see Wedin, Chapter 2 concerning children as asylum seekers in Sweden). Angela even points out how much easier the situation was in the mid-1960s and tells how different humanitarian organizations even competed for her to come to their country, including a Norwegian organization that she decided to go along with. At that time, she was assigned a host family. Nowadays, however, no one competes for refugees anymore.

In the focus group conversation, Sarah and Angela co-construct an extended narrative of the type that Baynham (2011: 66) refers to as a 'generic or iterative narrative', which deals with what typically happens or what happens repeatedly. Refugees are said to move from one country to another, just looking for a place where they might live, as Sarah (S) points out in the excerpt presented in Example 1, and Angela (A) blames the system for the problem.

Example 1

1. S: Men så kommer det.
2. Gjør du ett eller annet, også kommer det massa papirer
3. og "yes, he has been in that and that country ja,
4. han har varit i det og det landet, det og det landet".
5. Men har jo forsøkat å bosette seg bara.
6. Og få lite fritt=
7. Anne: Mm

8. S: =fritt område der han kan få bli.
9. A: Og Schengen blir at han sklir ut.

Example 1 (English translation)

1. S: But then it comes.
2. If you do something or another, and then there's a lot of paperwork
3. og "yes, he has been in that and that country yes",
4. "he has been in that and that country, that and that country".
5. But has just tried to settle down.
6. And get little free=
7. Anne: Mm
8. S: =free area where he can remain.
9. A: And Schengen is why he slips out.

Sarah's switch to English in the direct speech cited in Example 1 indexes an institutional treatment of refugees. The current Dublin II Regulation[1] decrees that the asylum seeker's case be treated by the first country of arrival in Europe, a regulation that complicates the situation for refugees. Initially, Sarah refers to refugees in the third person, as 'the *ones* who do not have a choice'. She then states that she sees the refugees' problem and takes the stance that this is 'våra problem' ('*our* problem'), and 'our' refers to all former refugees, also despite the fact that 'we' are integrated, as noted in Example 2. In lines 3–7, she points out that despite identities as Scandinavians in the system, refugees will always be refugees, a point she reasserts several times in the interaction.

Example 2

1. S: Og derfor sitter vi her nu, [når vi er vel integrerade]=
2. A: [jo, jo, jo, jo]
3. S: = og, og har alt og vi er svensker og nordmenn og allting=
4. A: Mm
5. S: = i systemet=
6. A: Mm
7. S: = men vi i sjelen er vi flyktninger.

Example 2 (English translation)

1. S: And that is why we are sitting here, [while we are well integrated]=
2. A: [yeah, yeah, yeah, yeah]
3. S: =and have everything and we are Swedes and Norwegians and everything=
4. A: Mm

5. S: = in the system =
6. A: Mm
7. S: = but we in our souls we are refugees.

As De Fina (2003: 23) points out, 'Through pronominal choice, narrators express personalized or depersonalized views of experience and construct themselves in stories as socially or personally oriented individuals'. Sarah foregrounds her identity as a refugee, bringing it to the front stage, through the use of inclusive first person pronouns, concluding that being a refugee is an inalienable part of her soul. Angela co-constructs this identity through her persistent positive backchannelling. Sarah identifies with various unproblematic categories in the system such as Swedes and Norwegians, yet she considers her implicitly 'true' identity as a refugee is still present, as part of her soul. According to Sarah then, refugees will always construct a refugee identity despite their construction of other socially acceptable identities.

Identity Negotiation as Categorization: *We* and *Them*

In Example 3, talking about Norwegian language and culture, Sarah reflects on her way of living in Scandinavia about five years after her arrival as a refugee. The researcher, Anne, had initiated the topic for both Sarah and Angela by asking about their lives in Scandinavia. Sarah engages in a narrative about a literacy event that occurred after her return to Africa. Through the narrative of this event, she negotiates her identity as both an African and a Scandinavian woman. Sarah was waiting in line to get a visa, and as the line was long, she started reading, as she points out in line 1; however, her expectations about reading and standing in line are not matched by the others in line, as we note in her narrative (line 5).

Example 3

1. S: Jag kan ta min bok og stå i kø og lesa min bok.
2. A: Mm
3. S: Og jag kan se at flere går forbi meg bara. Og jag sejer: "Hva er det som skjer".
4. A: Mm
5.→S: "Ja, men du står der og leser", sier dom. "Men jag står og leser i kø"
           =
6. A: Mm
7. S: = "jeg går inte utanfor".
8. Anne: Ja

9. A: [Mm]
10. S: [Og] da kan dom inte forstå at jag inte passar på min plats, hva.
11. A: Mm
12. S: Men når jag står der, da passar jag min plats, så tenker jag va?
13. Anne: Ja.
14. S: Inte at [jag]=
15. A: [Mm]
16. S: = ska kriga for den platsen.
17. A: Mm
18. S: Men det [er]=
19. A: [Mm]
20. S: = ikke så dom tenker=
21. A: Mm
22. S: = "når hon sitter og bara leser og slappar av, betyder det at [hon har @ hela dagen]"
23. A: "[hon bryr seg ikke]"
24. S: "Hele @ =
25. Anne: Hele [dagen]
26. S: = [dagen] @ og står der hva".

Example 3 (English translation)

1. S: I can take my book and stand in line and read my book.
2. A: Mm
3. S: And I can see that several people are just walking past me. And I say: "What's happening".
4. A: Mm
5. →S: "Yes, but you are standing there and reading", they say. "But I am standing and reading in line" =
6. A: Mm
7. S: = "I am not going out of it".
8. Anne: Yeah.
9. A: [Mm]
10. S: [and] then they cannot understand that I am not watching out for my place, what.
11. A: Mm
12. S: But when I am standing there, I am watching out for my place, that's how I think right?
13. Anne: Yeah.
14. S: Not that [I]=
15. A: [Mm]
16. S: = am going to fight for the place.

17. A: Mm
18. S: But it [is]=
19. A: [Mm]
20. S: = not how they think =
21. A: Mm
22. S: = "when she is sitting and just reading and relaxing, that means [she has @ the whole day]"
23. A: "[she doesn't care]"
24. S: "Whole @ =
25. Anne: Whole [day]
26. S: =[day] @ and stands there what".

    Sarah polarizes two views on literacy practices through her narrative of this literacy event, and thereby negotiates an identity that contrasts with that of those in her home country. Once again pronominal choice, as noted above, accentuates this contrast as Sarah contests being passed up in line, saying that *they* cannot understand (line 10). *They* think that reading is a full-time activity that cannot be combined with any other activity. Indirectly, drawing on common knowledge among the participants in the focus group conversation, Sarah indicates that she is engaged in a Scandinavian practice and it is natural for her to read while waiting in line. In short, she constructs a Scandinavian identity. The local African understanding of the literacy practice of reading that is implicit in Sarah's narrative associates reading as a separate activity, which is not relevant in the visa application context. Sarah, however, evaluates that she can do both activities at once, as she points out in line 12: 'så tenker *jag* va?' ('that's how I think right?'), while this is 'ikke så *dom* tenker' ('not how they think') (line 20). The use of pronouns (*jag* 'I' - *dom* 'they') reveals her sense of belonging in this regard, as she marks contrasts in personal stances to literacy practices. As Jaffe (2009: 9) notes, '… personal stance is always achieved through comparison and contrast with other relevant persons and categories' as speakers '… lay claim to particular social and/or moral identities'. Interestingly, in line 16 Sarah, who was a war refugee, uses the verb *kriga* ('fight'; literally 'wage war') in her description of reacting to those passing her up in the line. By indicating her reticence to react, she negotiates an identity of one who has cross-cultural understanding in contrast to 'dom' ('them').

    Sarah's use of constructed dialogue (Tannen, 2007) is also worth noting. In lines 3–5, the conflict or complication of the narrative is highlighted by constructed dialogue enacted out by Sarah and includes both her own and the others' voices. Among the many forms constructed dialogue can take, Tannen (2007: Chapter 4) names the following: dialogue representing what was not said, dialogue as instantiation, summarizing dialogue, choral dialogue, dialogue as inner speech and as inner speech of others, dialogue constructed by a listener, dialogue fading from indirect to direct, dialogue including vague referents and dialogue involving nonhuman speakers, for example, pets. In lines 22–26, Sarah refers to what the others are supposedly thinking. Both Angela and Anne chime in and co-construct the purported inner dialogue, and hence co-construct Sarah's stance towards literacy, an activity that can co-exist with other activities. This conception of literacy is in sharp contrast with that of the others in the line. Hence through constructed dialogue and pronominal choice, Sarah identifies herself with a certain literacy practice which is at odds with that of her original home country, and it is through her narrative that she negotiates with the other participants in the focus group conversation a Scandinavian identity.

Identity as Being Different

Subsequent to Sarah's narrative account in Example 3, Angela reflects upon her way of living when she was a student in Norway and compares this to Sarah's patience with the people in line with her. Angela says that she has always felt herself as different even if she sees herself as well-integrated, engaging in Norwegian cultural activities salient for certain groups at a certain time of history (going to a particular club, participating in the feminist movement). Norway during the 1960s, before the discovery of oil in the North Sea, was very different from the Norway of today. Angela arrived into a very 'white' society, but it was a society in which people liked to think of themselves as very socially engaged. Angela went to a rural area where her dark skin was even more salient. In rural areas in Norway in the mid-1960s, the average knowledge of African culture was often very stereotypical, merely lots of animals and very primitive life. Angela recalls how some boys uttered 'hongabongahonga' when she passed by, and she interpreted this as 'monkey talk'. Angela highlighted a feeling of being different, as having a non-Norwegian component to her identity, as always being part of her, an identity she constructs through her *choice* of narratives.

Prior to her other narratives concerning literacy, Angela provides a backdrop for how she herself felt she was different in Norwegian society. She was well-integrated, but there was 'alltid det der, at jeg er ikke norsk' ('always that there, that I was not Norwegian'). And it was this difference that she always tried to accentuate. Accordingly, Angela reveals the tension between the categories of being well-integrated in society but not being Norwegian. She further explained that her solution for dealing with her feeling of isolation was to emphasize the differences by engaging in socially unusual activities, by highlighting her difference, in order to defend herself: 'det var en måte å forsvare meg selv til å bli borte i- i den norske' ('it was a means to defend myself to disappear in - in the Norwegian (context)'). One of those activities Angela engaged in was to read English language newspapers, an activity she enjoyed. Although this is a commonplace activity today, at the time the events took place in Angela's story, such practice was quite marked in Norwegian society. Angela opens her narrative by saying that she went to a rather fashionable café to read the newspaper, the Grand Café on the main street of Oslo.

Example 4

1. A: Og det var ikke en eneste svart jente som dro der=
2. Anne: Nei.
3. A: = på den tida. Ja. Og jeg gjør det enda.
4. Anne: Ja.
5. A: Og jeg er en av de få svarte som enda er der.
6. Anne: Ja.
7. A: Så jeg likte å provosere fram de her (.) hva kan man kalle det da, ikke hindringer, men (.) de ytterpunktene.
8.   Men allikevel når jeg kommer der, så ville jeg vise at jeg er sørafrikansk (.)
9.   Og jeg leste engelske aviser (.) Til og med enda i dag, men i den tiden jeg var student.

Example 4 (English translation)

1. A: Og there wasn't a single black girl that went there =
2. Anne: No.
3. A: = at that time. Yeah. And I still do it.
4. Anne: Yeah.
5. A: And I am one of the few blacks who are still there.
6. Anne: Yeah.
7. A: So I liked provoking those (.) what do you call it then, not obstacles, but (.) the extremes.
8.   But anyway when I get there, then I wanted to show that I was South African (.)
9.   And I read English newspapers (.) Even still today, but back then I was a student.

Angela summed up her reading activities: 'Så det ble en vane. Og jeg begynte å merke at jeg hadde en vane som (.) som definerte meg da. Som ikke-værende' ('So it became a habit. And I started noticing that I had a habit

(.) that defined me then. As not present'). Angela highlights her black South African identity in lines 5 and 8, and constructs a rebel identity by using the verb 'provosere' ('provoke') (line 7) and implicitly by noting she was a student (line 9) during a time when there was student unrest in society. Through this, Angela expresses her lack of assimilation into mainstream Norwegian society. And this she couples with a literacy event.

Literacy in English and reading English language newspapers was a very exclusive activity in Norway around 1970. In Oslo of that time, only a few places sold international newspapers since there were not many people who would read English for pleasure nor were there many tourists. At that time, there were still not many black people even in Oslo and according to her it was very rare to see a black woman in a café. Through her behavior, she attempted to negotiate an identity of independence; she went to places where she was one of a kind – and as such, highly visible – and she performed an act that could be interpreted either as foreign/international or as intellectual/well-educated – she read a newspaper in a language that not many people felt comfortable with, and it was a prestigious language. As Blommaert (2005: 205) points out, 'In order for an identity to be established, it has to be *recognized* by others'. And Angela sought to have this side of her recognized. Through her activity, she engaged in an act of identity that implicitly attributed to her a high degree of agency.

In line 7 Angela further negotiates an empowered agency in interaction with the interviewer and Sarah when she states that she likes to provoke in order to bring out what she calls 'ytterpunktene' ('the extremes'). Nonetheless, these provocations, these acts, positioned her as an outsider. Even though Angela participated in the feminist movement and radical student life with the so-called 1968 generation, there was still something different with her way of living, as she was always eager to point out.

Literacy in English, particularly at the time Angela refers to in her narratives, was particularly prestigious, not only in Norway but also in African countries. As Purcell-Gates (2007: 3) states:

Being ideologically bound, different literacies are recognized by the established institutions of time and place as more or less legitimate. Some literacies provide access to power and material well-being, others are marked as substandard and deficient.

This relates, furthermore, to what Blommaert (2005, 2010) refers to as *orders of indexicality*, whereby, for example one language may be on a higher order on a scale and thus have more prestige. As Blommaert (2010: 6) notes, 'Orders of indexicality define the dominant lines for senses of belonging, for identities and roles in society... '. And English carries 'the heavy ideological load it has acquired in contemporary globalization: it is the language of upward globalised mobility' (Blommaert, 2008: 195). Moreover, literacy in English is indeed perceived as a key to power and material well-being. In Example 5, this stance-taking towards English as a prestigious language is further revealed in Angela's narrative in which she introduces her father's reaction to her first husband, who had been a student in her home country.

Example 5

1. Anne: Men, men, eh, mannen din, snakket han engelsk eller?
2. A: Engelsk.
3. Anne: Ja. Mm.
4. A: Og da jeg gifta meg med min mann nummer én (.) så spurte min pappa (.) da han fikk vite at Angela har tenkt å gifte seg med Pete i Oslo.
5. Anne: Ja.
6. A: Så sa min pappa: "Hvem er denne Pete?" (.)
7. Og så sa (.) min fetter som studerte medisin (.)
8. "He was, he's the best English-speaking student in the University". Og da likte pappan min det.
9. Anne: [Ja]
10. S: [Mm]
11. A: Selv om han ikke visste hvilken [familie]=
12. S: [Ja]
13. A: = han kom fra.

Example 5 (English translation)

1. Anne: But, but eh, your husband, did he speak English or what?
2. A: English.
3. Anne: Yeah. Mm.
4. A: And when I got married with my husband number one (.) then my daddy asked me (.) when he got to know that Angela was thinking about getting married with Pete in Oslo =
5. Anne: Yeah.
6. A: Then my daddy said: "Who is this Pete?" (.)
7. And then my cousin said (.) who studied medicine (.)
8. "He was, he's the best English-speaking student in the University". And then my daddy liked that.
9. Anne: [Yeah]
10. S: [Mm]
11. A: Even though he didn't know what [family]=

12. S: [Yeah]
13. A: = he came from.

In lines 8 and 11 we learn that Angela's choice of a future husband has approval from her father even though he knows nothing of the man's family. And this is due to the fact that he is purportedly 'the best English-speaking student in the University' (line 8). Interestingly, Angela flags her cousin's response to her father's question in line 8 in this constructed dialogue by actually uttering it in English. Moreover, we note in line 7 that Angela points out that her cousin was studying medicine, a prestigious subject. As Pennycook (2010: 32) points out, 'Language practices are repeated, social and meso-political practices that mediate between social structure and individuated action'. In Example 5, we see that the practice of English is highly socially evaluated by Angela's father. This narrative serves to further Angela's identity construction through highlighting her differentness as prestigious. She uses competence in English and literacy practices involving English as a platform for this identity construction.

Literacy as a Reaction to Social Injustice

Some time before the focus group conversation, there had been an incident in an Oslo park involving a black man who had a malaise and felt badly treated by the ambulance drivers when they arrived. This incident was interpreted by many as racism, and it was at the top of the news for weeks. In Example 6, the interviewer had initially referred to the category of Norwegian and ethnic identity, a topic that clearly agitates Sarah to tell about her reaction to the media event. Sarah had been greatly upset by this event as she thought of something potentially happening to her children, as they are not only 'svarta' ('black') (line 5) but also 'afrikanere' ('Africans') (line 7), as Sarah points out, and 'det er gutter' ('it's boys') (line 8), as Angela was quick to add to the litany of identifying characteristics. Sarah repeats that it's boys and adds 'og de er unga' ('and they are young') (line 9). Moreover, they could 'havna i masse konfliktar' ('end up in a lot of conflicts') (lines 9-11). Sarah's choice of the verb 'havne' ('end up in') accentuates how her sons could be victims.

Example 6

1. S: Altså min første reaksjon når jeg hörde om den her ambulansen på Sofienbergsparken (.) var jag hadde så lyst å skrive til Tove Strand. Jag jobbade på X da =
2. A: Mm

3. S: = og seja. "Vet du hva? Det kunne ha varit mina barn". (.) Det er en sånn følelse en har, hva?
4. Anne: Ja.
5. S: Mina barn er svarta=
6. A: Mm
7. S: = men dom er inte bare [afrikanere]
8. A: [og det er gutter]
        Det er [gutter]
9. S: [og] det er gutter. Og de er unga. Dom kan havna i [masse]=
10. Anne: [Ja]
11. S: = konfliktar og [sånt]her =
12. Anne: [Ja]
13. S: = Og då bli dom dömnde på grunn av deras farg=
14. Anne: [Ja]
15. A: [Mm]
16. S: = inte på grunn av hva dom gjör.

Example 6 (English translation)

1. S: So my first reaction when I heard about that ambulance at Sofienberg Park (.) was I wanted to write to Tove Strand. I was working at X then =
2. A: Mm
3. S: = and say: "You know what? That could have been my children". (.) It is the feeling one has, isn't it?
4. Anne: Yeah
5. S: My children are black =
6. A: Mm
7. S :   = but they are not only [Aficans]
8. A: [and it's boys]
        It's [boys]
9. S: [and] it's boys. And they are young. They can end up in a [lot]=
10. Anne: [Yeah]
11. S: = conflicts and [stuff]=
12. Anne: [Yeah]
13. S: = And then they will be judged on the basis of their color =
14. Anne: [Yeah]
15. A: [Mm]
16. S: = not on the basis of what they do.

When Sarah talks about this incident, she initially says that she was provoked and wanted to *write* to Tove Strand (line 1), who at the time was the director of one of the hospitals in Oslo where Sarah was working and also a former minister in the Norwegian government. Sarah felt that not to be met professionally because of skin color could have happened to her children (line 3), as she points out in constructed dialogue. The way she thought of contesting such an outrageous event in her eyes was through writing. Literacy had become part of her way of reacting to injustice, a practice that is highly salient in Norwegian society. People often write to various public institutions to complain about things they disagree with or find unjust, and the addressees are obliged to answer such written inquiries within a certain deadline. There is a common belief in the Nordic countries that conflicts can be resolved by authorities and hence formal inquiries are taken seriously. In Norway now the catchphrases are *dialogue* and *transparency* both in politics and in public/government offices. Literacy plays a key role in society and the socialization of migrants into these literacy practices is important. Through her stance-taking in her personal narrative of such practice in her own life, Sarah negotiates an identity of inclusion in Norwegian society and by addressing herself directly to the director of the hospital, a high-profile public figure, she constructs an identity of empowerment – that her involvement could potentially mean something for society.

About Learning the Language and the Culture

As doctors, Sarah and Angela have patients, both Norwegians and those originally from other countries, as pointed out in Example 7 (lines 1–3). They are both very concerned with migrants, and particularly refugees, and their need to learn about Norwegian language and culture. Migrants have a need to read and write in Norwegian so that they can be agents in their own lives, able to understand the system and participate in the society in which they live. As Sarah points out in line 10, these individuals usually realize this necessity after a while.

Example 7

1. S: Jag mener jag har, jag kjenner folk. Jag har pasienter som er analfabeter som ikke kan lese og skrive, [folk fra].
2. A: [Jo]
3. S: = Somalia. Som har varit her i 10–12 år. (.)
4. S: Og da tenker jeg. Det er det første man skal man skal satse på.
5. A: Mm
6. S: At dom kan lære seg [å lese og skrive].
7. A: [Jo mm]
8. S: At man får jo så mycket beskjeder på papir her.

9. Anne: Mm mm
10. S: Hva ska dom gjöra liksom? Då går dom rundt til andre venner som kan lese. Og det er på måfå.
11. Dom vennerna som leser, kanskje inte beherskar heller og da får dom inte [uppfatta det].
12. A: [De gjør det].

Example 7 (English translation)

1. S: I mean I have, I know people. I have patients who are illiterate who cannot read and write, [people from] =.
2. A: [Yes]
3. S: = Somalia. Who have been here for 10-12 years. (.)
4. And then I think. That is the first thing one should focus on.
5. A: Mm
6. S: That they can learn [to read and write].
7. A: [Yes mm]
8. S: That one gets so many messages on paper here.
9. Anne: Mm mm
10. S: What are they supposed to do? Then they go over to other friends who can read. And that is random.
11. Those friends who read maybe don't master it either and then they don't [understand it].
12. A: [They do that].

To be an agent of one's own life means that the individual is capable of initiating practices that may bring them out of any situations that seem to be disadvantageous. As Baynham (2006: 27) puts it, 'Agency is typically evoked as a response to and challenge to the determination of social structuring'. As Sarah and Angela see it, the only way their patients may get out of their difficult situation in Norway is to learn the Norwegian language and get educated, as pointed out in Example 7. In line 4, Sarah accentuates her stance to the importance of learning the language and culture of the host society as the first thing one should focus on. Many of Sarah and Angela's patients are what Connell (1987: 92) calls 'up against something', an experience caused by social structuring that constrains possible agency, and 'to describe the constraints of the particular situation to which the active individual responds is to describe structure' (Baynham, 2006: 27). Learning a new language, a new semiotic tool, opens up the possibility for agency in the sense described by Norton (2000) and Relaño Pastor and De Fina (2005), highly advantageous resources, particularly for migrants. Sarah constructs a Norwegian identity in her emphasis of the importance of literacy in Norwegian by reiterating in the conversation a common Swedish expression: in order to understand the system, she states, 'det med språket i alle fall, det er a og ø' ('that with language in any case, it is a to z'). She continues, 'For du ska bare kunne språket for om du skal leve her altså' ('For you must learn the language if you are going to live here then'). The emphasis on language and literacy as the key to success in Norwegian society is a salient ideology that both Sarah and Angela espouse.

Empowering the Patient through Literacy

Both Sarah and Angela treated many immigrants and were determined to help their patients deal with their lives in Norway and to participate more effectively in society. One important obstacle to this, they noted, was literacy, a topic brought up in Example 8, a narrative that is actively co-constructed by both Sarah and Angela, with Anne providing positive backchannelling.

Example 8

1. S: Så jag har sendt tre av mine pasienter, fire av mine pasienter til voksenopplæring.
2. Anne: Mm
3. S: Det er jo en del av behandlingen, sejer jag.
4. Anne: Ja [ja]
5. A: [Å ja] Det er viktig.
6. Anne: @
7. A: Det er den psykososiale.
8. S: Ja visst. Du ska klara deg ute=
9. A: Mm
10. S: = og en ting som gjør at du klarar det, er jo å lære deg, lære å [skrive]=
11. A: [Mm]
12. S: = og [lese]=
13. Anne: [Mm]
14. S: = og lære deg [norsk]
15. Anne: [Ja]
16. S: = så går det. (.)
17. A: Fordi det er en vei, og det er en måte å finne seg gjennom det her innviklede systemet.

Example 8 (English translation)

1. S: So I have sent three of my patients, four of my patients to adult education.

2. Anne: Mm
3. S: That is a part of the treatment, I say.
4. Anne: Yeah [yeah]
5. A: [Oh yes]. That is important.
6. Anne: @
7. A: That is the psychosocial.
8. S: Of course. You have to manage out there =
9. A: Mm
10. S: = and one thing that makes you manage is to teach yourself, learn to [write]=
11. A: [Mm]
12. S: = and [read]=
13. Anne: [Mm]
14. S: = and teach yourself [Norwegian]
15. Anne: [Yeah]
16. S: = and there you go. (.)
17. A: Because it is a road, and it is a means to find yourself through this complicated system.

Both doctors assert their empowered agency when dealing with their patients with diminished agency by prescribing adult education, and implicitly, literacy, as part of therapy (lines 1–3) – that in order to manage, the patients needed to learn to read and write and learn Norwegian. Angela concludes in line 17 by referring to literacy as 'en vei' ('a road') their patients must take to manage the complicated system of society, as well as through their illness.

Angela expresses concern about how to make her patients see that education is the way out of their problems, about how to get them motivated, because as she says, the women think 'når de er 40, at livet er over for de' ('when they are 40, life is over for them'). Her goal was to prevent them from going on disability pension, which in essence is to give up and to be disempowered. As a response to this passiveness among her patients, Angela started to act like a teacher, 'to bring the outside in' (Baynham, 2006: 25, 37), as illustrated in Example 9.

Example 9

1. A: Jeg (.) tok kart over land. Jeg underviste geografi i min @ i min behandlingstime. Kart=
2. Anne: Ja
3. A: = over land hvor de kom fra.
4. Anne: Ja

5. A: Og spurte: "Hvilken del er du fra? Bashra?" Også fortalte jeg det jeg visste Bashra=
6. Anne: Ja
7. A: = også viste jeg Sør-Afrika der, og Norge der.
8. Anne: Ja
9. A: Og prøvde å vise den her bevegelsen.
10. S: Mm
11. A: Hvordan de klarte å gå så langt hit.
12. Anne: Ja
13. A: Og så gikk vi gjenom de byene (.) Fra Eritrea hvis hun er fra Eritrea og Bashra.
14. S: Mm
15. A: Så jeg prøvde å være lærer samtidig.

Example 9 (English translation)

1. A: I (.) took a map of countries. I taught geography in my @ in my therapy sessions. Map=
2. Anne: Yeah
3. A: = of countries where they came from.
4. Anne: Yeah
5. A: And asked: "What part are you from? Bashra?" And then I told them that I knew Bashra=
6. Anne: Yeah
7. A: = and then I showed South Africa there, and Norway there.
8. Anne: Yeah
9. A: And tried to show them this here movement.
10. S: Mm
11. A: How they managed to go so far to get here.
12. Anne: Yeah
13. A: And then we went through the cities (.) From Eritrea if she is from Eritrea and Bashra.
14. S: Mm
15. A: So I tried to be a teacher at the same time.

In Example 9, we see how Angela maintains the attention of her interactants, as documented in their continual backchannelling. In her narrative, she portrays how she wanted to empower her patients through lessons in geography by using maps. She uses trajectories of time and space (lines 9 and 11) to highlight their accomplishments. This activity is what resembles 'contingent interaction' (Baynham, 2006: 26), not as a task or a topic but rather as a way to meet them, as a zone where she might be in contact with their experiences. This way of reacting is to be 'locally responsive answerable in a Bakhtinian sense' (Baynham, 2006: 26). Classrooms can be seen as a 'figured world', as Holland *et al.* (1998) state,

> ... an 'as-if' domain; a simplified, parallel world in which positioned human agents carry out a manageable range of meaningful acts aided by material and symbolic artefacts. Its significance lies in the context it provides for the formation of social identities and institutions.

Through her narrative in Example 9, Angela negotiates a teacher identity as she 'underviste geografi' ('taught geography') during her therapy sessions. Through constructed dialogue in line 5, she highlights her role as a teacher. Literacy involves many semiotic resources; through the use of maps and by mapping the trajectories of her patients' migration to Norway, Angela attempted to negotiate an empowered identity for her patients. Through 'reading' maps, her patients would become more aware of their accomplishments and more aware of their sense of place, then and now. And this would be the means to get them on the road to literacy.

Conclusion

Migrants' narratives on literacy foreground the actor or agent in literate and social practices. They can provide insight into the stance that individuals take to the transition to new literacies in a new homeland and hence to their identity construction. Moreover, such narratives display local understandings of the meaning of certain culturally specific literacy practices. The high value attributed to literacy is expressed not only outrightly in the focus group conversation but also implicitly in the two doctors' accounts of how they deal with patients with a migrant background. Their stance-taking in their narratives on literacies reveals their ideologies towards language and literacy, and in the case of Angela, the prestige attributed to literacy in English as well. Through and in their narratives, the two migrant adults actively engage in constructing identities with a high degree of agency. In the case of Angela, who highlights her differentness, we witness in her narratives how she portrays herself as an empowered agent. She does not portray herself as a victim, but rather as someone who accentuates her differentness in such a way that it can be perceived as prestigious, notably through her invoking of literacy practices. Nonetheless, the embedding of the two doctors' identity constructions in the interaction reveals that agency is indeed co-constructed and an interactional achievement, as Al Zidjaly (2009) so clearly points out. Sarah and Angela each provide important feedback to each other's identity constructions and hence contribute, along with the interviewer, to the construction of an empowered identity in the conversation (cf. Lanza, in press).

We suggest that our results have implications for language education, both for the teachers and for the learners/students. Encouraging students to tell their stories in small groups with the teacher is a way for the teacher to give the students the possibility to negotiate different identities, not only as receivers of knowledge but also as experts on their own lives. This will in turn have an impact on the students' own perception of themselves. Small focus groups as the ones in this study prove to be positive environments for triggering the performance of narratives and their evaluation. Through these narratives participants are offered insight into complex blendings of cultural and linguistic diversity in various communities and institutions and of new cultural identities and practices.

In technologically advanced societies such as Scandinavia, reading and writing activities are embedded in all kinds of everyday activities and are also a common way to react to injustice. This might not be the case for all the communities from which the refugees/migrants have their background experience and hence in many cases, migrants will experience a transition to different understandings of literacy. Teachers' awareness of the different literacy practices the students bring with them to the classroom may contribute to the prevention of misunderstandings and hence provide an environment more conducive to learning a new language. Learners with a migrant background, including refugees, cover an enormous span of literacy competence as the narratives on literacy in this chapter have shown – from a lack of literacy to literacy in higher education. In the classroom, students can become learning resources for one another as individuals often wish to teach and not just learn for themselves. By placing students in such a learning situation is to empower them and a means for them to exercise higher degrees of agency. And it is through their narratives of their personal migrant experience that learners can attempt to negotiate an empowered identity for themselves and others as they move along the road to initial literacy or transitional literacy in a new language.

Transcription Conventions

-	self-interruption
@	giggle or slight laughter
@@@	marked laughter
(.)	short pause
[ ]	overlapping speech
=	latching

52 Part 1: Literacy and Identity in Transition

" "   bracket constructed dialogue
→   indicates the segment in focus
[...]   indicates short segments that have been taken out of the transcription

Notes

(1) http://europa.eu/legislation_summaries/justice_freedom_security/free_movement_of_persons_asylum_immigration/l33153_en.htm

References

Ahearn, L. (2001) Language and agency. *Annual Review of Anthropology* 30, 109–137.
Al Zidjaly, N. (2009) Agency as an interactive achievement. *Language in Society* 38, 177–200.
Bamberg, M., De Fina, A. and Schiffrin, D. (2007) *Selves and Identities in Narrative and Discourse.* Amsterdam: John Benjamins.
Barton, D. and Hamilton, M. (2000) Literacy practices. In D. Barton, M. Hamilton and R. Ivanič (eds) *Situated Literacies: Reading and Writing in Context* (pp. 7–15). New York: Routledge.
Baynham, M. (2006) Agency and contingency in the language learning of refugees and asylum seekers. *Linguistics and Education* 17, 24–39.
Baynham, M. (2011) Stance, positioning, and alignment in narratives of professional experience. *Language in Society* 40, 63–74.
Benwell, B. and Stokoe, E. (2006) *Discourse and Identity.* Edinburgh: Edinburgh University Press.
Blommaert, J. (2005) *Discourse.* Cambridge: Cambridge University Press.
Blommaert, J. (2008) *Grassroots Literacy: Writing, Identity and Voice in Central Africa.* London: Routledge.
Blommaert, J. (2010) *The Sociolinguistics of Globalization.* Cambridge: Cambridge University Press.
Brockmeier, J. and Carbaugh, D. (2001) *Narrative and Identity: Studies in Autobiography, Self and Culture.* Amsterdam: Benjamins.
Bucholtz, M. and Hall, K. (2005) Identity and interaction: A sociocultural linguistic approach. *Discourse Studies* 7 (4/5), 585–614.
Connell, R.W. (1987) *Gender and Power.* London: George Allen & Unwin.
De Fina, A. (2003) *Identity in Narrative: A Study of Immigrant Discourse.* Amsterdam: John Benjamins.
Georgakopoulou, A. (2006) The other side of the story: Towards a narrative analysis of narrative-in-action. *Discourse Studies* 8(2), 235–257.
Georgakopoulou, A. (2007) *Small Stories, Interaction and Identity.* Amsterdam: Benjamins.
Goffman, E. (1981) *Forms of Talk.* Philadelphia: University of Pennsylvania Press.
Holland, D., Lachicotte, W. Jr., Skinner, D. and Cain, C. (1998) *Identity and Agency in Cultural Worlds.* Cambridge, MA: Harvard University Press.
Jaffe, A. (2009) *Stance. Sociolinguistic Perspectives.* Oxford: Oxford University Press.
Johnstone, B. (2009) Stance, style, and the linguistic individual. In A. Jaffe (ed.) *Stance: Sociolinguistic Perspectives* (pp. 29–52). Oxford: Oxford University Press.

Krueger, R. A. (1994) *Focus Groups: A Practical Guide for Applied Research.* Thousand Oaks: Sage.
Labov, W. and Waletsky, J. (1967) Narrative analysis. In J. Helm (ed.) *Essays on the Verbal and Visual Arts* (pp. 12–44). Seattle: University of Washington Press. Reprinted in *Narrative and Life History* 7, 1–38.
Labov, W. (1972) Chapter 9: The transformation of experience in narrative syntax. In *Language in the Inner City.* Philadelphia: University of Pennsylvania Press.
Lanza, E. and Svendsen, B.A. (2007) Tell me who your friends are and I *might* be able to tell you what language(s) you speak: Social network analysis, multilingualism, and identity. *International Journal of Bilingualism* 11 (3), 275–300.
Lanza, E. (in press) Empowering a migrant identity: Agency in narratives of a work experience in Norway. *Sociolinguistic Studies.* Special issue on "Agency and Power in Multilingual Practices".
Lewis, C., Enciso, P. and Moje, E.B. (eds) (2007) *Reframing Sociocultural Research on Literacy.* New York & London: Routledge.
Marková, I., Linell, P., Grossen, M. and Orvig, A.S. (2007) *Dialogue in Focus Groups. Exploring Socially Shared Knowledge.* London: Equinox.
Miller, S.J. and Kirkland, D.E. (eds) (2010) *Change Matters: Critical Essays on Moving Social Justice Research from Theory to Policy.* New York: Peter Lang.
Moje, E.B., Luke, A., Davies, A. and Street, B. (2009) Literacy and identity: Examining the metaphors in history and contemporary research. *Reading Research Quarterly* 44 (4), 415–437.
Norton, B. (2000) *Identity and Language Learning.* London: Longman.
Ochs, E. and Capps, L. (2001) *Living Narrative: Creating Lives in Everyday Storytelling.* Cambridge, MA: Harvard University Press.
Pavlenko, A. (2007) Autobiographical narratives as data in applied linguistics. *Applied Linguistics* 28 (2), 163–188.
Pennycook, A. (2010) *Language as a Local Practice.* London: Routledge.
Prinsloo, M. and Baynham, M. (eds) (2008) *Literacies, Global and Local.* Amsterdam: John Benjamins.
Purcell-Gates, V. (2007) Complicating the complex. In V. Purcell-Gates (ed.) *Cultural Practices of Literacy: Case Studies of Language, Literacy, Social Practice, and Power* (pp. 1–22). Mahwah, NJ: L. Erlbaum.
Relaño Pastor, A.M. (2010) Ethnic categorization and moral agency in 'fitting in' narratives among Madrid immigrant students. *Narrative Inquiry* 20 (1), 82–105.
Relaño Pastor, A.M. and De Fina, A. (2005) Contesting social place: Narratives of language conflict. In M.
Baynham and A. De Fina (eds) *Dislocations/Relocations: Narratives of Displacement* (pp. 36–60). Manchester: St. Jerome.
Riessman, C.K. (1993) *Narrative Analysis.* Newbury Park: Sage.
Street, B. (1984) *Literacy in Theory and Practice.* Cambridge: Cambridge University Press.
Street, B. (ed.) (1993) *Cross-Cultural Approaches to Literacy.* Cambridge: Cambridge University Press.
Tannen, D. (2007) *Talking Voices. Repetition, Dialogue and Imagery in Conversational Discourse.* Cambridge: Cambridge University Press.

2 Literacy in Negotiating, Constructing and Manifesting Identities: The Case of Migrant Unaccompanied Asylum-Seeking Children in Sweden

Åsa Wedin

Introduction

This chapter is concerned with the issue of unaccompanied children who seek asylum in Sweden and the roles literacy plays in their negotiation of identities. Foucault's views of identities as fluid and complex (Canagarajah, 2004; Ivanič, 1997) are taken as a starting point, and the focus is on agency and voice as instruments of power. Unaccompanied asylum-seeking children tend to be regarded as victims in need of assistance. This view may be benevolent, but in this chapter such children will instead be treated as agents, as individuals actively taking part in creating and negotiating their space and future lives. The boys referred to in this chapter take hold of literacy in their negotiation, manifestation and resistance in relation to identities – both identities that are ascribed to them by the surrounding society and identities that they themselves choose to claim. The chapter shows how literacy is part of the practices in which the boys are involved. It looks at how literacy is woven into different modes of interaction, constituting a complex fabric of oral and written language through different media and in different languages, in an extended process in which the boys' agency is exhibited.

Unaccompanied asylum-seeking children in contemporary Sweden, as a group, are highly involved in various processes of transition, such as the physical migration from one setting to another. The boys in this case include literacy strategies among the tools they use to grapple with frustrating situations. This chapter describes how, when faced with situations which they did not choose and in which their identities are threatened or questioned, the boys use literacy strategies to negotiate, construct and manifest identities.

The Migration of Unaccompanied Asylum-Seeking Children to Sweden

The term 'unaccompanied child' can be defined in various ways. Sweden uses the EU definition, which states that an unaccompanied minor is a child or adolescent under 18 years of age who arrives in the country without a legal caretaker (Hessle, 2009). It is difficult to get a clear picture of the migration to Sweden of children who are not accompanied by close adult relatives. Probably, migration throughout the ages has involved unaccompanied children, but their existence has seldom been documented. Children have migrated to Europe for centuries (Hessle, 2009). There are several reasons behind the migration of unaccompanied children; they may be fleeing armed conflicts; ethnic, political or religious oppression; poverty; sexual abuse; forced labour, or health problems causing death in their extended families. One example of child migration is the mass evacuations of children during the Second World War. Sweden was particularly involved, accepting children who were transferred from Finland and also Jewish children who were evacuated to Sweden.

According to Hessle, there are no reliable statistics regarding the arrival of unaccompanied children in Sweden prior to 1996. The children who have come to Sweden since 1996 arrived from 98 different countries – from Africa (e.g. Rwanda, Congo, and Somalia), Asia (e.g. Afghanistan), the Middle East (e.g. Iran) and Europe (e.g. Rumania). The official number of asylum-seeking unaccompanied children who came to Sweden in 2008 was 1510 (Hessle, 2009). Not all of the unaccompanied children who come to Sweden are asylum seekers, however. Children also come to apply for residence permits or they come without being registered. It is important to remember that not all of the children have come of their own free will, and that some have been forced (Hessle, 2009). This chapter deals only with children who are asylum seekers. Two-thirds of unaccompanied asylum-seeking children who arrive in Sweden are boys (Ayotte, 2000), and there are various possible explanations for this. First, in some settings boys are more often faced with violence than girls are, for example, as child soldiers in active war. Second, many children come by the way of smugglers, and when their families can afford to send only one or some of their children, usually boys are chosen. Third, it is often perceived as more risky for girls to migrate unaccompanied than it is for boys.

According to UN conventions on children's rights, and according to Swedish law, the priority in the treatment of asylum-seeking children should be to act in the children's best interests. In Sweden, the children are initially placed in refugee camps. Since 2006, they have been placed in municipalities all over the country as soon as possible. From then on, the responsibility for the care of the children is on the municipalities, which may apply to the migration authorities for reimbursement of their costs. The process of applying for asylum starts as soon as the children arrive in Sweden and is supposed to be given priority. When a child arrives, he or she is appointed a lawyer and a guardian. The asylum process continues when the child has moved to the municipality, through the social services, which may place the child in a group home, a 'family home' or a separate apartment. If the child is granted asylum, the guardian will be replaced by a specially appointed custodian (although in some cases, this may be the same person, so only the title is changed). The child's legal status should then be equal to that of other children who live permanently in Sweden. Schooling is supposed to start at the camp and continue in the municipality. The children have, according to school regulations, the right to be educated in and to receive social support in their mother tongue; however, this is far from always implemented (Skolverket, 2008).

The asylum-seeking children are likely to meet actors representing the following authorities and organizations who provide support from the society: the migration department, the municipality (social services, group home or housing personnel and school personnel), the county council (asylum health service, psychiatric care for adolescents and children and health workers), guardian, lawyer, voluntary organizations (Red Cross, Save the Children, etc.) and various religious congregations.

Unaccompanied asylum-seeking children have not been the focus of much research, and it is only in recent years that research has shown, for example, that many of the children in earlier evacuations, such as the Finnish children, suffered severely. Many of them suffer from lifelong effects of traumas from their experiences in exile. However, Hessle (2009), as a psychiatrist, stresses that it should be taken into consideration that many of these children may have suffered more had they not been evacuated.

Theoretical Framework

The children who are the concern of this chapter are situated in a process of migration that includes different levels of transition. This process is affected by local and global factors, and it entails the children renegotiating their identities, a process in which they may or may not have a great deal of influence themselves. When analyzing relations between literacy and identity in such complex settings, the notions of literacy events and literacy practices are particularly useful. The term 'literacy event' is here used according to Heath's definition: 'any occasion in which a piece of writing is integral to the nature of the participant's interactions and their interpretative processes', and 'any action sequence, involving one or more persons, in which the production and/or comprehension of print plays a role' (Heath, 1982: 93). These events may then be investigated as literacy practices, which refers to 'both behavior and the social and cultural conceptualizations that give meaning to the uses of reading and/or writing' (Street, 1995: 2) and 'the general cultural ways of utilizing written language which people draw upon in their lives' (Barton *et al.*, 2000: 7). Street (2003: 79) has further elaborated on the distinction between events and practices so that 'literacy practices' refers to 'the broader, cultural conception of particular ways of thinking about and doing reading and writing in cultural contexts'. Thus, events are here perceived as embedded in practices and as the tools that enable the study of practices as ideological problems that tell us something about how literacy is related to the negotiation of identities.

Language in transition

Linguistic processes and phenomena, of which literacy is a part, become more complex and less predictable in times of globalization and could be characterized as fluid and ephemeral (Gee, 2005) or as messy, complex and unpredictable (Blommaert, 2010). Thus, globalization results in a growth in linguistic variety, variability and diversity. According to Lo Bianco (2000), a necessary consequence of globalization is the need for both personal bilingualism and societal multilingualism. Blommaert (2003) refers to globalization as a *world system*, stressing that this is not a uniform system but should instead be viewed as a system consisting of different specific groups of people and specific discourses in specific contexts that are spread all over the world. These specific discourses may be fragmented but interconnected through different types of networks that hold them together. Blommaert gives the discourse of worldwide élites as one example of a discourse that is spread globally. Discourses of this type take place in specific spaces that are interrelated through networks in which exchanges through literacy activities are central. He refers to a world system where situated events are connected to worldwide patterns and processes. Through globalization processes, these discourses are reallocated to new spaces, as are the resources they contain.

Blommaert (2003) stresses that this complex world system is characterized by inequality. When such systems are reallocated, the resources placed in them may become dysfunctional in their new contexts. In this way, he characterizes globalization as series processes in which systems reallocated.

Following globalization, we have seen new migration structures with extreme diversity (Blommaert, 2010), where migrants have intensive contacts both locally and translocally through networks that are both real and virtual. This results in repertoires where resources from a variety of languages and genres are used – what Blommaert (2010) calls truncated repertoires. These repertoires combine different developmental levels of language ability; they comprise a mix of 'unfinished' and correctly expressed chunks of information that, as a whole, can result in quite successful communication.

As written texts are particularly useful for interaction over long distances, literacy is a crucial component in these networks, and the reallocation of systems and resources includes reallocation of literacy practices, the social practices associated with the written word. This also results in literacy repertoires that may have similar truncated characteristics.

Identity and migration

Migration is one of the reallocation processes mentioned by Blommaert (2003), and the specific type of migration that this chapter is concerned with, the migration of unaccompanied children, has increased since the beginning of the third millennium. When children are sent to Western countries such as Sweden, they are reallocated from one specific discourse where they have developed certain identities to another discourse where their identities will be reconstructed. A useful framework for studies of identity has been developed by Holland et al. (1998: 270) who '... take identity to be a central means by which selves and the sets of actions they organize form and re-form over personal life-times and in the histories of collectives'. According to Ivanič (1997), identities are not socially determined but socially constructed, which means that the children face new possibilities that are open for contestation and change. Pavlenko and Blackledge (2004) rely on social constructivism when they stress the role of power relations and argue that particular identities are legitimized or devalued in the context of global and local political economies. They distinguish between imposed identities, assumed identities and negotiable identities.

Canagarajah (2004) refers to identity, together with roles and subjectivity, as comprising selfhood, a selfhood that is multiple, conflicted, evolving and negotiated on two levels, macro-social and micro-social. Macro-level selfhood is imposed mainly in relation to historic identities, institutional roles and ideological subjectivity. This is manifested and negotiated at a micro-social level through the individuals' agency through which they resist, modify or negotiate the identities they are ascribed through larger social structures. Canagarajah sees voice as a rhetorical construction of selfhood, negotiated in relation to identities. Following Foucault, one can thus regard voice as being manifested on a micro-social level and in relation to selfhood that is imposed on a macro-social level. People use language – and literacy – in their struggle for voice by resisting and modifying dominant resources in personal communication. It is at the level of voice that we gain agency to negotiate identities. On a macro-social level, selfhood is mainly imposed or ascribed in relation to historic identities, institutional roles and ideological subjectivity. Canagarajah relates this to Foucault's concepts of instinct versus institutions, and voice in relation to selfhood.

The unaccompanied asylum-seeking children who arrive in Sweden and settle here face a situation that is particularly complex and that affects different aspects of their identities, both identities that they are ascribed by structures on a macro-level and identities that they themselves want to claim on a micro-level. First, the majority are between 13 and 18 years old, which means that they are in some ways already involved in processes of identity change related to the transition from child to adult. This may include having already achieved identities commonly associated with adulthood in earlier contexts, for example, that of family provider, guardian of younger siblings or soldier in active war. In such cases, their immigration to Sweden entails their being reallocated as children in need of protection. Ahmadi (2003) stresses that the notions of youth and childhood are products of a certain historic period in the Western world and do not exist in many collectivistic societies. He relates the notion of youth to the emergence of individualism.

Second, the migration affects the children's identities related to ethnicity and nationality as they settle in Sweden. In most cases, earlier perceived identities such as belonging to a specific group, family, clan or ethnic or religious group are, in Sweden, replaced by more general perceived or ascribed identities such as Afghan, African and/or Muslim. Their categorization as unaccompanied asylum-seeking children is another example of an identity ascribed from outside.

Third, settlement in Sweden includes socio-economic changes affecting identity. As migrating to Sweden from war zones such as Afghanistan is very costly and often organized by smugglers, many of the children come from high-status and well-off groups. Once in Sweden, they have to rely on the welfare system for support, and they receive the status of children in need of protection and support, a prerequisite for this group to obtain a permanent residence permit. Many of them come from settings where the welfare system is largely the responsibility of informal powers, which contrasts with the Swedish welfare system, where the overall responsibility for security, care and safety for all rests on the municipality.

Fourth, the migration also includes identity-related changes in lifestyle. In some cases, the children come from traditional ways of life far from what is, in Sweden, perceived as normal modern facilities, such as refrigerators and flush toilets. In other cases, the children come from homes where household work was mainly carried out by others, such as servants or female family members, while in Sweden they are expected to carry out domestic work in ways that are new to them. Some come from lifestyles were people mainly relied on oral personal exchanges of information, whereas in Sweden they become involved in using multiple modalities for communication, such as electronic information technology. For many of the children, migration also includes reallocation from a Muslim society under Muslim laws to a secular Christian-dominant society in which religion is considered a private issue. Their migration may also present them with conflicting views on masculinity and femininity, of what it means to be a man or a woman.

Fifth, the children also experience change in educational identity. When they arrive in Sweden, some of them have already developed identities such as 'good student' or as 'illiterate'. In Sweden these identities undergo dramatic change, as all of the children are expected to start to learn Swedish from a basic level, including reading and writing Swedish, which for most of them includes learning a new writing system.

Finally, there are cultural factors and cultural encounters that may affect the children's identities. This may include reallocation from one institutionalized cultural pattern to another, from a collective community to individualism. Ahmadi (2003) refers to societies where relations between people are stressed and the individual human being is part of an indivisible whole, in contrast to societies where the individual is central and self-reliance is important; along with self-reliance often comes loneliness.

Identities and literacy

The reallocation also means that identities the children developed earlier in relation to literacy will be contested and affected. In some educational settings in Sweden, all students who do not know how to read and write Swedish, or at least Latin script, are treated as illiterate; as students with severe deficiencies which need to be attended to before they may start with other types of education. This may include strict teacher control over literacy activities in school. Teachers may have explicit expectations about what types of reading and writing activities the children should engage in.[1] School curricula set out specific reading and writing skills and also how and when they should be learned. However, as Dyson (2003) highlights, children draw on different literacy practices and textual materials from their social worlds, where identity and agency are interrelated. Language learners are engaged in finding a voice through a variety of practices, which means that they struggle for voice through their literacy practices while negotiating identities in their new setting. These are processes where power becomes visible.

Methodological Considerations

Ethnography offers relevant tools to create deeper understanding of fluent and transforming phenomena such as literacy and identities in sensitive settings, as in this case. The data in this study is a result of close involvement with three boys, ranging in age from 15 to 18, during their first 14 months in the municipality where they were placed. Blommaert (2008) refers to an ethnography of process, transfer and mobility; a process that spans communities. Data consists of field notes from participant observations and written artefacts such as SMS messages, emails, forms, protocols and electronic data from interactions of different types related to the boys. Artefacts also include written materials in their environment, such as written notes and statements in their home. Due to the sensitive nature of the subject, most of the artefacts collected are from interactions between the boys and the officials or other adults. Any of the artefacts used for analysis of private interactions between the boys and the mates of their age are used with the boys' explicit permission. No oral interaction has been recorded other than through field notes. The text excerpts and examples have been anonymized and pseudonyms are used.

Although the focus here is on the boys' agency, it should be noted that they are in a vulnerable situation. Their experiences include coming to Sweden with the help of smugglers in dramatic circumstances, living in a refugee camp, uncertain waiting for a permanent residence permit, placement in a setting not of their own choosing over which they have little control and having to rely on various persons in Sweden without themselves having much choice. Many asylum-seeking children have also left their families, friends and relatives behind in unstable circumstances. It is clear that they live under high pressure and many of them suffer from post-traumatic stress disorder (PTSD). This vulnerable situation of the subjects of the study demands that the ethnographer pay close attention to ethical questions. The research has to be planned carefully to avoid any negative effect on the informants. Asking for informed consent initially was not an option. The situation the boys were in did not give them a fair chance to consider the effects of such research or to understand its implications for themselves. As the boys were in a completely new environment, in contexts they had never experienced before and faced with numerous adults who were unknown to them (e.g. lawyers, interpreters, police officers, group housing staff), I did not find it ethical to ask them to consider the effects of participation in research at the beginning of the observations. Instead, informed consent was obtained at the end of the study from the boys who were involved, and no data is presented that the boys have not approved of. Also, trustees and guardians have been informed and have given their consent.

Literacy Practices in Negotiating New Identities in Sweden

During their first year and a half in Sweden the boys were involved in many events involving literacy of different types, both in and outside of school. While literacy in school mainly consisted of literacy practices that are traditionally connected with classroom education, such as reading textbooks, filling in exercise books, writing lists of glossary terms, looking up words in dictionaries and so on, the out-of-school literacy activities were much more varied, and it is these literacies that will be considered here. The literacy events that were observed in this case study were frequently included in processes that were extended over time. This means that the understanding of the literacy practices that constitute the frame, or the context in which the events are situated, need to be understood as such. Thus, the literacy events that these boys are included in, initiate and involve themselves in will be analysed not only in their social and cultural contexts but also as they are included in processes that stretch over time.

In the different activities the boys were engaged in, literacy was present together with oral language practices. There were no clear-cut borders between oral and written language practices, and communication was carried out using a variety of media. Observations showed that the boys engaged in a multiplicity of literacy activities, both self-initiated and initiated by others, such as official persons, age-mates and relatives. From the observations and collection of artefacts, I constructed the following list of the types of literacy events they frequently participated in outside school:

- Sending and receiving SMS messages (frequently; started as soon as they arrived in their home)
- Using the internet (communicating via Facebook, chatting via MSN, visiting web pages, watching films and music videos from their home country or neighbouring countries)

- Sending and receiving emails (less frequently; only two of the three boys ever engaged in this mode of communication)
- Being involved with official documents such as reports, forms, registration (mainly in connection with the asylum process, receiving a permanent residence permit, applying for an identity card and passport, being involved in a search for lost relatives and immigration cases involving relatives); these documents are in both digital and hard copy formats
- Applying for money or other benefits
- Working towards obtaining a driving license (studying for the road test, filling in application forms)
- Being involved in literacies connected with travelling (e.g. applying for funds; buying tickets; using signs, timetables, maps and other relevant print material)
- Asking others to carry out literacy activities for them (e.g. friends, trustees, group home staff, social services personnel, health workers and dentists)
- Handling banking matters through cash cards and on the internet (the latter usually prompted by the trustee) and sending money to relatives abroad (with the help of relatives or friends)
- Being involved in literacies connected to health care (usually the writing was done by professionals, such as nurses, doctors, dental hygienists, psychiatric therapists, opticians, physical therapists and secretaries)

To analyse the role of literacy in the negotiation of identity among these boys, three processes where literacy events played an important part will be presented. The first two deal with two types of digital media: sending and receiving SMS messages and chatting on the internet. The third deals with literacy events related to the asylum-seeking process. They constitute examples of how the literacy events the boys were involved in were woven into processes that include other modalities, such as speech and digital communication. These three examples are chosen because they represent different types of literacy practices where the boys used literacy to struggle for voice in relation to identities, ascribed or assumed on macro-social levels.

Sending and receiving SMS messages

As soon as the boys arrived in their municipality and their new home, each one was given a mobile telephone with a SIM card with SEK 200. Every month they then received another SEK 200 on their cards. The boys immediately started to use their mobiles to communicate with friends from the camp where they had spent their first months in Sweden, and with relatives and other friends. This communication was mainly oral and was conducted in their mother tongue. However, they soon started to send SMS messages when they communicated in Swedish, for example with Swedish adults, such as trustees or group home personnel. This means that soon after their arrival, while they were still in the early stages of learning Swedish, they were sending and receiving messages in Swedish. As all three boys came from backgrounds in which Arabic script was used, and one had not even attended school in his home country, this meant that they were using literacy to communicate in Swedish before they had formally learned to read and write in Swedish.

The boys frequently used SMS messages when they needed to see or speak to their trustees or other adults. One of them, a boy who had not attended school in his country of origin and was categorized as 'illiterate' by school authorities, was sending and receiving SMS messages to his trustee after just two weeks in his new home. This means that he was already using literacy to meet his needs when he had just started schooling. One of the early messages he sent reads: *Lars du komer* (Lars you kome).[2] This was sent to his trustee, Lars, and the message was clear. Lars could understand that he was wanted there. Another early message read: *Komer briv* (Kome letr). This was also understood by Lars; a letter had arrived that Lars was supposed to see.

It is interesting to see that mobile interaction with friends usually took the form of speech, while mobile communication with Swedish-speaking adults in the beginning took the form of written SMS messages. One reason in the first case may be that the telephone used Latin script while their own languages, which they used with friends, used Arabic script. Another reason why they chose a written form for Swedish may be that reading and writing takes longer than speaking, allowing the writer more time to figure the text out; reading may also be carried out letter by letter. Oral speech, in contrast, requires more speed, particularly on a mobile telephone where one pays according to time used. The choice of speech versus SMS may also have been based on what was communicated, the content. Communication with friends may be more fluid. It may be mentioned that, after some time, one very strong motivation for writing in Swedish, both in SMS messages and chatting on MSN or posting on Facebook, turned out to be the opportunity to communicate with girls more or less secretly.

One example where literacy in the form of SMS messages was explicitly used to negotiate identity early on was when Mahmood, only four weeks after arriving in his new home, had been to a shopping centre together with some other boys and one of the group home staff members, Anneli.

At the shopping centre, Anneli and Mahmood had an argument about his shopping. As this was in early January, Anneli had insisted that Mahmood buy himself a warm jacket at a reasonable price, whereas he wanted to buy a more expensive jacket that was not as warm but, in his opinion, more smart-looking. The result of the argument was that he did not buy anything, but in frustration went out to the car and waited there for the others. When they got home, Mahmood refused to leave the car, claiming that he needed his trustee, Per, to come. Anneli and the other boys left the car and went inside, so Mahmood took out his mobile telephone and sent an SMS to his trustee urging him to come at once: *Du komer nu! Mahmood* (You kome now! Mahmood). As this was late on a Saturday afternoon Per could not come, so there was an exchange of some messages. In between, Per called the home and talked to Anneli to get a better picture of what had happened. Through SMS he asked Mahmood to leave the car and go in, and he indicated that he would come the next day so that they could solve the problem. Mahmood was very frustrated and it was getting very cold in the car (the temperature was below –10 degrees), and he finished the exchange with a last message: *Du komer nu eller aldrig* (You kome now or never). Then, he left the car and went inside, locking himself in his room. Per understood the message as a threat, that if he would not come at once Mahmood did not want to see him ever again. This was verified the next day by Mahmood, who had already applied for a new trustee and refused to meet Per at all.

In this example, we see that Mahmood struggled for voice in the negotiation of how his money should be used and what type of clothing he should wear, which he clearly considered to be important to his identity. This time Mahmood was writing in affect. He wanted to use his money in other ways than Anneli wanted him to, and he also wanted the right to make his own decisions about how to use his money and what type of clothing to wear. As he had just started in a new school, he found it important to look good. Mahmood was in the process of creating a new identity in his new context, and clothes were an important way to express part of that identity, as a smart-looking young man. Anneli, on the other hand, knew that Mahmood lacked warm clothes and that the money he had would not cover as much as he wanted. She had also been told by other people who were involved, including the trustee and personnel at the migration authorities and the social welfare services, to make sure the boys bought clothes that covered their needs. Also, in relation to the trustee, Mahmood claimed voice in negotiating his identity, either as someone with the right to demand that his trustee should come at once, or as someone required to wait until it suited the trustee. In this process, Mahmood made use of literacy as an important tool.

Chatting on the internet

In the home where the boys had been placed they had access to four computers, located in a corridor, set in a row on a long table. Here the boys started to use the Internet and to communicate with friends in other places in Sweden and in other countries. Figure 2.1 is an example of a chat between Amir and his friend Tahlil. (In the translation, unmarked text is in Somali in the original, **bold** is used for Swedish, underlined for English and *italics* for Arabic. In the translation, standard spelling is used regardless of original spelling.)

Original chat text	Translation	Comments
Amir: tjoo brorsan :) Tahlil: haa tja bro.	Amir: **hi** **brother** :) Tahlil: yes **hi** <u>bro.</u>	Refers to Swedish 'tja', a common greeting among Swedish youth. 'brorsan' is Swedish slang.
Amir: is every thing ok Tahlil: yes but i need mony	Amir: <u>is everything ok</u> Tahlil: <u>Yes but I need money</u>	('bro' could be an abbreviation of either Swedish 'brorsan' or English 'brother')
Amir: hahahahah hur mycket behöver du :) Tahlil: 1000 kr walh jag ska till Oslo	Amir: hahahahah **how much do you need** :) Tahlil: 1000 **SEK** *by Good* **I'm going to Oslo**	'Arabic figures'[3] Arabic with Latin letters, non-standard spelling
Amir: nääääääääää!!! waryaa! för mycket ! Tahlil: okej 500' kan jag få låna då ? ? Amir: runtaa miyaa or only joke	Amir: <u>noooooooo!!</u> You! **too much** ! Tahlil: ok 500' **may I borrow then?** ? Amir: is it true <u>Or only joke</u>	

Literacy in Negotiating, Constructing and Manifesting Identities 67

Tahlil: walah bilaah run ayee iga tahy Amir: goormee! waxaan ku helo aan ku siinaa bro don't worry Tahlil: olkay brow 15 waan iska tahriiba 15 bishaan marka barito ma imaani karta mise aniga ayaan kuu imaanaayo Amir: talaadada aan imaanaa !! Tahlil: taladada ma hubta ? mana isine waxa aa ii aboodid walh abowe dhab ayee iga tahy Amir: انشاالله Tahlil: oka insahlh waan ku kla barana maraxow walh dhab ayee iga thay Amir: okej wallah Tahlil: okay brow	Tahlil: by Good I swear I'm serious Amir: when! I'll lend you if I have anything bro don't worry Tahlil: ok bro 15 I'll go 15 this month can you come tomorrow or shall I come to you Amir: I'll come on Tuesday!! Tahlil: is that true ? Will you lend *By good* how much can you lend me Amir: *If Good wishes* Tahlil: Ok *if Good wishes* ?? Amir: Ok with Good Tahlil: Okay brother	 Exclamation mark as question mark Arabic with Arabic letters Non-standard spelling According to the boys 'bad language which is not translatable'

Figure 2.1 Chatting on the internet

This is an example of what Blommaert (2010) calls truncated repertoires. In this short chat, we see that the boys use a mix of four languages, Arabic, Somali, English and Swedish, and that they use what may be called standard language as well as slang and jargon in the fragmented way that is typical for chats. They use both Latin script and Arabic as well as figures and signs (such as question marks and smileys). There are many examples of non-standard spellings, such as an exclamation mark for a question mark and 'insahl' for 'inshallah'. There are also many examples of inconsistent spelling such as 'tjoo/tja' for 'tja' and 'olkay/oka/okay/okej'. Thus, there is a variety in languages, styles and semiotic expressions in the interaction where a lot of negotiation is taking place. The negotiation is explicitly about lending and borrowing money, the sum to be lent, when and where this transaction should be carried out and the reason for it, but one can assume that there is more under the surface that is not explicitly expressed here. As we have only this chat to go by, and as I decided not to interfere with the boys' private communication, we may only guess what may be hidden behind this explicit negotiation regarding money. As in everyday speech, only what is perceived as necessary by the interlocutors is represented in the text and much is implicit, which makes it impossible for us to understand things such as what the boys' relationship is, whether there has been lending and borrowing between them before and what the relevance is of mentioning going to Oslo. We can understand that the chat is part of a process of negotiating relations and that the boys use literacy without any apparent regard for standard norms.

Being involved in the asylum-seeking process

The asylum process involves a variety of literacy practices, most of them included in official discourses. When these boys first arrived in Sweden, this process was very significant in their lives. The process included the handling of many formal and official documents. For ethical reasons, they may not be shown in detail here. The boys took active part in the asylum process in different ways, arguing that their guardians should investigate why the process took so long, investigating whether they had been given a poorly qualified lawyer and so on. When the boys arrived at their home, they had already been provided with a lawyer and they had been interviewed about their arguments for seeking asylum. This interview had been written down in a protocol that was sent to each boy and his trustee. When Hussein received his protocol, he read it carefully. The protocol was written in Swedish, and Hussein had only been in Sweden for six months. Although he had started to learn Swedish, he discovered some mistakes that he realized were of importance for his case and should be corrected. He found this too complicated to explain by SMS, so he asked Mattias, one of the staff members in the home, to arrange a meeting with Maria, his trustee, and an interpreter so that he could explain the problem to her. Mattias did so, and after Maria listened to his explanations, she contacted Hussein's lawyer, who arranged a telephone meeting with Hussein, the trustee and an interpreter. At the meeting the protocol was the main topic. Hussein explained what parts he was not satisfied with and how he thought they should be changed. The lawyer listened and promised to make sure the changes were made. The corrected protocol was later sent by post to Hussein, who checked and approved the corrections.

This case is an example where the boy claimed voice in relation to an official document that was important for the outcome of his asylum process. By using advanced literacy strategies, including using as mediators two of the adults appointed to care for him, the lawyer and the trustee, and an interpreter, he was actively involved in the process. By reading the corrected protocol through and approving the text, he claimed voice in relation to the authorities on a macro-social level through this document that played a central role in his asylum process.

An important step in the asylum process is the delivery of the decision. It is always delivered orally, and the asylum seeker and his/her trustee receive a formal call through official letters that are sent out. The invitation is formally to come to the migration authorities at a certain point in time, but informally the lawyer usually calls the trustee beforehand if the result is positive. In this case, the asylum seeker may already have received the positive message orally through the trustee. When they meet the person in charge at the migration authority, he or she reads the decision from the formal decision protocol. Then the trustee is to take the asylum seeker immediately to the tax authorities to be registered as a resident in Sweden. This involves obtaining official documents, such as the document for appointing the trustee, and filling in various forms. This step in the process is another example of when dominant, official types of literacies are important.

After this step there are some changes in the children's situation affecting their identities. During the asylum process they received a certain sum of money each month, and if they were in need of extra resources, for example to buy winter clothes, they had to apply for them to the migration authorities through their trustee. After they receive a permanent residence permit, the local social welfare authorities take over all areas of responsibility. The children will receive between 40% and 100% more money every month, depending on the age,[4] but cannot apply for extra money except in certain extraordinary cases, such as being in need of glasses.

For the boys observed in this study, receiving a residence permit was an important step as it meant that they achieved more influence in economic matters and also because they perceived it as very important to receive a Swedish identity card and to have a bank account and bank card of their own. This involved filling in many forms, most of them downloaded and printed out from websites, and visiting different offices, some of them in neighbouring towns, such as the tax authorities. It also included seeking help from mediators. Another thing that some of the boys perceived as important to have was a passport. The authorities in the boys' municipality decided that it was not important that the boys have passports as they were not expected to travel abroad immediately. Thus, the trustees were instructed to leave this to the boys themselves to handle.

One of the boys, Amir, had a particular interest in getting a passport. To him, having his own passport was an important step in the process of creating his new identity. He asked his trustee where he could find the necessary information and was shown the web page of his home country's embassy, which is located in Oslo, Norway. He was also informed about the possibility of applying for an alien's passport, which would be less expensive and easier to obtain, but he rejected that at once as it was the Afghan passport that he thought it important to have. On the web page he found information about the application process in his own language, in Arabic script (Figure 2.2). Amir is among those who did not attend school until he came to Sweden and was thus among those labelled 'illiterate'. At the time he started the process of obtaining his passport, Amir had been attending school in Sweden for less than a year; all of his education was in Swedish. Still, he read the information in his own language, understood it and was thus able to prepare himself. When he was ready, and had collected the required sum of money, he contacted his trustee to get her permission. As an unaccompanied child having received a permanent residence permit in Sweden, one has to have the trustee's permission to travel, and written permission from the trustee was also required by the embassy. The whole process, which Amir undertook on his own, included finding friends of the same nationality over 20 years of age in Oslo who could guarantee his nationality, finding his way around Oslo and finding somewhere to stay. This also included bringing the required documents and photos as well as the required sum of money. Not least, it included finding the cheapest way to travel from the middle of Sweden to Oslo and making the necessary bookings.

This process is another example of how voice is used to contest assumptions imposed from macro-levels. This included the use of official types of reading and writing in Swedish and the boy's first language, with different scripts, through different modalities, including SMS messages, the internet, and printed and handwritten texts with or without a mediator. It also included using different types of symbols and written materials such

رهنمود صدور ویژه

سفارت کبرای افغانستان در اسلو برای کسانی که در کشور های ناروی، سویدن، دنمارک، فنلند با آیسلند سکونت داشته و درخواست ارائه نمایند، ویزه صادر مینماید. صدور ویژه (ورقۀ ورودی) برای افغان های مقیم کشور های اسکاندیناوی رایگان است.

براساس مقررات موجود، ما فقط ویزۀ یک ماهه یک بار مسافرت صادر می کنیم. کسانی که می خواهند برای مدت بیشتر در افغانستان باقی بمانند، می توانند جهت تمدید مدت اعتبار ویزۀ اقامت شان به ریاست امور قنسولی وزارت امور خارجه در کابل، مراجعه و درخواست ارائه نمایند. البته در حالات استثنایی ویزه های کثیرالمسافرت و سه ماهه فقط برای منسوبین رسمی دولت و قوای مسلح کشور های ناروی، سویدن، دنمارک، فنلند و آیسلند و دارندگان پاسپورت های سیاسی، در صورتی که هدف سفر شان رسمی بوده و در زمینه دلایل قانع کننده ارائه کنند، صادر شده می تواند.

متقاضیان ویزه می توانند درخواست های شان را از طریق پست ارسال کنند و یا جهت درخواست به بخش قنسولی سفارت افغانستان در اسلو مراجعه نمایند. درخواست های ویزه بر اساس نوبت دریافت و اجرا میگردد. درخواست هایی که معلومات شان ناقص باشد و یا اسناد لازم را با خود نداشته باشند، مورد اجرا قرار نمی گیرند.

Figure 2.2 Part of the information on the web page of the Embassy of Afghanistan in Oslo, describing the services of the embassy

as bus schedules and web pages. What motivated Amir to carry this out and to go to Oslo on his own was, as he explained it, that he thought that somebody always has to be the first, a pioneer, and that he wanted to be that someone. If he succeeded in doing this, then others could follow his example. By interacting and navigating his way through different modes, different languages and different scripts, he reached his goal, becoming an Afghan who has a passport and at the same time someone who is an example for others. He may also have managed to be someone who showed that having a passport may be an important matter even though the Swedish authorities claimed otherwise.

Discussion

The analysis of these events and processes gives us an image of the literacy practices the boys participate in and shows that identities that may be assumed on a macro-social level, such as being vulnerable and in need of help, are contested on a micro-social level, where the boys claim what they consider to be more positive identities for themselves. Thus the boys construct voice in the transition process they are involved in, which includes reallocation and renegotiation of identities. When one wants to be perceived as a good-looking young man rather than as someone who wears practical clothes, one tries to negotiate given conditions in whichever ways are available. When one comes upon written documents that are important for one's own life conditions, one takes necessary measures to make sure that they are in accordance with one's own interest. When one perceives having a passport as important and this demands the use of advanced multiple literacies, one finds a way to manage them, regardless of authorities who deem the task unimportant. When one finds that the benefits offered do not meet one's needs or wishes, one tries to find ways to solve this problem. When one wants to negotiate one's identity in relation to peers, one uses literacy in the languages, scripts and modes one finds suitable. In short, what we have seen is that the boys in this case do not passively accept the roles and identities that are ascribed to them from a macro-social level, by the surrounding society and various authorities; instead, they creatively negotiate them on a micro-social level, resisting some and claiming others. This also means that they themselves construct voice in the reconstruction of their identities. To do this they use the modalities they find useful, and written language is an important part of this.

It is also clear that the discourse they are in is a multilingual one and that they competently use the variety of linguistic skills they have access to, not only their own individual skills but also others' skills, in their negotiation of identities. The boys showed complex literacy awareness and talent, including the ones who had not had previous schooling and had been categorized as 'illiterate' by authorities. They used multiple literacies, including multiple scripts, multiple languages and multiple modes where they showed sensitivity to diversity regarding ethnicity, language, language varieties and identity. The literacy practices they involved themselves in to navigate their way through different discourses included both standard and non-standard types and also mastery of effective strategies. These strategies included creating and using different networks and seeking help from mediators, and they revealed multilingual, multimodal and multilateral competence. The examples also revealed the interactive character of the literacy practices the boys initiated. Through literacy, in combination with other modes, the boys created, used and maintained different types of networks and affinity groups, on inter- and intra-ethnic levels and on local, national and global levels.

Notes

(1) Most teachers of Swedish as a second language in Sweden have little or no education in teaching literacy in a second language and have no personal experience learning literacy in a second language (Wedin, 2010). They tend to fall back on their past experiences, for example adopting the teaching strategies their own teachers used when they were in school, or using the same strategies they have used in their own teaching of young Swedish children.
(2) Non-standard spelling has been represented as non-standard spelling in the English translation.
(3) 'Arabic figures' refers to figures used in Latin script. These are not the figures used in Arabic script.

(4) Actually, he will receive the child allowance until the age of 16 and thereafter will receive support in the form of study allowances.

References

Ahmadi, N. (2003) Om jaguppfattningens betydelse för tolkningen av sociala roller [About the meaning of I-view for the interpretation of social roles]. In N. Ahmadi. (ed.) *Ungdom, Kulturmöten, Identitet* [Youth, Cultural Encounters, Identity] (pp. 49–78). Stockholm: Liber.
Ayotte, W. (2000) *Separated Children Coming to Western Europe: Why They Travel and Why They Arrive*. London: Save the Children.
Barton, D., Hamilton, M. and Ivanič, R. (2000) *Situated Literacies: Reading and Writing in Context*. London: Routledge.
Blommaert, J. (2003) Commentary: A sociolinguistics of globalization. *Journal of Sociolinguistics* 7 (4) 607–623.
Blommaert, J. (2008) *Grassroots Literacy: Writing, Identity and Voice in Central Africa*. New York: Routledge.
Blommaert, J. (2010) *The Sociolinguistics of Globalization*. Cambridge: Cambridge University Press.
Canagarajah, A.S. (2004) Multilingual writers and the struggle for voice in academic discourse. In A. Pavlenko and A. Blackledge (eds) *Negotiation of Identities in Multilingual Contexts* (pp. 266–289). Clevedon: Multilingual Matters.
Dyson, A.H. (2003) *The Brothers and Sisters Learn to Read and Write*. New York: Teachers College Press.
Gee, J.P. (2005) Semiotic social spaces and affinity spaces: From the Age of Mythology to today's schools. In D. Barton and K. Tusting (eds) *Beyond Communities of Practice: Language, Power and Context* (pp. 214–232). Cambridge: Cambridge University Press.
Heath, S.B. (1982) Protean shapes in literacy events: Ever-shifting oral and literate traditions. In D. Tannen (ed.) *Spoken and Written Language: Exploring Orality and Literacy* (pp. 99–117). Norwood: ABLEX Publishing Corporation.
Hessle, M. (2009) Ensamkommande men inte ensamma: Tioårsuppföljning av ensamkommande asylsökande flyktingbarns livsvillkor och erfarenheter som unga vuxna i Sverige [Unaccompanied but Not Alone: A Ten-Year Follow-up Study of Unaccompanied Asylum-Seeking Refugee Children's Life Conditions and Experiences as Young Adults in Sweden]. PhD thesis, Stockholm University.
Holland, D., Lachicotte, W., Skinner, D. and Cain, C. (1998) *Identity and Agency in Cultural Worlds*. Cambridge, MA: Harvard University Press.
Ivanič, R. (1997) *Writing Identities: The Discoursal Construction of Identity in Academic Writing*. Amsterdam: John Benjamins Publishing Company.
Lo Bianco, J. (2000) Multiliteracies and multilingualism. In B. Cope and M. Kalantzis (eds) *Multiliteracies: Literacy Learning and the Design of Social Futures* (pp. 92–105). London: Routledge.
Pavlenko, A. and Blackledge, A. (eds) (2004) *Negotiation of Identities in Multilingual Contexts*. Clevedon: Multilingual Matters.
Skolverket (2008) *Med Annat Modersmål. Elever i Grundskolan och Skolans Verksamhet* [With Another Mother Tongue: Students in the Compulsory School and the School System]. Stockholm: Fritzes.

Street, B. (1995) *Social Literacies: Critical Approaches to Literacy in Development, Ethnography and Education.* New York: Longman Publishing.

Street, B. (2003) What's new in new literacy studies? Critical approaches to literacy in theory and practice. *Current Issues in Comparative Education* [online] 5 (2), 1523–1615. Available at *http://www.tc.columbia.edu/cice/Issues/05.02/52street.pdf.*

Wedin, Å. (2010) *Vägar till Svenskt Skriftspråk för Vuxna Andraspråksinlärare* [Roads to Swedish Literacy for Adult Second Language Learners]. Lund: Studentlitteratur.

3 Privileging Identity Positions and Multimodal Communication in Textual Practices: *Intersectionality* and the *(Re)Negotiation of Boundaries*

Sangeeta Bagga-Gupta

Introduction

This chapter focuses upon the *situated, distributed* and *multimodal* ways in which oral, signed and written language varieties, other symbolic systems and dimensions of human interactions more broadly are used in everyday life in a *range of institutional settings*. The analytical aim is to highlight the contributions of finely tuned understandings of human *ways with words* and *ways of being* (Bagga-Gupta, 2006a, 2010a, in press; Heath, 1983). This work also *highlights* what can be called 'the oral language bias' (compare with Linell, 2005) in the analytical reporting from studies of social practices, a bias that has more recently become visible in research on multimodal languaging from a range of settings including deaf arenas.[1] Such emerging work suggests that analysis of audio/video recordings of social life continues to privilege representations of oral language use in scholarly writings, eclipsing a range of other significant aspects of human behaviour including written communication.

Juxtaposing different types of empirically driven examples, the work presented here theorizes issues related to how identity and languages are made (in)visible in social practices and policy textual worlds. Irrespective of the concepts used to describe and discuss different dimensions of human life *evoked by, attended to* or *conferred upon* individuals or communities of practices (Lave & Wenger, 1991; Säljö, 2005), the analytical approaches employed here recognize the need to (re)conceptualize identity and languages from poststructuralist positions (see e.g. Bagga-Gupta, 2010a, in press; Berger & Luckman, 1967; Blommaert, 2010). Such positions question the dominance accorded to *borders* in the analysis of life inside and outside institutions. Inspired by intersectionality approaches (De los Reyes & Mulinari, 2005; McCall, 2005; Staunaes, 2003), *crossroads* and *transitions* – that is the *borderlands* themselves – are recognized as analytically relevant spaces in their own right; they constitute potentially rich sites for understanding ways in which identity and language varieties are privileged and/or made obscure; they enable an exploration of tensions and challenges that analysis of textual worlds and everyday life in institutional settings gives rise to.

Framed within sociocultural[2] and postcolonial[3] perspectives, including multimodal[4] frameworks, the analytical focus in this chapter is on *written-language-varieties-in-use* in three empirical sets of data from distinct social practices, in addition to *policy textual worlds*. Empirical examples from a range of settings – traditionally discussed in separate areas of research, not least identity-related research – are brought together with the aim of taking on challenges involved in operationalizing *intersectionality* at the empirical level. Highlighting the dual dimensions of languag*ing* and of human*ness* through the analytical lenses of (written-) language-in-use in different settings *within the framework of a single study* enables transcending a narrower view of identity, languages and the monological monolingual bias (García, 2009; Linell, 2009) in the language sciences and the educational sciences (see also Bagga-Gupta, 2011, 2012b).

Section 2 considers a textually based empirical example of written-language-in-use from a large non-government organization (NGO) that caters to the education and welfare of migrant families and their children in a Southern setting. This example focuses on the collaborative processes involved when the contents and design of a magazine are negotiated in an office setting. The second and third analytical sections focus mundane aspects of life at educational institutions in Northern settings: Section 3 zooms into a mainstream grade 7 classroom where 2 adults and 19 youngsters participate in a routine language-focused exercise; Section 4 considers everyday interactions from a grade 9 social studies classroom in a segregated 'special school for deaf/hearing-impaired' where 2 adults and 5 youngsters discuss some English words available on the whiteboard from the previous lesson. Explorations in Sections 2, 3 and 4 situate written language varieties against the backdrop of different types of multimodal slices of everyday life. Section 5 presents analysis of educational policy documents spanning over half a century with the aim of identifying the range of categorizations that frame language varieties and identity across time in one geopolitical space in the North.

The analysis of micro-level interactions, 'thick descriptions' (Geertz, 1973) of different types of social practices and studies of educational policy can be envisaged in terms of different 'scales' (Scollon & Scollon, 2004) that constitute the central analytical sections in this chapter. The concluding Section 6 brings together salient features that arise when mundane human behaviour from different institutional settings is focused upon and juxtaposed with analysis of policies.

Multiauthored *Process Texts*: Fluidity in Work Place Social Practices

Process texts are documents that often get created in the course of multiparty communication in institutional settings. Zooming into such a process text in Figure 3.1,[5] attention can be drawn to a number of issues. This (re)presentation of the notes created by the 'magazine group' made up of four to six women employees during the course of an office meeting – the third in a linked sequence of meetings over a month – takes place at an NGO where school education and a range of community services like child care and health support are made available to migrant communities at construction sites in an emerging economy.[6] Discussing the various ways in which an institutionally significant artefact gets conceptualized when adults who communicate orally in at least six language varieties necessitates that the participants (as well as the analyst) have an in-depth knowledge of what the NGO does, who its members and clients are, what the envisaged purpose of the proposed magazine is going to be, etc. In addition, the textual artefact focused here frames the ways in which written language varieties are used for recording the course that the discussions take and that create the contents of the magazine. This record constitutes at least one layer of what is at specific moments considered important by the participants and what they orient towards becomes available in the notes that they themselves maintain as a 'collective record or memory' (Middleton & Edwards, 1990; Wertsch, 2002) of their discussions.

The record displays signs of being authored by different members: different handwritings, scripts and language varieties used allow us to surmise this and are reflected in the 'Guide to translation' in the lower right section of Figure 3.1. At least three written scripts (Devanagari, Latin and Roman), three recognized language varieties (English, Hindi and Marathi) and transliteration of Hindi and Marathi words from Devanagari to Latin can be noted. Latin letters are written in both capital and small case. Furthermore, traces of the flow of oral language discussions can be discerned: the striking off of words (e.g. NEW (new Information), held, conducted), a section (e.g. II]) and section markings (e.g. e, f). A list of seven proposed names for the magazine in two language varieties and one script is listed on the top left-hand corner. The chosen title (the fourth name in Hindi, Devanagari script) – 'Parivartan' (English: Change) is underlined and highlighted in this list.

Between the first and the third office meeting, the group has requested the teachers at its 50 education centres spread across the megacity of Mumbai to send in contributions for the new NGO magazine. The materials sent in are piled into four heaps in the centre of the group and the piles are represented with the roman numerals I, II, III and IV in the record available in Figure 3.1. There is thus a symbiotic relationship between the oral talk, the organization of physical artefacts (the piles created) and the note-work. The titles of the four sections are noted primarily in English (Latin script); section III (b) is presented in Hindi (Devanagari script). One member of the group authors this part of the record in two language varieties and two scripts.

The work that the women do in the slice of life analysed here gets recorded through collective authorship where *different language varieties* and *scripts* are used at times collaboratively by different adults and at times by one adult in different sections of the record. The situated nature of the magazine work and the distributed nature of the authoring of the record are framed by the

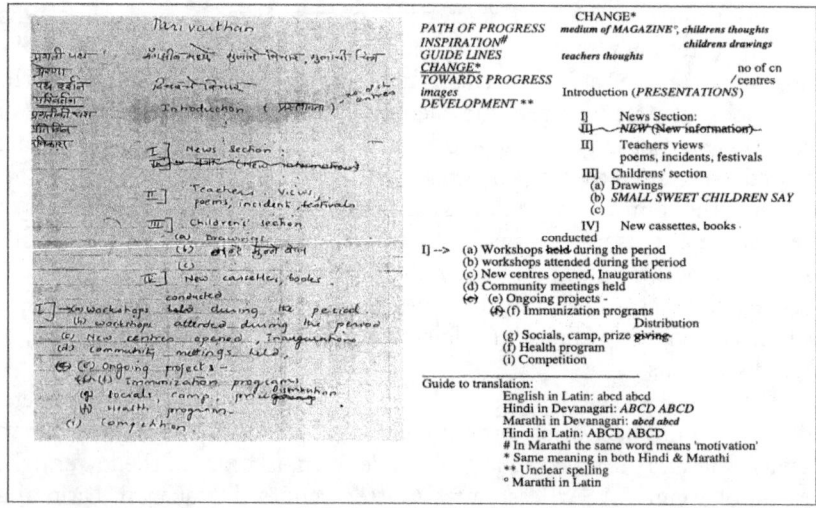

Figure 3.1 Scanned process text (including translation and 'Guide to translation') from an office site meeting – 'Notes to reorganize the magazine' (from Bagga-Gupta, 1995: 174)

participants' collective engagement. These participants are reported to have different exposure to the language varieties and scripts used: two members have no formal school-type learning experiences in English and one has limited formal learning experiences in Hindi and none in Marathi. Nevertheless, the contents of the magazine are collectively authored in all these language varieties and the record is used as a point of reference in upcoming meetings. Furthermore, one of the participants has a brief employment record at the NGO. She participates more passively in the oral discussions and takes a more active role in the position of a scribe. The *ways with words* thus authored are contingent both upon the *ways of being* of the social practice in the institutional setting and on the individual experiential histories of members of this specific languaging event.

Knowing how to author a text during a meeting is thus not contingent upon individual skills in one, two or three language varieties or scripts. It is the *distributed* nature of particular kinds of knowledge bases (among the participants) that are significant. The identification processes involved in what the participants do during the course of this specific activity could be specified in terms of traditional identity categories like gender, age, formal education, competencies in specific languages, socioeconomic circumstances, etc. However, the analysis of this process text allows us to instead become sensitive to the participants 'identity work and performance' (Butler, 1993; Goffman, 1959; Schieffelin & Ochs, 1986) in terms of the situated and shifting nature of social positions that the doing of the note-work itself entails.

Becoming a member in a work setting or a task force like a magazine group is contingent upon the positions that the institution makes possible or confers (in)formally and that participants accord one another. What the members make salient in their interactions is contingent upon the novice–expert status tensions that socially (re)produces an activity system or a specific task. Here, it is not identity based on the notion of knowledge about a specific language or a specific writing system that is significant. Expertise lies in collectively authoring and (re)using records for specific outcomes. This means that when limited experiences with a specific language variety disadvantages a specific member during the course of the activity (or later when ideas noted in the record need to be operationalized), then other members make these salient; when knowledge of field operations from the geographically dispersed centres become salient for creating the subsections, then old-timers at the NGO provide the necessary framework for joint accomplishment of the task at hand. Apprenticeship into various competencies relevant for the NGO allows participants to gain membership into a range of activities and it is shifts in situated experiences at the borderlands of the known and the unknown that socialization into specific competencies and identity positions become relevant. The written language varieties used and the process text thus produced itself play a crucial role in coordinating and managing the overall activity in focus and it at the same time allows for different types of knowledge – linguistic, textual, managerial, identity-related, etc. – to emerge. This *fluidity of languaging and social positioning* is a fundamental aspect of all social practices particularly in settings characterized by diversity and where the written modality is drawn upon. Let us now consider slices of life from two different settings in Northern contexts. Diversity becomes salient in and through the language varieties in use in both the settings.

Ways with Words: Discursive Technologies in Mainstream Classrooms

Zooming into a grade 7 classroom,[7] Figure 3.2 presents a thick description of everyday interaction from a language-focused lesson. Reading aloud is a common activity in language-focused lessons and the social practice of listening to parts of a text (sometimes in a language variety that participants have limited experiences with) on an audio-player and then reading the same sections aloud from a textual artefact (a textbook) is also a regular feature of many classrooms (in parts of the North). This is a routine feature in the grade 7 setting that is focused upon in Figure 3.2.

The representation of the social practice in this German lesson in a school in the geopolitical spaces that constitute Sweden illustrates a recurring pattern that the 19 pupils and two adults engage in. An adult assistant is usually seated in the far end where a large computer and printer stand on one of the pupil tables. A variety of other discursive technologies and literacy tools like the whiteboard, an audio-player, ceiling maps, various written instructions in Swedish including fire-safety instructions, class timetable, etc. are visible at the front – teachers' – end of the classroom.

Some issues regarding the *multimodal, discursive technological nature of languaging* and *literacies* emerge related to the ways in which participants use tools and artefacts in the course of this mundane classroom activity. There is an important link between the written, oral, tactile and listening modalities – all of which converge on a central artefact, a text. While the teachers' initial remarks explaining a routine classroom behaviour is delivered in oral Swedish, the subsequent oral, written, tactile listening–reading-aloud behaviour takes place in German. This routine cyclic literacy practice entails that participants listen collectively to a taped voice read one sentence from a German textual artefact while attending to the sentence in their individual texts in the visual or tactile mode, read orally the same sentence collectively,

> The teacher asks all the pupils to open their books and asks if Jonny has found the correct page on his Braille-Text Display*. She then proceeds to explain that they will listen to a text on the audio-player and read aloud when she stops it at the end of each sentence. This *listening – silent reading – reading-aloud* activity proceeds without a hitch and as envisaged by the teacher initially. It appears that all pupils manage to both silently read the text in their individual textbooks and read aloud when the teacher shuts the audio-player. However, after a few minutes, it appears that Jonny is not able to keep pace with the temporal phases of the activity. He is unable to read his Braille-text and stops reading silently and appears to listen and subsequently 'reads aloud' with the rest of the class.
>
> *Jonny's Braille-Text Display functions so that it can 'read off' the digital text that has been fed into his computer. What is visible on the computer screen gets displayed as raised signs on the Braille-Text Machine and the attached printer has the possibility to print texts with Braille signs. The 'word-display strip' on the machine is short and makes available a few words at a time. The user – here Jonny – is required to give a command to shift reading rows frequently. The computer takes time to move between different rows when a command is given.
>
> (Winther, 2000: 48, my translation from Swedish, emphasis added).

Figure 3.2 Thick description of a listening–reading activity in a language-focused lesson in a mainstream school

listen again to another recorded sentence and so on. The *intertwined* nature of the languaging behaviour is an intrinsic element of the *multimodal chaining* where technologies and tools (including oral and written language) play a central role. This highlights the *discursive technological nature* (see also Bagga-Gupta, 2004b) of multimodal languaging where boundaries converge and overlap in everyday life in classrooms. 'Doing classroom work' (cf. Bergqvist, 1990) during a language-focused lesson thus links participants' use of different language varieties and modalities in ways that are similar to the women's work discussed in the first empirical example in Section 2. Furthermore, the Swedish language used during the introduction phase of the lesson and the subsequent multimodal literacy practice in German illustrate a regular routine where one language variety familiar to the participants is *used to talk about* the business of the lesson and another language variety – the target language for learning – is *used in the listening–viewing–reading-aloud phase* of the social practice.

Here some salient issues related to identification processes can also be raised. The teacher uses a discursive technological tool to both introduce and augment her own adult role in the classroom. The voice that gets broadcast from the audio-player has a distinctive 'german*ness*' to it. Thus, teaching occurs through the distributed collective instruction made available through at least four agents: the teacher and assistant who are present, the reader whose voice is transmitted and the author whose text is available through two literacy artefacts. The cyclic nature of the activity focuses both receptive and active production skills of the participants in collective mode. The teacher orients especially towards the 'differently-abled' (Corbett, 1996) nature of the discursive technologies that frame the participation of one pupil, Jonny. Finding the correct page on a textbook as compared to on a Braille display machine appears to entail different time frames. What is interesting here is that highlighting the 'special needs' that Jonny has in whole-class discourse confers a specific position while simultaneously explicitly 'including' him in the common framework of the activity.

Evoking Jonny's otherness is a common aspect of classroom public behaviour by adults here. This othering not only draws attention to the special discursive-technological situation that frames Jonny's participation, but the teachers specific oral attention also temporally creates space for him to keep pace with his "able-bodied" (Corbett, 1996) peers. When such micro-interactional spaces subsequently become unavailable in the course of the activity, he does not keep pace and completely stops reading in the tactile mode. Going beyond traditional identity categories such as 'blind 14-year-old boy', it can be suggested that the teacher evokes and attends to Jonny's 'pupil*ness*'. The *interactional complexities* involved in negotiating a text via a Braille display machine highlight and make visible through this slice of social life some of the finely tuned issues that members of 'inclusive' educational settings encounter and negotiate in mundane activities. One can say that traditional othering categories like blind, handicapped, etc. perhaps blur the interactional dimensions involved in learning and instruction. This has key significance for discussions on equity generally and marginalization processes more specifically (see Bagga-Gupta, 2002, 2006b, 2007a; Hjörne & Säljö, 2008). Winther and Bagga-Gupta (2007) capture the interactional dimensions involved in such processes through the title of their study: 'The Acquisition of Blindness in Communicative Spaces'.

How dimensions of identity positions and multimodal communication are both privileged and downplayed are illustrated through a different micro-interactional slice of classroom life from a segregated school for a specific pupil category in the next section.

Visual-Orientations: Synchronous Multimodality in Segregated Classrooms

Micro-level analysis of video-taped life from secondary classrooms in 'special schools' from the geopolitical space of Sweden are focused in this section.[8] While these segregated schools for the deaf build upon a 'bilingual' model, previous and ongoing analysis from three large ethnographic national projects[9] demonstrate that members here communicate using a variety of resources from more than two written, oral and signed languages in patterned ways.[10] Studying these social practices makes visible the *complex* nature of mundane communication and also the ways in which participants link language varieties that frame work in deaf educational arenas.

Figure 3.3a represents mundane aspects of the fluidity of languaging and identification processes in a slice of data taken from a whole-classroom discussion phase of a social science lesson in grade 9. Five pupils and two adults – a subject teacher and a resource aide – have momentarily shifted attention from the primary focus of the lesson to some words on the whiteboard (see Figure 3.3b) from a previous language-focused English lesson.

Figure 3.3a illustrates the *visual-orientation* (Bagga-Gupta, 2004b) that characterizes routine languaging in many (not all) lessons in these segregated schools. Visually-oriented communication is characterized by the use of different modalities – primarily sign and textual, and also oral language resources including 'mouthing' – that members in such small communities of practices employ in patterned ways.[11] Here, participants are discussing the subtle differences related to variations of the concepts woman and girl. Figure 3.3a and b including the 'Transcription key' suggests that at least three recognized language varieties (SSL, Swedish and English) and at least three–five different linguistically significant modalities (signed, fingerspelling, written, oral and mouthing) are in use in this slice of life. Furthermore, the synchronous multimodal languaging occurs in a couple of specific ways. First, the signed modality is chained to the written modality explicitly when the teacher (lines 2 and 5) uses the visual dimensions of signing and highlights the visuality of words on the whiteboard to explicate issues related to the situated need of drawing attention to the similarities and differences between the gendered concepts in focus.

Second, the teacher in lines 2, 3 and 5 links resources from signed, oral and written language varieties, illustrating ways in which oral language is woven into the communicative practice. Third, fingerspelling (lines 1, 2, 3 and 6) constitutes another significant resource that explicitly links the written and the signing modalities. Furthermore, mouthing (lines 1, 3 and 5) highlights and connects different language varieties and modalities and, like fingerspelling, constitutes an important resource in visually-oriented communication. It draws attention to silent mouth formation in conjecture with resources from signing or written modalities. The teacher exaggerates mouth formations of words like woman, lady and lass *silently* (lines 1, 3 and 5) linking them *simultaneously* to other aspects of the multimodal interaction.

84 Part 1: Literacy and Identity in Transition

(a)

Teacher:
1a. L-A-D-Y OTHER WOMAN (.) [accompanied with exaggerated mouthing of woman]
1b. *(Fingerspelled word lady) is different from woman*
1c. *L-A-D-Y ANNAN KVINNA*

2a. L-A-D-Y=**lady** FINE WOMAN **can say** <woman> <aristocrat> FINE WOMAN L-A-D-Y
2b. *(Fingerspelled word lady) lady is a fine woman, one can say (writes woman on whiteboard; points to word aristocrat on whiteboard) (fingerspelled word lady) is a fine woman*
2c. *L-A-D-Y=**lady** FIN KVINNA **kan säga** <kvinna> <aristocrat> FIN KVINNA L-A-D-Y*

3a. L-A-D-Y WOMAN (.) L-A-D-Y W-O-M-A-N [accompanied with exaggerated mouthing of lady woman] **adult female aristocrat**
3b. *(fingerspelled word lady) woman (fingerspelled words lady woman) is an adult female aristocrat*
3c. *L-A-D-Y KVINNA L-A-D-Y K-V-I-N-N-A **vuxen kvinnlig aristokrat***

Pupil:
4a. GIRL DIFFERENT LASS=**lass** SAME=**same** DIFFERENCE=**difference** (asks questioningly)
4b. *Girl is different from lass (signed and oral simultaneous talk) is this the same difference (parallel signed and oral talk)*
4c. *FLICKA OLIKA TJEJ=**tjej** SAMMA=**samma** skillnad=**skillnad***

Teacher:
5a. NONO [shaking head] LASS=**lass is slang** (.) LASS [accompanied with mouthing of word lass] INFORMAL LANGUAGE
5b. *nono lass is slang lass is informal language*
5c. *NEJNEJ TJEJ=**tjej är slang** (.) TJEJ VARDAGSSPRÅK*

6a. <lady> L-A-D-Y EVERYDAY LANGUAGE NO <aristocrat> [pointing toward lady on whiteboard] FINE WOMAN
6b. *(Written word lady on whiteboard that is fingerspelled like this) is informal language (the written word aristocrat on the whiteboard) is a fine woman*
6c. *<lady> L-A-D-Y VARDAGSSPRÅK NEJ <aristocrat>*

Transcription key:
SSL TALK IN ENGLISH; *SSL TALK IN ORIGINIAL*; F-I-N-G-E-R S-P-E-L-L-E-D W-O-R-D; **oral talk**; SSL=**oral talk** i.e. two modality parallel talk; <writing word/s or pointing to words/s on white-board>; [significant body, face or mouth movements/actions of members in interaction]; (presentation of clarifying information); (.) micro pause

Line a. SSL (visually-oriented) TALK IN ENGLISH
Line b. Translated into English talk
Line c. SSL (visually-oriented) TALK IN ORIGINAL

(b)

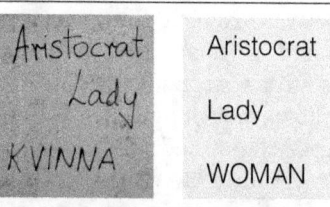

| Aristocrat |
| Lady |
| WOMAN |

Figure 3.3 (a) Micro-interactional transcript of language varieties in concert in a segregated special school for the deaf and transcription key. (b) Digital representation of written words on whiteboard (including translation)

She and a pupil chain oral talk to signing and written resources (lines 2, 3, 4 and 5). The use of written language on the whiteboard – when the teacher writes an English word (woman, line 2) or highlights some specific concepts (aristocrat, lines 2 and 6; woman, line 6) – occurs not in isolation but as part of the communicative flow where three language varieties and four modalities are employed. Specific words on the whiteboard are privileged through pointing (lines 2 and 6). Body orientations including pointing constitutes an important resource in much classroom talk in both mainstream and segregated settings (see also Bagga-Gupta & St-John 2010, submitted; Goodwin, 2003). Understanding classroom communication without attending to the fluidity of languaging neglects the complex ways in which participants regularly chain language varieties and modalities in everyday interaction. Together with the empirical examples presented earlier in Sections 2 and 3, the social practice (re)presented in Figure 3.3a and b illustrates again the symbiotic relationship between different linguistic varieties, modalities and resources.

Discussing the participants in this segregated setting in terms of their audiological and hearing levels neither informs nor illuminates the complex linguistic behaviour that becomes visible in the micro-level analysis presented above. The use of oral language in a 'deaf' classroom setting has, in the segregated school settings in Sweden, been a touchy issue since the 1990s (see Section 5). The organizational placements of deaf pupils in segregated classrooms have become confounded with the normative idea that spoken language – including mouthing – does not (or rather should not) have any place there. This idea is at odds with the communicative behaviours that have been reported from 'signing bilingual' deaf classroom-based [12] studies in other geopolitical settings as well.[13] Issues regarding identification processes can also be raised in terms of participants' positions as experienced members of visually-oriented languaging, rather than in terms of either bounded essentializing categories such as deaf, hard-of-hearing, Cochlear Implanted (CI), normal/hearing humans *or* the separate language varieties that are ad hoc, since the 1990s, positioned as deaf peoples' 'first' and 'second' languages – SSL and Swedish primarily in the geopolitical spaces of Sweden (see Section 5). The analysis of a mundane activity like a classroom discussion of the meaning potentials of different gendered concepts illustrates how participants become apprenticed into different *zones of identity-cum-linguistically related potential development* (compare with Vygotsky's popularly quoted concept 'zone of approximate development'). Such apprenticeship into different types of competencies relevant for the immediate ongoing discussion contributes to and enables membership into a range of activities and areas.

Knowing how to participate in classroom talk is not primarily contingent upon individual skills in a specific language variety or modality. Similar to what was illustrated previously in the adult work-place example in Section 2, it is the distributed nature of particular kinds of knowledge (among the members) that is significant. Visually-oriented languaging is accounted for here in terms of the tensions that arise in the access that participants have to *different* communicative resources: experiences with SSL resources (signing, fingerspelling and mouthing), experiences with the Latin-based Swedish and English varieties in use, hearing and oral resources, experiences with lip reading and mouthing strategies, etc. The point that again becomes salient is that it is not identifications based on the notion of 'knowledge about a specific bounded language', or a specific writing system that is significant. Rather it is the *ways with words* illustrated in Figure 3.3a and b that are contingent upon the *ways of being* and on the individual experiential histories of the members of a community of practice. This questions the rationale that continues to allow for the segregation of a specific pupil category in the organization of education in a Northern context (for further discussions on this theme, see particularly Bagga-Gupta, 2007b, 2010b and the next empirical section).

The fluidity of written, signed and oral resources can be surmised through the concept 'visual-orientation', rather than in terms of hearing (levels), deaf or related other*ness* concepts. The distinction accorded to the concepts 'Deaf–deaf' in the literature adds another dimension to the othering processes in the deafness academic fields. Membership in *linguistically imagined* communities of practices, irrespective of hearing status, rather than audiologically determined functionally dis/abled human beings, constitutes the perspectives that have been focused via the Deaf/deaf dichotomy. The multimodal linked ways in which language varieties are used in visually oriented settings has been reported in the literature primarily since the mid-1990s. Researchers who report micro-interactional analysis and contribute to this academic literature have been identified as experienced users of the different language varieties that are employed by members inside and outside classroom settings (see Bagga-Gupta, 2004a, 2007b, 2010b).

Shifting scales by moving to macro-levels, the final empirical deliberations in the study presented here focus educational policy texts with the intention of highlighting how identities and language varieties are conceptualized in national school syllabi in a Northern context *over time*.

Boundaries and Categories: Codes and Identities in Textual Worlds

Policy materials like national syllabi frame ways in which education gets conceptualized in and across time.[14] Compulsory education became a mandatory provision in policy (at least) in many geopolitical spaces across the globe during the post-World War II period. Analysing such provision across time makes visible the kinds of identity positions and language varieties that are privileged and shifts, if any, that may have occurred. *Different language varieties* like Swedish, English, Norwegian, Spanish, Hindi, Turkish, etc. including some signed languages like New Zealand SL, Spanish SL, Venezuelan SL and Finnish SL have received political (and academic) recognition in different geopolitical spaces. World language varieties like English and Spanish have further received political and academic recognition in terms of different English*es* and Spanish*es* (see Bagga-Gupta, 2010a, in press). To illustrate the overarching point here, different varieties of English e.g. Australian English, American English, Indian English and British English (or varieties of other world languages like Chinese, Spanish, etc.) are recognized in terms of their uniqueness, history, literature base, etc. and different oral and written varieties are used by members of different geopolitical spaces like Australia, United States of Amercia, India, England, etc. The issue that is of interest here relates to how language varieties and human identity, for instance, *language learner categories* are conceptualized in policies across time.

Zooming into national syllabi for mainstream and segregated schools in the geopolitical space of Sweden during the past 50 years gives rise to some important issues of relevance to the overall aims of the study presented in this chapter. A range of language varieties and young peoples' identity emerge in the formulation of the 'titles of course plans' in the mainstream/general syllabi[15] on the one hand and the syllabi for the segregated special schools[16] on the other hand for the period 1960–2011 (see Appendices A and B).

Divisions in terms of different linguistic codes for different pupil categories emerge in the syllabi across six decades. The language landscape expands from two language varieties in 1962 to at least six 'areas' by 2011. The total number of individual language varieties made available through the national syllabi and thereby accessible for pupils, however, is much greater by 2011. The introduction of 'foreign languages' and 'home languages' accounts in part for this large increase. Another specific expansion occurs due to the shifts in how a central subject in the curricula, Swedish, gets (re)conceptualized over time. Within the 'one-school-for-all' institution, the language-focused subject 'Swedish' is conceptualized in the early 1960s in terms of an *all-encompassing* language subject *for all pupils*. Two decades later in 1980, it becomes divided into two – 'Swedish' and 'Swedish as a foreign language'. A further shift occurs in the next national syllabi in 1994, with the foreign language terminology being discarded in favour of a numerical conceptualization: 'Swedish as a second language', a course title in use today. The bifurcation pertaining to Swedish in 1980 becomes further expanded in the mid-1990s when 'Swedish as a second language for the deaf/hearing-impaired' emerges. 'Neighbouring' language varieties like Danish, Norwegian and Icelandic are made available within the Swedish language course syllabi.

Some specific shifts in the language landscape across time can also be seen vis-a-vis pupils with functional disabilities in general and the segregated special schools for the deaf/hearing-impaired more specifically. The language-focused/related courses/areas available through the formal titles in the national syllabi show that while five courses/areas are available in the syllabi in 1970 (Lgr 69), the total number expands considerably during the next four decades. Three important shifts can be noted. First, the syllabi from 1983 (Lgr 80) has a clear cut bilingual language block. Second, an explicit numerical and categorical terminology emerges in the mid-1990s (Lpo 94) and remains in place in Lgr 11 (2011). Of the 11 language-related courses listed in the syllabus in 1996, five are specified 'for deaf/hearing-impaired' pupils, one is specified 'for hearing' pupils, while the remaining five are non-marked. Third, the latest national syllabi in 2011 become available digitally for both mainstreamed and segregated school settings simultaneously.

To summarize a central point here, specific identity positions are both implicitly and explicitly marked in how the language varieties are framed in the course titles. Specifications regarding the *different types of Swedish* for different *implicit* or *explicit* learner categories are significant in this respect. Lgr 11, for instance, continues to make available the courses 'Swedish' (for native ethnic Swedish pupils), 'Swedish as a second language' (for first-, second-, etc. generation immigrant pupils) and 'Swedish for deaf/hearing-impaired' (for pupils who are members of the segregated special schools[17]). This analysis of course titles across half a century suggests that while the first couple of national syllabi can be said to be oriented towards 'language learn*ing*', the national syllabi from the mid-1990s onwards have a 'language learn*er*' orientation that is essentialistic both in terms of bounded language units and in terms of bounded learner categories.

Some further issues can be raised vis-a-vis the categorizations in the course titles of the syllabi and assumptions regarding the learning needs of specific groups. The rationale used for the subject Swedish as a 'foreign language' in Lgr 80 or a 'second language' in Lpo 90 is diffusely legitimized as a pre-theorized fact. The terminology employed since the mid-1990s, 'second language', is targeted towards pupils, many of whom are already at least bi- and trilingual. In addition, targeting the subject 'Swedish as a second language' in terms of biological lineage defies not just basic democratic doctrines but also post-structural analytical understandings of identity, culture and difference. Recent discussions by national education authorities also raise concerns since less than a fifth of the pupil population whose otherness in terms of immigrant*ness* can be evoked is reported as studying this subject (Swedish Authority for School

Improvement, 2005). However, 'native' minority[18] pupils are not recognized as potential candidates for studying 'Swedish as a second language', explained perhaps by the fact that the latter's minority status builds upon a unifying recognized 'other' language. English remains unmarked and is not offered as a (using the previous logic of a 'second language') 'third language' and the foreign languages are not offered in terms of a 'fourth language' to pupils who are offered 'Swedish as a second language'. The point that is salient is the reductionism and the unclear rationale that has created subjects like 'Swedish as a second language' and 'Swedish as a second language for the deaf/hearing-impaired' in the mid-1990s. This reductionism encompasses all pupils: while some get reduced to a bilingual position, the vast majority get reduced to an implicit monolingual status.

Reserving a language course for a category of pupils in a segregated school setting or a language course for pupils whose ancestors have moved across geopolitical boundaries is pre-theorized and contentious. Boundaries in the area of language education and specific language learnership liaisons, as is illustrated here (see Appendices A and B), draws upon a reductionistic rationale and a discourse of other*ness*. Such boundaries have been previously discussed in terms of a *horizontal division* that separates language codes or varieties or creates three Swedish language subjects and a *vertical division* where implicit or explicit categories are envisaged and connections made between language learners and a bounded language unit (Bagga-Gupta, 2004b, 2010a, 2011, 2012b). Such boundary marking is at odds with both recent theoretically informed shifts in the fields of human learning, languaging and identity and empirically driven analysis of languaging and identification processes during the last three decades (as also analysis presented in Sections 2, 3 and 4 testify). The boundaries that emerge in the policy data are closely related to 'webs of understandings' and interconnected conceptualizations that exist in the area of bilingualism (see Bagga-Gupta, 2012b). Such ideas not only are at odds with the fluidity of languaging and identification processes that emerges when social practices are scrutinized but they also operationalize and fortify specific ways of demarcating language and identity in other institutional areas. Thus, for instance, the three different Swedish subjects in the educational language landscape illustrated here live demarcated lives within higher education and research arenas as well. Thus, Swedish is offered as *three separate areas of specialization* for professionals and becomes legitimized as areas of linguistic research within academia. Such divisions *mediate* and *function as structuring resources* for specific ways of understanding identity, learning and development in educational institutions. An administrative/organizational logic legitimizes a problematic pre-theorized vertical division in research, higher education and the school syllabi.

Fluidity and Intersectionality: *Privileging Positions*

A key idea that has emerged in the study presented here is that while different language varieties and modalities are linked and chained in the meaning-making enterprise in everyday life, categorizations play *significant meditational roles* that account for and simultaneously shape membership into formal institutional language educational settings. Another issue that arises is related to the ways in which oral, written, tactile, signed communication, and human behavior including the use of tools and artefacts both conserve and challenge categorizations in institutional contexts. Members of different communities of practices in both Southern and Northern contexts can be marked though a range of *potential* identifications. Children and adults in institutional settings are not *merely* the labels (e.g. woman, bilingual, newcomers/old-timers, blind/normal, deaf/hearing, immigrant/multilingual or disadvantaged/poor/displaced) that are highlighted in discourses of specific contexts – an urban educational-cum-community facility for children of migrant labourers, a 7th grade mainstream or a 9th grade segregated classroom. The significant point is that paying attention to the *dynamic, micro-level* and *fluid* nature of the ways in which humanness and humanhood get (co-and-re)constructed in and through languaging dislodges the mythical stability of static bounded identities.

Intersectional positions challenge the static boundaries that dominate analysis and the naturalized points of departure that focus marginalization (not least in the educational and language-related literature). Thus, for instance, human diversity is pre-theorized and gets compartmentalized in and through the (re)cycling and 'looping' (Hacking, 1995; Hjörne & Säljö, 2008) of concepts such as 'functional disability', 'woman/girl', 'immigrant' (including first-, second- and third-generation immigrants), 'class', etc. Linguistically defined groupings and other communities of practices (bounded in terms of institutional contexts or their typical routines or rituals rather than in terms of historically significant categories) can never be pure, original or exclusive for any one group over time. While such a position is privileged in post-structuralist thinking, it appears to be alive and thriving in educational policy and the organization of education as the analysis presented in Sections 4 and 5 suggest.

The segregated deaf education institution that has survived different methodological swings over the last century in the geopolitical space called Sweden is an illustrative example. At present, legitimacy is granted to this segregated institution because of assumptions regarding deaf 'pupils' needs' vis-à-vis 'their' two languages, that is SSL in terms of the 'first language of the deaf' and Swedish in terms of a 'second language of the deaf'. In other words, privileging a vertical organizational division has naturalized the need for a segregated bilingual school 'for the deaf'. Such static boundaries make invisible the diverse nature of deaf pupil's primary language experiences[19] and homogenizes all pupils based upon hearing levels. Fluid and intersectional perspectives draw attention to the fallacy inherent in the idea 'different language codes for different categories of learners' and allow for an *inverted inclusive* institution where SSL and Swedish can be privileged as *primary language* varieties in schools for all pupils irrespective of their hearing status.[20]

Another example regarding the mismatch between a post-structural position on identification and languaging and the boundaries that are privileged in some educational contexts in the North (including academia) lies in the recurring use of the concept 'bilingual'. Echoing Heath's (1983) observations based on large-scale ethnographic studies from the 1970s in southern United States, the empirical discussion in Sections 2–5 highlight that categories related to socioeconomic status, educational backgrounds, race, ethnicity, mobility, functional disabilities, etc. ignore and make invisible the fluidity of communication and the identification processes that are (co- and-re)created in everyday life. The stratification made visible through the analysis of the shifts in the national policy materials – the vertical division in the language sciences including the organization of the learning and instruction of languages – is thus a normative selective position that is at odds with the fluidity that emerges in the analysis of social practices. The segregated organization of instruction for deaf pupils is an explicit illustration of the inherent reductionism that such stratification implies.

The empirical analysis of a range of social practices presented in this chapter from research projects that are traditionally kept apart in the analytical reporting highlights the complex chained ecology of *modalities-cum-language-varieties-in-use* and the fluid nature of identification processes or *ways of being* across settings. Communication that is traditionally conceptualized in terms of bi- and multilingualism can, in light of the analysis presented in Sections 2–4, be extended in a couple of specific ways. First, recognizing the oral language bias in empirical reporting requires that analysis attends to the multimodal nature of perhaps all institutional learning and instruction. Here, written, digital and technological resources including participants' body orientations across time and space constitute important dimensions that for a variety of reasons remain invisible in the majority of reporting. Second, the complexities of languaging implies that bilingualism and biliteracies need to be re-conceptualized by going beyond the dominant view of competencies in two (or more) separate language codes/modalities. Third, the distributed nature of competencies and the experiential histories of members in multilingually framed social practices calls for revisiting the dominant cognitive view of individually owned skills. Finally, the empirically driven analysis of the three very different slices of everyday life from different institutional settings highlight that human identity is fluid and situated and cannot be framed as a pre-theorized category divorced from social practices.

These empirical discussions illustrate the intricate ways in how the 'Self' and 'Other' are represented in and/or oriented towards in everyday communication and through the sociohistorical discourse about language, and human identity in policy documents. Furthermore, the study presented in this chapter has explicated the *complex* nature of language-in-use including the fluid nature of chaining in different types of institutional settings. These analyses suggest that while the mediation of particular world views and of an 'imagined and pure homogeneity' is privileged in policy, understanding linguistic competencies and language teaching in educational settings on the one hand and human usage of language varieties on the other hand is a very different phenomenon. Together, these empirically grounded analyses highlight a tension between human *ways of being*, that is their actions and orientations in social practices, and human *ways of understanding* and conceptualizing human*hood*–human*ness* on the one hand and *mono* and *bi*lingualism in educational settings on the other hand.

Notes

(1) See, for instance, Bagga-Gupta (2000, 2004a, 2010b), Bagga-Gupta and St-John (2010, submitted), Jewitt (2009), Kress *et al.* (2005).
(2) Chaiklin and Lave (1993), Lave and Wenger (1991), Linell (2009), Scribner and Cole (1981), Säljö (2005), Vygotsky (1934/1986), Wertsch (1985, 2002), Wertsch *et al.* (1995).
(3) Bhabha (1994), De los Reyes and Mulinari (2005), Eriksson *et al.* (2002), Said (1978), Young (2001).
(4) See note 1.
(5) From a 3-year multisite ethnographic study conducted in the early 1990s (see Bagga-Gupta, 1995, 2012a).
(6) A more elaborate and detailed analysis of the chained literacies and social practices that constitutes the processes involved in the creation of the magazine are available in Bagga-Gupta (1995), Chapter 5, "The social (re)production and (re)distribution of knowledge at MC's different public arenas". Recordings and texts from these office meetings constitute the empirical data that have been revisited for the present analysis (see also Bagga-Gupta, 2012a).
(7) Empirical reporting from research presented in Winther (2000) and Winther and Bagga-Gupta (2007) are drawn upon.
(8) Data are drawn from the multi-site ongoing project, Languages and Identities in School Arenas.
(9) For an overview of these projects, see Bagga-Gupta (2004c, 2007b, 2010b).
(10) See also previous reporting from related studies in Bagga-Gupta (2000, 2002, 2004b).

(11) Empirical reporting that illustrates what I call visual-orientation can be seen in studies from Norway, Sweden and the United States in, for instance, Bagga-Gupta (2000, 2002, 2004b, 2010b), Bailes (2001), Erting (2001), Hansen (2005), Padden (1996a, 1996b).
(12) See also the literature that addresses the languaging behaviours in home settings of "deaf children of deaf adults" (e.g. Blumenthal-Kelly, 1995; Chamberlain *et al.*, 2000; Lartz & Lestina, 1995; Marschark, 1997; Masataka, 1992; Maxwell, 1983).
(13) See note 11.
(14) The analysis in this section is part of a larger study, within the ongoing Research project, Languages and Identities in School Arenas.
(15) Lgr 60 (1962), Lgr 69 (1969), Lgr 80 (1980), Lpo 94 (1994, 2000) and Lgr 11 (2011).
(16) Lgr 69 (Skolöverstyrelsen, 1970), Lgr 80 (Skolöverstyrelsen, 1983), Lpo 94 (Skolverket, 1996, 2002) and Lgr 11 (2011).
(17) It is unclear whether this language course is available for individually placed deaf/hearing-impaired pupils in mainstream school settings. Language courses targeted "for deaf/hearing-impaired" have not been available through the previous syllabi in mainstream settings. Given the fact that today almost all deaf/hearing-impaired pupils receive CI and are mainstreamed (at least initially), the present discussion is particularly relevant.
(18) Five minority groups have received political recognition as a result of the ratification of the European charter of regional/minority languages at the end of the 1990s in the geopolitical space of Sweden. The groups and the languages identified in this process include Sami (Sami), Finns (Finnish), Tornedalers (Meänkeili), Roma (Romani) and Jewish (Yiddish).
(19) It is often estimated that 95% of the deaf children are born into non-signing, that is non-SL environments. Furthermore, ethnic minority deaf pupils in the geopolitical space of Sweden may come from both non-SSL and non-Swedish speaking home environments. This diversity is made invisible in educational institutional settings.
(20) Individual schools have and continue to be organized on the principle of inverted inclusion and "visually-oriented" bilingualism (see Teruggi, 2003). In addition, an inverted inclusive idea rests on the historical fact that entire societies have existed where a SL has been used by all members of society.

References

Bagga-Gupta, S. (1995) Human development and institutional practices: Women, child care and the mobile creches. Linköping Studies in Arts and Science 130. PhD thesis, Linköping University, Sweden.
Bagga-Gupta, S. (2000) Visual language environments: Exploring everyday life and literacies in Swedish Deaf bilingual schools. *Visual Anthropology Review* 15 (2), 95–120.
Bagga-Gupta, S. (2002) Explorations in bilingual instructional interaction: A sociocultural perspective on literacy. *Journal of the European Association on Learning and Instruction* 5(2), 557–587.
Bagga-Gupta, S. (2004a) *Literacies and Deaf Education: A Theoretical Analysis of the International and Swedish Literature*. Research in Focus N. 23. Stockholm: Skolverket. http://www.skolverket.se/publikationer?id=1843
Bagga-Gupta, S. (2004b) Visually oriented bilingualism: Discursive and technological resources in Swedish deaf pedagogical arenas. In M. van Herreweghe and M. Vermeerbergen (eds) *To the Lexicon and Beyond: Sociolinguistics in European Deaf*

Communities (Vol. 10), The Sociolinguistics in Deaf Communities Series (pp. 171–207). Washington DC: Gallaudet University Press.

Bagga-Gupta, S. (2004c) Bilingual talk and talk about bilingualism: A bird's eye view of research and developmental projects in the Swedish deaf educational landscape. In G. Hie and A-E. Kristoffersen (eds) *Inkluderende eller Ekskluderende Klasserom: Doveundervisningen – et Case å Laer av?* [Inclusive or Excluding Classrooms: Deaf Education – a Case to Learn from?] (pp. 167–198). Oslo: Skådalen Publication.

Bagga-Gupta, S. (2006a) Theme Opening-speech of the 34th NERA Congress: "Education Widens Democracy –Or?" *34th Congress of the Nordic Educational Research Association.* Örebro, March 9–11 2006.

Bagga-Gupta, S. (2006b) *Att förstå delaktighet utifrån forskning som fokuserar deltagande och interaktion*[Understanding involvement and participation through research that has focused participation processes and interaction]. Special pedagogiska institutet [The Swedish Institute for Special Needs Education]. http://www.spsm.se/Forskning-ochutveckling/Delaktighet/Litteraturstudier/Att-forsta-delaktighet-/

Bagga-Gupta, S. (2007a) Aspects of diversity, inclusion and democracy in education and research. *Scandinavian Journal of Educational Research* 51(1), 1–22.

Bagga-Gupta, S. (2007b) Going beyond the Great Divide: Reflections from deaf studies, Örebro, Sweden. *Deaf Worlds. International Journal of Deaf Studies* 23 (2&3), 69–87. Special theme issue: The meaning and place of "Deaf Studies".

Bagga-Gupta, S. (2010a) Representations as mediation: Revisiting understandings of language and identity in present day Northern settings. Plenary lecture at the International conference on Language, Culture and Diversity – Issues and Challenges, 8–10 February 2010, Department of Linguistics, Aligarh University, India.

Bagga-Gupta, S. (2010b) Creating and (re)negotiating boundaries: Representations as mediation in visually oriented multilingual Swedish school settings. *Language, Culture and Curriculum* 23 (3), 251–276.

Bagga-Gupta, S. (2011) Re-thinking human diversity and multilingualism in Europe: Critical reflections from empirical research on oral, written and signed communication. Invited keynote at the International Conference on Multilingualism in Europe, March 2011, Budapest, Hungary.

Bagga-Gupta, S. (2012a) Scaffolding identities and learning at construction sites: Literacies and representations as mediation across time and space in an Indian NGO. Paper in panel "Asian Mediation 1: South Asia" at the Norwegian and Swedish Anthropology Conference on the theme "Mediation" – SANT-NAF, May 2012, Stockholm University, Sweden.

Bagga-Gupta, S. (2012b) Challenging understandings of bilingualism in the language sciences from the lens of research that focuses social practices. In E. Hjörne, G. van der Aalsvoort and G. de Abreu (eds) *Learning, Social Interaction and Diversity: Exploring School Practices* (pp. 85–101). Rotterdam: Sense.

Bagga-Gupta, S. (in press) The boundary-turn: Relocating language, identity and culture through the epistemological lenses of *time, space* and *social interactions*. In I. Hasnain, S. Bagga-Gupta and S. Mohan (eds) *Alternative Voices. (Re)searching Language, Culture and Identity.* England: Cambridge Scholars Publishing.

Bagga-Gupta, S. and St-John, O. (2010) Making complexities invisible? Contributions to the representation of social interaction in scholarly writings. Presentation at the Biennial EARLI joint-SIG Social Interaction, Learning and Diversity meeting: "Moving through Cultures of Learning", 2.–3 September 2010, Utrecht, The Netherlands.

Bagga-Gupta, S. and St-John, O. (submitted) Making complexities (in)visible. Empirically-derived contributions to the scholarly (re)presentations of social interactions.
Bailes, C.N. (2001) Primary-grade teachers' strategic use of American sign language in teaching English literacy in a bilingual school setting. Unpublished PhD thesis, University of Maryland, College Park.
Berger, P.L. and Luckman, T. (1967) *The Social Construction of Reality: A Treatise in the Sociology of Knowledge*. London: Allen Lane Penguin.
Bergqvist, K. (1990) Doing schoolwork: task premises and joint activity in the comprehensive classroom. Linköping Studies in Arts and Science 55. PhD thesis, Linköping University, Sweden.
Bhabha, H. (1994) *The Location of Culture*. London: Routledge.
Blumenthal-Kelly, A. (1995) Fingerspelling interaction: A set of deaf parents and their deaf daughter. In C. Lucas (ed.) *Sociolinguistics in Deaf Communities* (pp. 62–73). Washington DC: Gallaudet University Press.
Blommaert, J. (2010) *The Sociolinguistics of Globalization*. Cambridge: Cambridge University Press.
Butler, J. (1993) *Bodies That Matter: On the Discursive Limits of "Sex"*. New York: Routledge.
Chaiklin, S. and Lave J. (eds) (1993) *Understanding Practice: Perspectives on Activity and Context*. Cambridge: Cambridge University Press.
Chamberlain, C., Morford, J.P. and Mayberry, R. (eds) (2000) *Language Acquisition by Eye*. Mahwah, NJ: Lawrence Erlbaum Associates.
Corbett, J. (1996) *Bad-Mouthing: The Language of Special Needs*. London: Falmer Press.
De los Reyes, P. and Mulinari, D. (2005) *Intersektionalitet: Kritiska Reflektioner över (O) jämlikhetens Landskap* [Intersectionality: Critical reflections of the landscape of (in)equality]. Malmö: Liber.
Eriksson, C., Eriksson Baaz, M. and Thörn, H. (eds) (2002) *Globaliseringens Kulturer. Den Postkoloniala Paradoxen, Rasismen och det Mångkulturella Samhället* [Cultures of globalisation: The post-colonial paradox, racism and the multicultural society]. Nora, Sweden: Nya Doxa.
Erting L. (2001) Book sharing the deaf way: An ethnographic study in a bilingual preschool for deaf children. Unpublished PhD thesis, University of Maryland, College Park.
García, O. (2009) *Bilingual Education in the 21st Century*. Chichester: Wiley-Blackwell.
Geertz, C. (1973) Thick description: Toward an interpretive theory of culture. In C. Geertz (ed.) *The Interpretation of Cultures: Selected Essays* (pp. 3–30). New York: Basic Books.
Goffman, E. (1959) *The Presentation of Self in Everyday Life*. New York: Doubleday.
Goodwin, C. (2003) Pointing as situated practice. In S. Kita (ed.) *Pointing: Where Language, Culture and Cognition Meet* (pp. 217–241). Mahwah, NJ: Lawrence Erlbaum Associates.
Hacking, I. (1995) The looping effect of human kinds. In D. Sperber, D. Premark and A. J. Premark (eds) *Causal Cognition: A Multidisciplinary Debate* (pp. 351–394). Oxford: Clarendon Press.
Hansen, A.L. (2005) Kommunikative praksiser i visuell orienterte klassrom: En studie av et tilrettelagt opplegg for döve laerestudenter [Communicative practices in visually oriented classrooms: A study of an adapted education for teacher–students]. NTNU 2005:132. PhD thesis, Trondheim: The Norwegian Technological–Natural Sciences University.
Heath, S.B. (1983) *Ways with Words: Language, Life and Work in Communities and Classrooms*. Cambridge: Cambridge University Press.

Hjörne, E. and Säljö, R. (2008) *Att Platsa i en Skola för Alla. Elevhälsa och Förhandling om Normalitet i den Svenska Skolan* [To be part of the common school. Pupil health and negotiation of normality in the Swedish school]. Finland: Norstedts Akademiska Förlag.
Jewitt, C. (ed.) (2009) *The Routledge Handbook of Multimodal Analysis*. London: Routledge.
Kress, G., Jewitt, C., Bourne, J., Franks, A., Hardcastle, J., Jones, K. and Reid, E. (2005) *English in Urban Classrooms: A multimodal Perspective on Teaching and Learning*. London: Routledge Falmer.
Lartz, M. and Lestina, L.J. (1995) Strategies deaf mothers use when reading to their young deaf or hard of hearing children. *American Annals of the Deaf* 140(4), 358–370.
Lave, J. and Wenger, E. (1991) *Situated Learning: Legitimate Peripheral Participation*. Cambridge: Cambridge University Press.
Linell, P. (2005) *The Written Language Bias in Linguistics: Its Nature, Origins and Transformations*. Routledge Advances in Communication and Linguistic Theory. London: Routledge.
Linell, P. (2009) *Rethinking Language, Mind, and World Dialogically: Interactional and Contextual Theories of Human Sense-Making*. Charlotte, NC: Information Age Publishing.
Marschark, M. (1997) *Raising and Educating a Deaf Child: A Comprehensive Guide to the Choices, Controversies and Decisions Faced by Parents and Educators*. New York: Oxford University Press.
Masataka, N. (1992) Motherese in a signed language. *Infant Behaviour and Development* 15, 453–460.
McCall, L. (2005) The complexity of intersectionality. *Signs: Journal of Women in Culture and Society* 3(3), 1771–1800.
Maxwell, M. (1983) Language development in a deaf child of deaf parents: Signs, sign variations, speech and print. In K. Nelson (ed.) *Children's Language* (Vol. 4, pp. 283–313). Hillsdale NJ: Lawrence Erlbaum Association.
Middleton, D. and Edwards, D. (eds) (1990) *Collective Remembering*. London: SAGE.
Padden, C. (1996a) Early bilingual lives of deaf children. In I. Parasnis (ed.) *Cultural and Language Diversity and the Deaf Experience* (pp. 99–116). New York: Cambridge University Press.
Padden, C. (1996b) From the cultural to the bicultural. The modern deaf community. In I. Parasnis (ed.) *Cultural and Language Diversity and the Deaf Experience* (pp. 79–98). New York: Cambridge University Press.
Said, E.W. (1978) *Orientalism*. New York: Pantheon Books.
Schieffelin, B.B. and Ochs, E. (1986) *Language Socialization Across Cultures*. Cambridge: Cambridge University Press.
Scollon, R. and Scollon, S. (2004) *Nexus Analysis: Discourse and the Emerging Internet*. London: Routledge.
Scribner, S. and Cole, M. (1981) *The Psychology of Literacy*. Cambridge, MA: Harvard University Press.
Staunaes, D. (2003) Where have all the subjects gone? Bringing the concepts of intersectionality and subjectification. *NORA* 11 (2), 101–110.
Swedish Authority for School Improvement (2005) *Slutrapport. Uppdrag till Myndigheten för skolutveckling att arbeta för förbättrad förskole- och skolsituation i segregerade områden* [Final report. Assignment to the Swedish Authority for School Improvement for improvement of preschools and schools in segregated areas]. Stockholm.
Säljö, R. (2005) *Lärande och Kulturella Redskap. Om Lärprocesser och det Kollektiva Minnet* [Learning and cultural tools. On learning processes and the collective memory]. Falun: Norstedts Akademiska Förlag.

Teruggi, L.A. (ed.) (2003) *Una Scuola, due Lingue. L'esperienza di Bilinguismo della Scuola dell'Infanzia ed Elementare di Cossato* [One school, two languages. Experiences of bilingualism from the preschool and school in Cossato]. Milano: FrancoAngeli.

Vygotsky, L.S. (1986[1934]) *Thought and Language.* Translated by A. Kozulin. Cambridge: Harvard University Press.

Wertsch, J.V. (1985) *Culture, Communication, and Cognition: Vygotskian Perspectives.* New York: Cambridge University Press.

Wertsch, J.V. (2002) *Voices of Collective Memory.* Cambridge: Cambridge University Press.

Wertsch, J.V., del Rio, P. and Alvarez, A. (1995) (eds) *Sociocultural Studies of Mind.* New York: Cambridge University Press.

Winther, Y. (2000) Vardagsliv i och utanför klassrummet. En explorativ studie om hur man görs till blind i skolan [Everyday life inside and outside the classroom. An explorative study of how one is made blind in school]. MA thesis in Education with a focus on youth culture and school, Linköping University, Sweden.

Winther, Y. and Bagga-Gupta, S. (2007) The "acquisition" of blindness in communicative spaces. Presentation at the 12th Biennial Conference of EARLI, European Association for Research on Learning and Instruction in Budapest, August–September, 2007.

Young, R.J.C. (2001) Postcolonialism. An Historical Introduction. Oxford: Blackwell.

Appendix A Language-Focused Course Plans and Implicit/Explicit Language-Learner Categories in the Swedish National Syllabi for Mainstream Schools, 1962–2011

National syllabus (year)	Language-focused/related courses/areas – formal titles (in contents page)	Implicit/explicit language learners
Lgr 60 (1962)	i. Swedish ii. English/German/French	i. and ii. All pupils (except those in 'remedial' settings)
Lgr 69 (1969)	i. Swedish ii. English and German/French iii. Sign language	i. and ii. All pupils iii. Pupils in segregated special schools
Lgr 80 (1980)	i. Swedish ii. Type writing iii. English and German/ French iv. Swedish as a foreign language v. Home language	i. Native ethnic Swedish pupils ii. and iii. All pupils iv and v. Pupils with special needs v. Immigrant pupils.

Lpo 94 (1994)	i. Swedish ii. Swedish as a 2nd language iii. B- and C-languages iv. English v. Home language vi. Sign language	i. Native ethnic Swedish pupils ii. 1st, 2nd, etc. generation immigrant pupils iii. and iv. All pupils. v. Minority or immigrant pupils vi. Normal hearing pupils
Lpo 94 (2000)	i. Swedish ii. Swedish as a 2nd language iii. B- and C-language. iv. English v. Home language vi. Sign language	i. Native ethnic Swedish pupils ii. 1st, 2nd, etc. generation immigrant pupils iii. and iv. All pupils v. Minority or immigrant pupils vi. Normal hearing pupils
Lgr 11 (2011)	i. Swedish ii. Swedish as a 2nd language iii. English iv. Foreign languages v. Mother tongue vi. Sign language for hearing	i. Native ethnic Swedish pupils ii. 1st, 2nd, etc. generation immigrant pupils iii. and iv. All pupils v. Minority or immigrant pupils vi. Normal hearing pupils

Appendix B Language-Focused Course Plans and Implicit/Explicit Language-Learner Categories in the Swedish National Syllabi for Segregated Special Schools or Groups of Functional Disabled Pupils, 1962–2011

Agency, National syllabus (year)	Language-focused/related courses/areas – formal titles (in contents page)	Implicit/explicit language learners
Skolöverstyrelsen 1969, A. Lgr 69:II Spsk (1969) B. Lgr 69:II Sp (1969)	A. I. i. Swedish. ii. English. iii. Speech training and speech correction. iv. Hearing training. v. Training for perception of speech with tactile means. vi. Lip reading. vii. Sign language II. i. Swedish. ii. English B. (no course titles)	A. I. Hearing and speech-impaired pupils. Hearing-impaired with additional handicaps. Speech- and language-impaired pupils II. Visually-impaired pupils B. i. Pupils with reading and writing difficulties. ii. Hearing-impaired pupils. iii. Visually impaired pupils. iv. Pupils with speech difficulties
Skolöverstyrelsen 1983, Lgr 80 (1980)	I. Language block: i. Bilingualism – Sign language and Swedish. ii. Sign language. iii. Swedish. iv. English. v. French/German II. i. Swedish. ii. Reading and technical support	I. Deaf and hearing-impaired pupils II. Visually-impaired pupils

Skolverket 1996, Lpo 94 (1994)	i. B- and C-languages for deaf/hearing-impaired. ii. B- and C-languages. iii. English for deaf/hearing-impaired. iv. English. v. Home language for deaf/hearing-impaired. vi. Home language. vii. Swedish for deaf/hearing-impaired. viii. Swedish. ix. Swedish as a 2nd language. x. Sign language for deaf/hearing-impaired. xi. Sign language for hearing	i., iii., v., vii. and x. Deaf and hearing-impaired pupils (including immigrant pupils) ii., iv., vi., viii., ix. and xi. Normal hearing pupils in mainstreamed schools ix. Immigrant normal hearing pupils in mainstreamed schools
Skolverket 2002, Lpo 94 (2000)	i. B- and C-languages for deaf/hearing-impaired. ii. B- and C-languages. iii. English for deaf/hearing-impaired. iv. English. v. Home language for deaf/hearing-impaired. vi. Home language. vii. Swedish for deaf/hearing-impaired. viii. Swedish. ix. Swedish as a 2nd language. x. Sign language for deaf/hearing-impaired. xi. Sign language for hearing	i., iii., v., vii. and x. Deaf and hearing-impaired pupils (including immigrant) pupils ii., iv., vi., viii., ix. and xi. Normal hearing pupils in mainstreamed schools ix. Immigrant normal hearing pupils in mainstreamed schools
Lgr 11 (2011)	i. Swedish for deaf and hearing-impaired ii. Sign language for deaf iii. English for deaf and hearing-impaired iv. Foreign languages for deaf and hearing-impaired v. Mother tongue	i., ii., iii. and iv. All deaf and hearing-impaired pupils in segregated schools v. Deaf and hearing-impaired minority or immigrant pupils in segregated schools

Part 2
Local Practices in Transition

Introduction

After taking a look at how individuals construct their identity through and around literacy, we focus our attention on practices, texts and interactions. The societal changes described in the introductory chapter inevitably have an effect on how we relate to each other and to texts, how we make sense of our social realities in interactions with others and with texts (and other semiotic signs) and how we construct, demonstrate, transform and reinterpret competences and membership in communities in and across different spaces.

The four chapters in this part examine literacy practices in school and higher education. The chapters focusing on schools investigate language and literacy education and science education in primary and secondary schools. The chapter with a focus on higher education explores an international master's programme. These spaces may appear very different from each other, but the phenomena examined are similar, as in all of them literacy is at the core of making sense of the social space, the objects and the means of learning, as well as of claiming membership and displaying competence. This sense making takes place in interactions in particular settings and with the texts and other modalities involved in interactions, but beyond that, we must appreciate how far the local settings are shaped by global discourses. The close analyses of interactions, texts and discourses show, however, that the participants in the practices are not 'at the mercy of the global'; instead, global discourses and categorizations are (re)interpreted, contested and appropriated by the participants, and thus local practices also shape global practices and discourses. The local and global become mixed, and global practices get a local manifestation, thus becoming *glocal* (see e.g. Pennycook, 2010).

One central theme in this part is the challenge to existing concepts and categorizations. One such categorization is the bilingual student, which is challenged by the empirical analyses in Chapter 4 by Daugaard and Larsen. The social reality of the classroom clashes with the globally established label, and close examination of local practices shows that pupils have agency and, building on their lived linguistic realities, create a multilingual space for themselves in the classroom. This chapter, as well as Chapter 7 by McCambridge and Pitkänen-Huhta, also challenges the notions of space and local practice. The spaces we operate in today are not simple and clear-cut, with neat boundaries and homogeneous communities of practice, but rather they are messy, indeed increasingly so, with a range of languages, modalities and other resources. Moreover, local practices are more often not just glocal but also translocal, thus reaching across spaces in multiple ways, especially with the help of new technologies. Discourses around and of literacy are (re)created in these translocal spaces to meet the needs of the emergent mobile communities. Related to the concept of space are the notions of formal and informal, which are reinterpreted in Chapter 5 by Halonen. The pupils in the classroom examined by Halonen are navigating in the fuzzy borderland between formal and informal writing practices. They are skilfully drawing on different linguistic, semiotic and textual resources to show multiple competencies in and orientations towards both formal and informal practices. Yet another concept that is challenged in Chapters 5 and 6 (by Axelsson and Danielsson) is the notion of text. In different disciplines and in our technologically saturated settings, the notion of text needs to include different modalities, and learners need to be able to draw on various semiotic resources in order to gain and display knowledge and membership in our postmodern societies.

Reference

Pennycook, A. (2010) *Language as a Local Practice*. London: Routledge.

4 Multilingual Classrooms as Sites of Negotiations of Language and Literacy

Line Møller Daugaard and
Helle Pia Laursen

Introduction

As a result of current globalization processes, many classrooms no longer look like the 'traditional' ones we once knew. Due to waves of immigration and other forms of mobility, a new form of sociolinguistic heterogeneity has entered many classrooms. When people move, they bring with them different linguistic resources reflecting their life trajectories (Blommaert, 2010). The mobility of speakers and linguistic resources also involves transitions across different spaces, in which speakers are placed in different discursive constructions and ascribed certain identities.

In a Danish context, 'the bilingual student' is an example of such a discursive construction. The bilingual student has become a more or less naturalized categorization, through which the increasing linguistic diversity in the educational system is perceived and evaluated. In public and policy discourse in Denmark, as well as in some research-oriented discourse, the label 'bilingual' refers to the child who speaks a language other than Danish at home, who does not master Danish at the same level as his peers and who comes from another (non-Western) country. Instead of looking at bilingualism as something that has to do with mastering a broad linguistic repertoire, bilingualism is looked upon in terms of a lack of competences in Danish and in terms of an individual's – or the individual's parents' – place of origin, thus linking bilingualism to a certain part of the immigrant population and invoking images of an inherently impoverished group or even an abnormal phenomenon. This broadly used conceptualization of 'the bilingual student' also rests on a model of sociolinguistic variation in which one can easily identify discrete well-defined languages in an individual's linguistic repertoire and link these languages to particular nations.

Variations within this conceptualization of 'the bilingual student' have set the stage for the general educational view of the multilingual classroom, and they contribute to the ongoing production of deficit and monolithic categories by offering and limiting opportunities for literacy learning and social identification. In official educational discourse, linguistic diversity seems to be associated with societal problems in society and education. 'The bilingual student' has come to symbolize problems in society, and these students are increasingly portrayed as being one of the primary reasons for Denmark's low international literacy rankings, and they are often thought of as posing a threat to a school's profile (Holm & Laursen, 2011).

The Changing Sociolinguistic Landscape

However, present sociolinguistic processes pose a challenge for the educational system, as the movement of people and the expansion of digital communication challenge predominant understandings of literacy and language. Blommaert (2003) points to linguistic changes, which he refers to as *sociolinguistic globalization* characterized 'as a matter of particular language varieties entering the repertoires of particular groups, creating new semiotic opportunities and commodities for members of such groups and indeed constructing them as groups' (Blommaert, 2003: 611).

When looking at literacy practices in urban multilingual settings, the notion of 'a language' or two or more separate languages becomes increasingly problematic. For example, two studies on linguistic practices among adolescents, one in London and one in Copenhagen, show how young people mix all kinds of linguistic and semiotic resources in their communicative activities (Rampton, 1995, 2006; Quist, 2009). In these linguistically diverse contexts, one can no longer assume a given link between ethnic or national categories and language use. In their meaning-making practices, individuals employ a broad repertoire of linguistic and semiotic signs.

In the multilingual classroom, children involved in different language and literacy transition processes meet. The children bring different language and literacy repertoires consisting of different 'ingredients' with them (Blommaert, 2003) and they assign different metapragmatic meanings and functions to these ingredients. For these children, even though they officially bear the label 'bilingual student', this does not necessarily mean that the language of their parents is their dominant language or that they are fluent speakers of this language. Nor does it necessarily mean that they have a special and intimate affiliation toward this language. On the other hand, even though they do not master their parents' language 'completely', or strive to master it completely, this does not mean that this language plays no role in their language practices, nor that it has no place in their linguistic repertoire and does not influence their self-representation and social identity.

These sociolinguistic changes both challenge traditional dichotomies, such as 'mother tongue' and 'second language', and the static and simplistic relationship between languages, speakers and places such as seen in the classic sociolinguistic concept of the speech community, which, in Quist's words (2009: 632), implies that '[l]anguages, speakers and places constitute a unity. Languages belong to specific speakers, and speakers belong to specific places.'

The Multilingual Classroom: A Messy Marketplace

In many respects, the school setting represents a forceful institution – also linguistically. Since language ideologies always affect language change (Blommaert, 2003), the classroom is also a setting in which language ideologies are negotiated: among children, among teachers and among children and teachers. In schools and other educational institutions, certain literacies will always be valued and supported, while others tend to be overlooked and devalued. Furthermore, in classrooms, some identity options are more available to students than others, and some linguistic practices are more valued than others (Miller, 2004). Doing and learning literacy is not only about mastering a code but also about knowing how to participate in language and literacy practices that are valued and recognized as legitimate. The classroom constitutes a site where students are introduced to socially sanctioned ways of being literate through cultural artefacts and interactional routines. It is also a place where the students' complex and fluid linguistic repertoires may conflict with the expectations associated with more static and essentializing models of language and literacy.

But the classroom, as a space of multilingualism, might also comprise what Baynham (2006) has called creative discourse (agency), a term which refers to 'the ways that students make their place and take their place in the classroom and the ways teachers contingently and responsively open up spaces where this becomes possible, and respond to interactive demands for space' (Baynham, 2006: 28). This creative discourse can, for example, be triggered when students claim interactive space, bringing their real or imagined linguistic worlds into the classroom discourse. Such instances might lead to, perhaps momentarily, destabilization of what counts as language and literacy knowledge. The multilingual classroom is also 'a site of dynamic pushes and pulls, with teacher and student agendas robustly shaping interaction, claiming space' (Baynham, 2006: 38).

In this sense, the multilingual classroom can be understood as an example of the 'messy new marketplace', which Blommaert (2010), with reference to

Bourdieu, introduces. This messy marketplace, resulting from the mobility of people and linguistic resources, is not uniform and unambiguous one with clear-cut normative orders. Rather, it is complex and polycentric, in the sense that different clusters of norms are at play simultaneously, thus offering students and teachers different centers of authority to which they can orientate themselves, even though these centers are of different order and do not carry the same value and even though not all participants have the same rights and responsibilities.

In this messy communicative space, linguistic resources and practices are subject to ongoing value attribution and negotiation. Different teacher and student agendas meet, sometimes resulting in immediately silencing the agendas of those parties who are not in control, sometimes in repressed tensions or intense clashes and sometimes in more or less open-ended negotiations of what counts as language and literacy (see also Chapter 7). Naturally, how much room for negotiation there is depends on the specific classroom and the specific situation. In the following section, we will analyse what happens when a particular multilingual classroom as a pre-eminent learning space (Soja, 2004) is opened up to this broader, real and imagined world of language and literacy.

The Study *Signs of Language*

This analysis draws on empirical data collected in the research project *Signs of Language* (Laursen, 2008, 2009, 2010, 2011). In search of a critical postmodern perspective on classroom studies, as advocated by Lin and Luk (2002), the project *Signs of Language* aims to investigate the possibilities of restructuring literacy practices in multilingual classrooms by focusing on the children's actual language and literacy use as well as understandings in concrete local sociocultural contexts. Thus, the ambition is not to reveal universal truths and general guidelines, but rather to analyse socially situated opportunities for change.

The project is a longitudinal study (2008–2014) involving five multilingual classes from five schools, which will be followed from Year 1 until Year 7. All the schools are located in urban areas and have in common that there is a considerable degree of linguistic diversity among the students and in the surrounding community.

The study aims at improving the understanding of children's complex uses of the linguistic and semiotic resources available to them by paying close attention to the perspective of the child – as a user and interpreter of literacy (Blackledge & Creese, 2010). It explores how multilingual children interpret and create signs in order to communicate and perform their social identity in different multilingual classroom settings.

With respect to literacy learning and teaching, the study applies a social semiotic approach focusing on the acquisition of sign systems as a process whereby children make meaning from the information available to them in their social environment (Hodge & Kress, 1988; Laursen, 2012; Kenner et al., 2004; Kress, 2001; see also Chapter 6, this volume). As Morgan and Ramanathan (2005) argue, this conceptualization of script learning as an active process of sign-making allows space, not only for information retrieval but also for creative and oppositional meaning making.

Through intervention studies in linguistically diverse classrooms, we investigate how teachers and students navigate in these often ambivalent sites of education, how they deal with linguistic diversity and how they negotiate the construction of language and literacy within the broader discursive climate. Thus, at the heart of the exploration are the language and literacy practices in the classrooms as they are accomplished through the processes of intervention and reflections on the interventions.

To investigate these language and literacy practices, we adopt an ethnographic approach which in Blommaert's words

> ... will allow us to unravel the details of how language varieties and discourses work for people, what they accomplish (or fail to) in practice and how this fits into local economies of resources. It also allows us to check, at the lowest level, how larger patterns and developments are set down in the actual realities of language usage. (Blommaert, 2003: 615)

This approach leads us to pay attention both to the local and the situated and to the processes through which the local use of sociolinguistic and semiotic resources is intertwined with globalized processes. In this perspective, language is conceptualized as a concrete resource that is mobile across time and space, shifting in meaning and value when moved from one space to another.

Literacy studies provides the framework for examining the issue of literacy. Within literacy studies, literacy is studied in terms of literacy practices and refers to 'the general cultural ways of utilizing literacy which people draw upon in particular situations' (Barton, 2007). Thus, focus is not on literacy as individual skills or competencies but on literacy as it is acted out in different settings with various functions and tied up with diverse values.

In addition to the investigation of classroom literacy practices, six focal children have been picked out in each class, and these focal children will be followed closely throughout the six years of the study. Data sources in this part of the study include classroom observations, informal interactions with the children, semi-structured interviews and collecting artefacts produced by the children as part of the teaching and as part of quasi-experimental activities.

This double focus enables us to combine different perspectives and thereby avoid one-sided focus on the individual by examining the individuals in their interactional and social context (Willett, 1995). This means that emphasis is, on the one hand, on the interaction between the children's creation of meaning, understood as a dynamic and changing phenomenon, and on the other hand, on the micro-interactions and the availability of, or access to, language and literacy resources in the classroom.

All five classrooms investigated in *Signs of Language* constitute sites of heteroglossic language and literacy practices. The examples in this chapter are taken from one of these classrooms. The classroom in question is located in a school situated in the suburbs of a large Danish town, in a neighbourhood that in public Danish discourse is labelled as a deprived residential area. The class in focus consists of 25 children, who are all officially labeled 'bilingual students'. All 25 children speak Danish and are learning to read and write in Danish, and most of them simultaneously meet and use a range of other languages in their everyday lives. Languages such as Arabic, Somali, Dari, Pashto, Romanian, Kiswahili, Urdu and Cantonese are spoken and sometimes read and written in the children's homes for a range of purposes, and many children learn Arabic in Qu'ranic class after school. In and out of school, the children engage with language and literacy in a range of ways and contexts: They listen to music, watch television, play computer games, read books, write letters, lists, and text messages and communicate with friends and relatives on the internet. Their language and literacy practices sometimes unfold in Danish, sometimes in English, sometimes in a variety of other languages – and often the children switch naturally between languages and language varieties (Daugaard, 2010).

Reading in Danish – with Reference to Urdu

> For literacy scholars and educators, the traditional confines of the classroom explode with new possibilities of interpretation, when this preeminent learning space is opened up to a wider, real and imagined world of ethnic, gender, and class consciousness, conflicting identity formations, creative cultural hybridities, new political positioning, an extensive microcosm of everyday life at multiple geographical scales, from the local to the global. (Soja, 2004: x)

The multiple geographical scales – and their linguistic correlates – find their way into the literacy classroom in various intricate ways. The teachers both strive and struggle to invite the diversity in languages and literacies into the classroom and to make a space for this diversity, but the children themselves also actively engage in creating a space for multilingual experiences – sometimes in ways which are contingent with the classroom agenda, sometimes in ways which interrupt the orderliness of classroom discourse and challenge established categories of language and literacy. The literacy classroom is not a neutral learning space void of valorizations and isolated from the discursive constructions in society, and classroom practices thus interchangeably reflect, enforce and sometimes contest and destabilize the discursive construction of 'the bilingual student'.

The excerpt below is taken from a structured reading activity conducted in all five classrooms as a part of *Signs of Language*. The reading activity was conducted when the children were half way through Year 2, and in the activity, each child was asked to read aloud a children's short book to the research assistant (RA). The reading and the interaction around the reading was videotaped and analysed in order to gain insight into the child's reading and reading strategies as they occurred in the particular situation.

The excerpt involves seven-year-old Naima, who has an Urdu background, reading aloud to the local RA. Naima carefully, and with some difficulty, makes her way through the text until she reaches the sentence *Far og Sofie går ud for at købe fisk* (in English: Daddy and Sofie go out to buy fish). The adverb 'ud' (in English: out) is pronounced [ut] instead of the correct pronunciation [ud] (turn 3). [Ut] has no immediately recognizable semantic content in Danish, and the research assistant offers the correct pronunciation [ud] (turn 4). Naima dutifully repeats [ud] and then reflects on the difference between [ut] and [ud] (turn 5).

Excerpt 1 Ut ut

Turn	Speaker	Original Danish wording	Rough translation into English
1	Naima	far (.) og (.) Sofie (.) gå (.) gå	dad (.) and (.) Sofie (.) go (.) go
2	RA	ja, de går	yes, they go
3	Naima	går (.) ud *((udtale [ut]))*	go (.) out *(pronunciation [ut])*
4	RA	ud *(udtale [ud])*	out *(pronunciation [ud])*
5	Naima	ud *(udtale [ud])* det er som om der står ut *(udtale [ut])* ut på pakistansk, det betyder, når der er nogen der siger ut ut, det betyder væk væk *(laver 'gå væk-bevægelse' med højre hånd)*	out *(pronunciation [ud])* it's as if it says ut *(pronunciation [ut])* ut in Pakistani, that means, when somebody says ut ut, it means go away *(makes 'go away' movement with her right hand)*

In the excerpt, Naima is involved in what can be considered an almost prototypical school literacy event in a Danish primary-school classroom: She is with a Danish-speaking adult who in Danish asks her to read aloud in Danish from a Danish-medium text in a classroom setting that signals literacy in Danish through the books and posters present in the room as well as the Danish alphabet that is hanging on the wall. This establishes a clear linguistic horizon of expectations in which Danish is the unmarked and thereby expected choice of language and linguistic reference. In the excerpt, however, Naima breaks with this expectation. She does not limit herself to reading aloud in Danish; she reads in Danish and makes references to Urdu formulated in Danish; and her reflection demonstrates her ability to activate knowledge about pronunciation and semantics in both Danish and Urdu, to compare knowledge across languages and literacies – and her willingness to make this relevant in the given situation. Even in a context where experiences with language and literacy other than those tied to Danish must be considered marked, Naima succeeds in opening up a space for multilingual experiences and hereby challenges a traditional understanding of what counts as relevant linguistic knowledge in a Danish primary-school literacy classroom.

Denmark, Manchester, Pakistan and Copenhagen

It takes Naima more than 30 minutes to carefully work her way through the book (consisting of 25 illustrated pages with a total of 280 running words). After finishing the reading exercise, Naima initiates a conversation evolving around her narrative of her linguistic world. When the research assistant asks Naima about her level of competence in and affinity with Urdu, Naima responds that she is not very good yet, but that she certainly has to learn more when she grows older. When asked how she will improve her Urdu, her answer is clear: She must go to Manchester, to her grandfather's place where there is ample opportunity to practice Urdu. Naima's arena of acquisition of language and literacy thus extends far beyond home and school in her own local neighbourhood and reaches out into a complex and globalized world. A world in which the relations between languages, speakers and places are not static and reducible to simple causal relations, but fluid and characterized by mobility and sometimes ambiguity. Naima's language-learning landscape is transnational and breaks down simplistic notions of the anatomy of the linguistic community. For a girl with roots in Pakistan growing up in Danish suburbia, Manchester may be an obvious site for acquiring Urdu literacy. Further dimensions of complexity are added to the picture of Naima's linguistic world in the excerpt below that occurs shortly after Naima's narrative about literacy learning in Manchester.

Multilingual Classrooms as Sites of Negotiations of Language and Literacy   111

Excerpt 2 Here in Denmark

Turn	Speaker	Original Danish wording	Rough translation into English
1	Naima	jeg skal også måske til Pakistan, om vinteren måske	I'm also going to Pakistan, in winter maybe
2	RA	skal du det	you are
3	Naima	ja, men det skal jeg ikke i dag	yes, but not today
4	RA	ikke lige nu	not right now
5	Naima	Nej	no
6	RA	det bliver spændende	that's going to be exciting
7	Naima	ja, næste gang (.) men ved du godt, RA, i Pakistan, ikke også, der er slippet nogle tyve fri derovre, så Pakistan tyve, ikke, de skal prøve (.) de prøver at (.) i Pakistan, ikke, der er det synd for dem, fordi børn og bedsteforældre fra Pakistan, de må kun være hjemme nu og lege	yeah, next time (.) but you know, RA, in Pakistan, right, some thieves got out over there, so Pakistan thieves, right, they must try (.) they try to (.) in Pakistan, right, there is, it's a shame because children and grandparents from Pakistan, they have to stay at home now and play
8	RA	nå, bor din bedstemor i Pakistan	oh, so your grandmother lives in Pakistan
9	Naima	ja, også min mormor, men ikke min farfar	yeah, also my grandmother, but not my grandfather
10	RA	nej, han bor i Manchester	no, he lives in Manchester
11	Naima	sammen med (.) sammen med (.) der hvor min største kusine også er (.) jeg kender også en baby i Manchester, ikke også, hende kan godt løbe nu	together with (.) together with (.) where my oldest cousin is too (.) I also know a baby in Manchester, right, her can run now
12	RA	så er hun ved at være stor	she's getting big then
13	Naima	ja, hun bliver to år snart, hun er et år nu, men jeg kender en fra Danmark, det er hende min kusine, hende er ikke så stor, men hun går i skole, ikke, jeg hørte hun var 13 år, ikke, før var hun 12, men nu er hun 13 (.) hun bor i en (.) hvad hedder det (.) hvad hedder det (.) i København	yeah, she turns two soon, she is one now, but I know one from Denmark, it's my cousin, her is not that big, but she goes to school, right, I heard she was 13, right, before she was 12, but now she's 13 (.) she lives in a (.) what is it called (.) what is it called (.) in Copenhagen

14	RA	nå, er hun flyttet derover	oh, she moved over there
15	Naima	ja, nu min onkel, han savner meget min kusine (.) og min storebror, ikke, han irriterer mig meget, han går snart ud og i københavnsk skole (.) min kusine, ikke, hende kan ikke lide det, hun vil gerne gå hen til sin egen skole her i Danmark	yeah, now my uncle, he misses my cousin a lot (.) and my big brother, right, he really irritates me, he will soon leave school and go to a Copenhagen school (.) my cousin, right, she wants to go back to her own school here in Denmark
16	RA	ja, er hun ikke så glad for den nye skole	right, she's not too happy about the new school
17	Naima	det tror jeg ikke måske (.) når de synger, så synger de bare københavnsk, så kan man ikke engang forstå det	I don't think so, maybe (.) when they sing, they just sing in Copenhagenish, then you can't even understand it

In Excerpt 2, Naima in one sense constructs the entire world as her linguistic playground. Both linguistically and interactionally, she moves with great ease and familiarity between talking about everyday life in her city in Denmark, Manchester and Pakistan. Copenhagen, however, appears distant and strange. Naima has difficulty even remembering (or formulating) the name of the capital, and Copenhagen is constructed as being in opposition to her own hometown, 'here in Denmark'. In equating her hometown with Denmark and using the deictic word 'here' signaling closeness (see Auer, 2012), Naima establishes a strong sense of homeliness or familiarity tied to her hometown. And language use seems to be at the heart of Naima's conceptualization of mental and emotional proximity and distance: in the Copenhagen school, they sing in 'Copenhagenish', a linguistic variant described as impossible to understand and therefore this contributes strongly to Naima's construction of Copenhagen as 'unheimlich'. Feeling at home is a many-faceted phenomenon (Winther, 2006), which among other aspects also has to do with language and literacy, and feeling at home linguistically cannot be understood within predefined patterns of and connections between speakers, languages and places.

On the contrary, in Naima's narrative of her linguistic world, we see a de-hierarchization of common understandings of concept pairs like near–far, home–away, center–periphery, well known–unknown and accessible–inaccessible. Traditional dichotomies dissolve, and new relevance structures are established; in Blommaert's words, we see a 'reordering of the locally available repertoires and the relative hierarchical relations between ingredients in the hierarchy' (Blommaert, 2003: 608). This unsettling of categories challenges traditional conceptions of what is local and what is global, and raises the question of where the suspense of the balance between the local and the global leaves the national? Naima's construction of her linguistic world cannot be adequately described with reference to the preconceived one-dimensional models of geography and linguistic and national affiliation that are at the heart of the discursive construction of 'the bilingual student'.

Rebelling Against Compartmentalized Categorization

Blommaert's challenge to sociolinguistic theory also has a classroom correlative. In Naima's classroom, the multilingual children themselves can be seen to be actively involved in the unthinking and rethinking which Blommaert appeals for. As mentioned earlier, the teachers in Naima's class both strive and struggle to open up the literacy teaching to a multilingual reality. Excerpt 3 is taken from a teaching cycle focusing on reading aloud in different languages using dual language books. In this lesson, the class is working with numbers in different languages. On the blackboard, there is a large grid with the numbers 0–10 written with Danish numerals, digital numerals and numerals written in a range of languages spoken by the children in the class. Together, the class is filling out the blanks, guided by the teacher. The writing of the Arabic numerals gives rise to intense negotiations of who has the rights to and ownership of Arabic between the teacher and a group of boys with Somali background – and within the group of Somali children.

Excerpt 3 You're not Arabic

Turn	Speaker	Original Danish wording	Rough translation into English
1	Teacher	vi mangler jo at få skrevet nogle tal på arabisk. Er der ikke nogen, der vil op og skrive nogle tal på arabisk? *(Farooq markerer ivrigt)*	we still need to write some Arabic numerals. Doesn't anybody want to come up and write some Arabic numerals? *(Farooq eagerly raises his hand)*
2	Gharib	Farooq, du er ikke arabisk	Farooq, you're not Arabic
3	Farooq	jo, jeg kan godt finde ud af arabiske tal, så... *(laver luk munden-tegn til Gharib)*	well, I know how to write Arabic numerals, so... *(makes shut up-sign to Gharib)*
4	Gharib	så luk din mund selv *(til Farooq)*	shut up yourself *(to Farooq)*
5	Abtidoon	må jeg så ikke på kinesisk?	can I in Chinese then?

6	Teacher	nej nej nej, fordi jeg kan høre, at I er jo meget inde i alle tallene, men er der ikke nogen af dem...	no no no, I can hear that you all know a lot about numbers, but doesn't one of you...
7	Farooq	jeg lærer arabisk *(vendt mod Gharib)*	I learn Arabic *(turned to Gharib)*
8	Teacher	... der kan de arabiske tal, der kommer op og skrive et arabisk tal? *(Farooq markerer stadig og rejser sig op)* Hvem er det? Jamen jamen, hvem er det? *(Farooq står stadig op, og han markerer fortsat. Abtidoon rækker også hånden op)*	... who knows Arabic want to come up and write an Arabic numeral? *(Farooq still has his hand up and stands up)* Who is it? Well, who is it? *(Farooq is still standing up, and his hand is still raised. Abtidoon also raises his hand)*
9	Abtidoon	mig! *(vifter med hånden)*	me! *(waves his hand)*
10	Teacher	hvem har vi? Hvem har vi, der kan arabiske tal herinde?	who have we got? Who have we got that knows the Arabic numerals?
11	Abtidoon	jeg kan, jeg kan godt	I do, I can do it.
12	Teacher	nej, jeg forstår ikke, hvorfor I siger, I kan? *(ser på Abtidoon og Farooq)*	no, I really don't understand why you guys say that you can? *(looks at Abtidoon and Farooq)*
13	Farooq	fordi jeg går til koran, og vi lærer arabiske tal *(taler med høj, insisterende stemme, står stadig op med armene over kors)*	because I go to Qu'ran, and we learn Arabic numerals *(speaks in a loud and insistent voice, standing up with his arms crossed over his chest)*
14	Teacher	dét var en god forklaring *(gør en bevægelse med overkroppen fremad og nedad)*. Det var en god forklaring. Farooq, værsgo at komme herop *(rækker et stykke kridt frem mod Farooq)*	now, that's a good explanation *(makes a sweeping movement forward and downwards with her torso)*. That's a good explanation. Farooq, please come up here *(hands a piece of chalk towards Farooq)*
15	Class	Jaaah	yeaaah
16	Teacher	hvad for et tal vil du skrive?	which number do you want to write?

When the teacher calls for volunteers to write Arabic numerals, Farooq who has a Somali background immediately raises his hand. However, the teacher does not immediately acknowledge Farooq as an appropriate candidate. Farooq does not seem to belong to the category 'one of you who knows the Arabic numerals'; a view shared by another Somali-speaking boy, Gharib, who objects to Farooq's candidature by saying 'you're not Arabic'. Farooq promptly objects to this, using both gestures and words, and now receives support from Abtidoon, also Somali-speaking, who volunteers to write both Chinese and Arabic letters, despite the fact that he is hardly identifiable as either Chinese or Arabic. However, the teacher maintains that Farooq and Abtidoon do not qualify as proper writers of Arabic numerals and explicitly asks the boys why they insist on wanting to write the Arabic numerals. Farooq now directly addresses the teacher and delivers a forceful argument, strengthened by his affirmative and determined body position and insistent voice, both of which signal calm perseverance: 'Because I go to Qu'ran, and we learn Arabic numerals'. Faced with this vigorous protest against compartmentalized categorizations of children, languages and literacies, the teacher immediately capitulates and invites Farooq to the blackboard. As he walks to the blackboard, he is greeted by cheers from the class, and when he has written an Arabic numeral, he smilingly returns to his seat in a triumphant victory dance.

Even in a curricular activity explicitly designed to make space for children's multilingual experiences, Farooq is not immediately recognized as legitimate writer of Arabic numerals. Having a Somali background, he seems to be automatically assigned the status as a native speaker of Somali, and the inclusion into this category seems to simultaneously exclude him from the category of legitimate writers of Arabic, which in this classroom context is cast as a desirable and exclusive community. Throughout the situation, Farooq struggles to claim an alternative space for himself. His determination to claim this space manifests itself in his body posture and his tone of voice, but his claim is not recognized until he delivers an apparently irrefutable argument: he goes to Qu'ran. Farooq's example shows how the multilingual classroom is a site for negotiation not only of values, identities, expertise in and ownership of the Danish language but also of a range of other languages – in this case, Arabic. In this messy marketplace, the commodity of Arabic is not only negotiated by the children who are assigned mother-tongue affiliations to Arabic within the discursive construction of 'the bilingual student', and the children themselves actively push to expand the marketplace.

Concluding Remarks: Studying Linguistic Space in a Messy Marketplace

The examples above with Naima and Farooq demonstrate the transitional processes involved when speakers and linguistic resources move across spaces. They also demonstrate the changing sociolinguistic landscape that characterizes many urban classrooms as well as the possible clashes between the sociolinguistic realities of such classrooms and the educational conceptualization of 'the bilingual student'. In a Danish context, linguistic diversity in school settings is typically perceived as a growing number of 'bilingual students' in an otherwise Danish environment. It is based on an understanding of 'the bilingual student' that is rooted in ideological positions which see the student either through the lens of a Danish-only ideology, ignoring any other linguistic resources the students might bring into the classroom, or through the lens of an essentialist-oriented bilingual model, resting on a simple equation of language, speaker and ethnicity.

In contrast, Naima and Farooq point to a linguistic heterogeneity that cannot be captured by the above conceptualization of 'the bilingual student'. The examples also illustrate how multilingual children actively claim linguistic space – in an assertive way of 'doing being' multilingual (see also Chapter 5). In different classroom settings and in different ways, they insist on making other linguistic identities and experiences relevant than those that seem to be expected. However, Naima and Farooq do not only claim interactive space but also push and pull for an extended linguistic space by creatively and persistently activating their lived linguistic experiences.

The multilingual classroom is not a neutral language and literacy learning space. There is more going on than just learning language and literacy. The classroom is also a messy marketplace, in which language ideologies and identity options are maintained, contested and negotiated. *Signs of Language* aims to provide insights into the complex and fluid linguistic worlds of multilingual students; How are these worlds acted out and negotiated in five multilingual classrooms and what are the locally situated opportunities for transformations in classroom practices? Observations from the study show the pervasive character of the dominant language ideologies associated with 'the bilingual student', but they also show moments of student agency and expertise like those demonstrated by multilingual children such as Naima and Farooq.

These observations point to an urgent need to discuss the classificatory practices and the conceptualization of 'the bilingual student' in education, and to the need for further ethnographic studies into linguistic practices of multilingual children as well as how these practices, repeating the words of Blommaert (2003), 'work for people, what they accomplish (or fail to) in practice and how this fits into local economies of resources'. The local economies of resources are not just local. They are also embedded in wider sociopolitical contexts that must be taken into account when analysing classroom practices and the local possibilities of changing these practices.

References

Auer, P. (2012) Spatial indexicalities and spatial pragmatics. In M. Meeuwis and J. Östman (eds) *Pragmaticizing Understanding* (pp. 53 – 76). Amsterdam: John Benjamins.
Barton, D. (2007) *Literacy: An Introduction to the Ecology of Written Language*. Oxford: Blackwell Publishers Ltd.
Baynham, M. (2006) Agency and contingency in the learning and of refugees and asylum seekers. *Linguistics and Education* 17, 24–39.
Blackledge, A. and Creese, A. (2010) *Multilingualism*. London: Continuum.
Blommaert, J. (2003) Commentary: A sociolinguistics of globalization. *Journal of Sociolinguistics* 7 (4), 607–623.
Blommaert, J. (2010) *The Sociolinguistics of Globalization*. Cambridge: Cambridge University Press.
Daugaard, L.M. (2010) Når flersprogetheden eksploderer... [When multilingualism explodes ...] In Helle Pia Laursen (ed.) *Tegn på sprog. Tosprogede børn lærer at læse og skrive. Tredje statusrapport* [Signs of Language. Bilingual children learn to read and write. Third status] (pp. 28–37). Accessed 8 January 2010. *http://didak.ucc.dk/public/dokumenter/UFEV/UC2/Statusrapport%20oktober%202010.pdf*
Hodge, R. and Kress, G. (1988) *Social Semiotics*. New York: Cornell University Press.
Holm, L. and Laursen, H.P. (2011) Migrants and literacy crises. *APPLES – Journal of Applied Language Studies* 5 (2), 3–16.
Kenner, C., Kress, G., Al-Khatib, H., Kam, R. and Tsai, K. (2004) Finding the keys to biliteracy: How young children interpret different writing systems. *Language and Education* 18 (2), 124–144.
Kress, G. (2001) Sociolinguistics and social semiotics. In P. Cobley (ed.) *The Routledge Companion to Semiotics and Linguistics* (pp. 66–82). London: Routledge.
Laursen, H.P. (ed.) (2008) *Tegn på sprog: Tosprogede børn lærer at læse og skrive. Første statusrapport*. [Signs of Language: Bilingual children learn to read and write. First status]. Accessed 8 January 2010. *https://didak.ucc.dk/public/dokumenter/UFEV/DIDAK/Statusrapport%20oktober%202008.pdf*
Laursen, H.P. (ed.) (2009) *Tegn på sprog: Tosprogede børn lærer at læse og skrive. Anden statusrapport*. [Signs of Language: Bilingual children learn to read and write. Second status]. Accessed 8 January 2010. *https://didak.ucc.dk/public/dokumenter/UFEV/DIDAK/Statusrapport%20oktober%202009.pdf*
Laursen, H.P. (ed.) (2010) *Tegn på sprog: Tosprogede børn lærer at læse og skrive. Tredje statusrapport*. [Signs of Language: Bilingual children learn to read and write. Third status]. Accessed 8 January 2010. *http://didak.ucc.dk/public/dokumenter/UFEV/UC2/Statusrapport%20oktober%202010.pdf*
Laursen, H.P. (2011) Lukket inde i et alt for lille alfabet [Trapped in a much too small alphabet]. *NORDAND. Nordisk tidsskrift for andrespråksforskning* [Nordic Journal of Second Language Research] 2, 35–58.

Laursen, H.P. (2012) Umbrellas and angels standing straight - a social semiotic perspective on multilingual children's literacy. *Journal of Bilingual Education and Bilingualism*. DOI: 10.1080/13670050.2012.709818.

Lin, A. and Luk, J. (2002) Beyond progressive liberalism and cultural relativism: Towards critical postmodernist, sociohistorically situated perspectives in classroom studies. *Canadian Modern Language Review/La Revue Canadienne des Langues Vivantes* 59(1), 97–124.

Miller, J. (2004) Identity and language use: The politics of speaking ESL in schools. In A. Pavlenko and A. Blackledge (eds) *Negotiation of Identities in Multilingual Contexts* (pp. 290–315). Clevedon: Multilingual Matters.

Morgan, B. and Ramanathan, V. (2005) Critical literacies and language education: Global and local perspectives. *Annual Review of Applied Linguistics* 25, 151–169.

Quist, P. (2009) Untying the language–body–place connection: A study on linguistic variation and social style in a Copenhagen community of practice. In P. Auer and J. E. Schmidt (eds) *Language and Space, Part 1: Theories and Methods. An International Handbook of Linguistic Variation* (pp. 632–648). Berlin/New York: Walter de Gruyter.

Rampton, B. (2006) *Language in Late Modernity: Interaction in an Urban School*. Cambridge: Cambridge University Press.

Rampton, B. (1995) *Crossing: Language and Ethnicity Among Adolescents*. London: Longman.

Soja, E.W. (2004) Preface. In K. Leander and M. Sheehy (eds) *Spatializing Literacy Research and Practice* (pp. ix–xvi). New York: Peter Lang Publishing.

Willett, J. (1995) Becoming first graders in an L2: An ethnographic study of L2 socialization. *TESOL Quarterly* 29 (3), 473–503.

Winther, I. (2006) *Hjemlighed. Kulturfænomenologiske studier* [Homeliness: Cultural–Phenomenological Studies]. København: Danmarks Pædagogiske Universitets Forlag.

5 Skills as Performances: Literacy Practices of Finnish Sixth Graders

Mia Halonen

Writing at School as a Sociocultural Situation and Performances as Social Actions

In the present-day Nordic, in this case Finnish, schools both formal traditional standards and informal registers for writing skills are practised. Pupils are informed of different genres and they practise to recognize them: which would be the suitable register and style of writing in each case. Thus, the line between the so-called school and out-of-school writing practice is blurred (Taalas *et al.*, 2008). Furthermore, in addition to basic skills required at school, many types of writing are done at school: notes to one another, text messaging and chatting (during those rare times pupils have an opportunity to use computers). Actually, school has for no reason often been regarded only as a monolithic and stable system of education (on the lack of school research and ethnographies, see Rampton, 2006: 3–4). In reality, pupils are very conscious of both different genres and expectations of teachers or researchers. Their performances in the tasks are choices where they move along the continuum of 'totally school adjusted formal writer' to 'totally informal writer'. Furthermore, they always have to choose to present some of their multiple identities, multiple positionings in the world. Writing as a presentation for a researcher is a multilayered, multi-ideological sociocultural situation, far from being simple gathering of knowledge about informants' skills; as Rampton (2006: 26) puts it

> ...people also **routinely** engage in more active intimations of perspective, **displaying a particular orientation to the situation and the social world** through innuendo, irony, prosodic emphasis and so forth... (bold font used for emphasis by the author).

In this chapter, the term 'performance' is used in the Goffmanian (Goffman, e.g. 1959, 1986 [1974]) framework of reference of studies in 'presentation[1]'. My synthesis of this way of perceiving the term and the concept is that in this framework[2], all social action is looked at not only as [profoundly] interactional but also, first and foremost, as 'actions for an audience'; the audience not even having to be present ('literacy as acted out', Chapter 5, this volume; or 'acting like someone', Chapter 6). Since language is profoundly social (see Vygotskij 1986 [1934]; also Wertsch 1991), situations without an audience are still imitations of social reality. Even though this type of a view on performance as the core of social action which draws on – and goes back to – the studies and theories of acting and the theatre, theatre is not – at least I am not using it as such – a mere metaphor for 'real' life acting, but rather a way to conceptualize 'the reality'. Ben Rampton has used the term 'performance' in his extensive school ethnography (2006) in very much the same way; the biggest difference lies in the type of data he analyses. The audiorecorded spoken data he uses are even easier to perceive as performances than writings at school in school genres. Even though the term performance is used, in this tradition, in a different sense than traditionally as part of a picture of one's skills (see e.g. Ellis, 2005), in the end, we are probably talking – or we could talk – about exactly the same kind of performing. The idea of performing and presenting oneself by writing comes also close to Ivanič's idea of writers' construction of identity. Every writing situation is a situated process of identification, and all the aspects of writing, ideational, interpersonal and textual, are used for identity making and heterogeneous positioning of self; all writings are polyphonic (Ivanič, 1998: 19; Ivanič & Camps, 2001).

In this chapter, I will analyse writing practices of sixth graders (12 years old) in Finland in a school context. My point of view is throughout sociocultural: writing at school for a researcher is a social situation which the participants orient to and construct with their actions. I will analyse how the writings of the pupils are constructed, and thus what resources they draw on.

School Writing Tasks in Ethnographic Focus

I will use data from two collections (2006 and 2009) of school data where different types of tasks – writing, listening and reading comprehension – were gathered among Finnish sixth graders (12 years old) in four suburban schools in Helsinki. The 2006 data form more like an informative background data (for me), my main focus being on the 2009 writing tasks. The data consist of writings from 146 pupils in four tasks: an essay, a chat answer and letters to the principal and to a friend on the same subject, approximately 600 writings in all.

The data were gathered in ethnically diverse and multilingual suburbs in Helsinki; the proportion of speakers of Finnish as L2 being about 30% of the whole. The biggest language groups consisted of Finnish and Somali L1 speakers. In this chapter, I will focus on these groups, and occasionally also discuss the cultural or linguistic background of the pupils. The final data thus consist of writings from 124 pupils. All the pupils had gone to school in Finland only, and they were variously multilingual.

In the letter to a friend, the pupils were asked to

Write your friend a letter where you suggest him/her a trip together to a concert, football match or whatever event you like. Your friend has not been as eager to go as you have – persuade him/her!

The other three genre types were (1) a letter to the principal to ask for a short extra leave (for the trip with the friend), (2) an answer to a chat question concerning racism or hobbies and (3) a traditional essay on 'My Helsinki'. The tasks were designed by me for the purposes of a research project studying the diversity of Helsinki Finnish[3]. All the writing was done with pencil and paper in the pupils' normal learning groups.

As discussed above, (in this chapter) the writings or texts are looked at as performances including the different types of skills and stances towards the school in general and the data gathering situation in particular. The writings were written for a researcher (me), which showed on the one hand as very school compliant writings and on the other hand as very rebellious writings with, for example, overrepresentation of swear words and pictures and comments in the task papers. The tasks – and consequently the writings – were different in nature, especially in relation to their context sensitivity as regards the relation to the audience, the readers. The essays dealing with Helsinki could have more easily been taken out of the context in which they were written, even though they were produced in the same sociocultural situation, and are full of identity work (the above mentioned works of Ivanič (1998) and Ivanič and Camps (2001)). However, especially the letter to a friend in a school context is already from the start an artificial genre which generates imaginary performances. Also, pupils are aware of them being performances – in all the meanings of the word. Described in terms of Goffman's participation framework (1986 [1974]), all readers other than the friends are inevitably bystanders or eavesdroppers – ones at whom the presentation was not directed in the first place.

For analysing the writings, I will apply ethnographically informed text analysis (see e.g. Barton & Papen, 2010; Marcus, 1995). Thus, my perceptions are based on the writings as such but I also have some background information on the pupils as well as field notes and observations. With regard to performing, what I think is of importance in this specific data is that they offer an opportunity to observe how the pupils see themselves as writers and language users. In this sense, this study is closely related to perceptual linguistics and dialectology (e.g. Preston, 1999) and especially folk (socio)linguistics (e.g. Vaattovaara, 2004); pupils themselves are their own analysts who show their skills in writing as much as they have decided to do. They are very skilled and sensitive writers who can both take into account and do a performance in relation to the expectations of the teachers and researchers and their own stances; their writings are complex hybrids of these diverse motivations.

Letters to a Friend as Performances

I have chosen the letter to a friend as the focus genre here. Of all the genres in the writing tasks, it is the one where different aspects of performing come into play (Scollon & Scollon, 2004). The genre is likely to be unfamiliar to most of the pupils as they do not write (paper) letters to their friends (even though some still do, they are a very small minority) but text or phone them or use some other digital device to keep in contact. Thus, the letters are probably the best examples to see how the pupils interpret what they are expected to do.

The first writer in focus is Siiri, a Finnish[4] as L1 speaker. Here is her letter[5]:

Mmmoi[6] Veera! =J

mmoi. How are you? I'm quite jees =)
We just had the autumn holiday, **when is yours**? or is it already?
I really can't stand waiting for the summer so that I could see you again ♥
But then I figured out that since this year I may go to a cruise with my big sister and her friend, would you like to come with us as my friend as we don't otherwise never see each other =(
We would leave in two and a half weeks on Saturday so that
if you'd come to our place for example already on Friday? We'll go to Sweden and be
there in Sweden in a hotel perhaps 1 or 2 nights? I hope you'd be able to come! And hopefully your parents will let you!
You can ask them for example **to contact my mother**

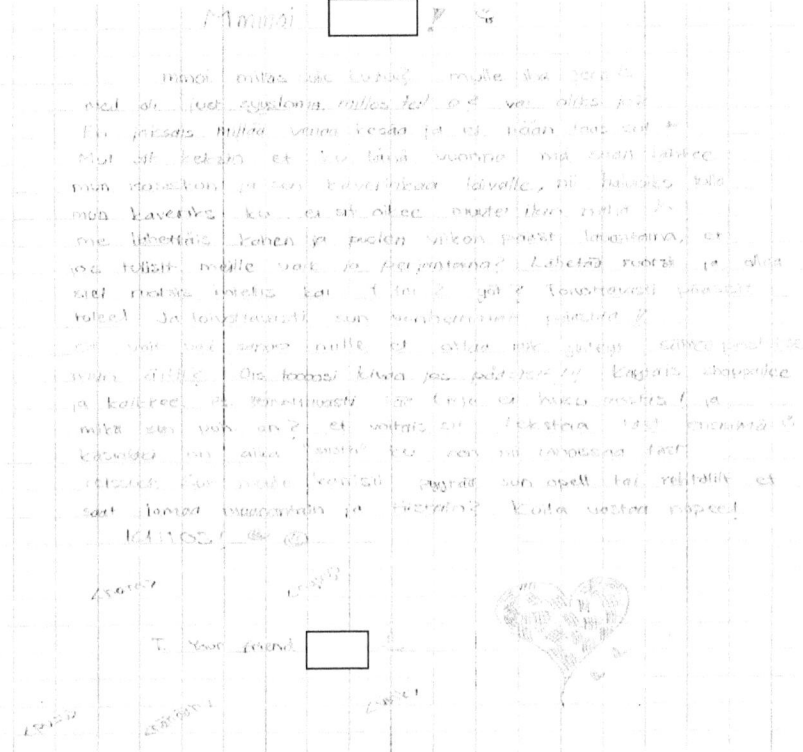

Figure 5.1 Siiri [43 T50A]

by email? It would be reaaaaally nice if you could make it!!! We would go shopping
and everything. PS. **Hopefully this letter does not get lost in the post**! And
what is your phone number? So that we could text more about this =)
Even my handwriting is quite 'neat' as I'm so excited over this
trip. By the way it would be good for you to ask permission from your teacher or principal so
that you would get a leave for Monday and Tuesday? Please try to answer quickly!

THANK YOU! =)
Your friend Siiri =)

In the brackets:
<nam>; <hymy> 'smile'; <pusu> 'kiss'; <nähään> 'see you'; <vink> 'wink' (referring to hinting at something).

This letter is extremely 'performative' in the sense that Siiri tries to fulfill very different types of expectations: a recognizable, quite long and 'old-fashioned' letter would fulfill the (assumed) expectations of the school, while writing in the Helsinki spoken variety and using smileys and 'typed' emoticons like <pusu> 'kiss', resources from the digital world, would fulfill the expectations of authenticity of her typical written communication with her friends. Furthermore, she manages in doing both; for example, asking about autumn holidays and her friend's phone number, as if not knowing about these, and 'missing her friend far away' makes her writing 'letterish' and quite phoney[7] when one has seen authentic messages for friends. The fear of the post losing the letter, the request for the parents to contact each other through email and commenting on her own handwriting are comments that index to the reader that this is not her typical mode of interaction. Then again, genre awareness and knowledge of registers are shown in a very accurate imitation of the spoken Helsinki variety in writing: for example, one very typical feature of this variety, dropping the word final letter *n* (or more strictly speaking, sound) (e.g. in the words *millää* [millään] 'in any way' or *ku* [kun] 'when') are perfectly 'correct' in the sense of writing phonetically (Halonen, 2009; see also Lappalainen, 1999; Paunonen, 1995 [1982]).

Compared to Siiri's writing, Henna's (a Finnish as L1 speaker) one is very similar: it is in the same way 'letterish' with again talk about the autumn holiday[8] and imitating to a degree the spoken Helsinki variety, even though not as consistently as Siiri; there are, for example, some very literal features such as writing some of the word final *n*-letters/sounds and the *ts*-combination in the word *katsomaan* 'to look at', which would typically be *kattomaa* or *kattoo* in the Helsinki spoken variety. Here is only the beginning of the letter.

Hi my dear friend!

How are you? I'm quite fine ☺
The autumn holiday is getting close and it would be nice to see the long awaited football match. **You already know that I play football just like you** and now there will be the Finland–Belgium match and **you do know that I have waited this match for a year**? It would be nice if you could come here to Helsinki for a couple of days, so that we could go to the match. Tickets have already been bought, you would only need to take money for candies and soft drinks =D.

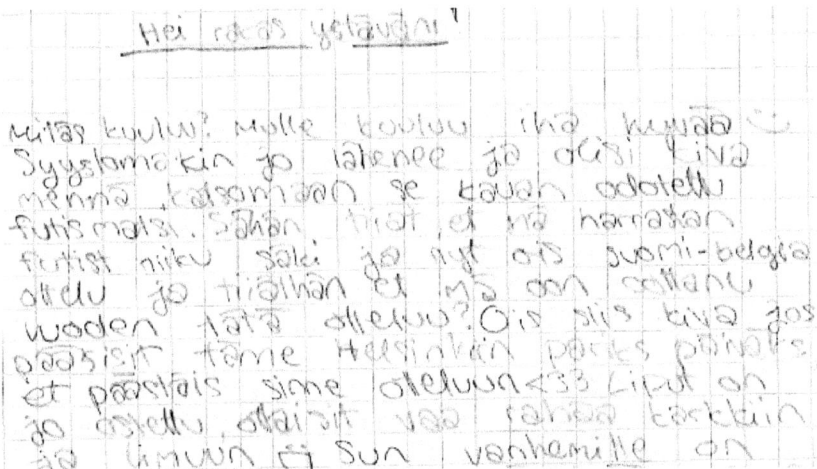

Figure 5.2 Henna [140 T86 D]

The writings of these two girls show a strong tendency and good skills of balancing between different types of expectations, whether real or assumed. In these writings, the unauthenticity of the genre is also highlighted. This might result from a (schooling) culture which often highlights and strengthens the stereotype of a 'good girl' who reacts – and is capable of doing that – to all (sometimes also only assumed) expectations; here the girls answer both to the expectations of writing in school context, fulfilling the task, and to the assumed expectations of showing their knowledge of the genre and the register associated with it. (About good girl stereotypes and general gender questions, see e.g. Beauvoir, 1964 [1949]; Grabrucker, 1985.)

Victoria's (a Finnish as L1 speaker) letter differs from the previous ones. It could be described as more authentic in the sense that it does not have the old-fashioned genre markers of a paper letter such as hellos and signatures, for in digital media senders are normally shown in some other way.

> Pliis, c'moon now. I'll buy you candy… and hello, if it is boring, we can just start to play around there oslt ['or something like that'; an acronym like an abbreviation]. PLIIS really don't be such a bastard!! I too come when you ask. PLIIIIS.

In this letter, Victoria is also making use of the spoken Helsinki variety. Furthermore, in addition to this, Victoria also uses intimate interactional

126 Part 2: Local Practices in Transition

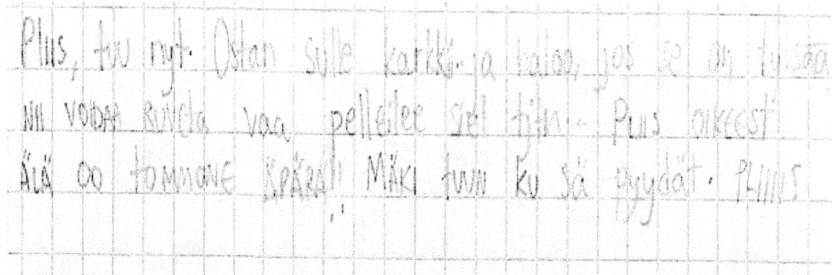

Figure 5.3 Victoria [75 T62 B]

practices of friends by mocking her friend by using the word *äpärä* 'bastard'. There has been for quite some time a trend to borrow English words and loaned meanings but to translate them into Finnish[9]. Mocking also indexes the entire discourse and the world of associated practices that have their roots in the (Black) rap and hip-hop culture (e.g. Alim & Pennycook, 2007). In this way, global practices acquire their local manifestation; the global and local converge as in the term *glocal* (Robertson, 1995; see also Alim & Pennycook, 2007; Androutsopoulos, 2010: 205–206). What is transferred varies: it can be a word acquiring new ways of usage or a practice that becomes localized. The global (e.g. Blommaert, 2010) and the local (e.g. Pennycook, 2010) are in constant interaction, and the 'scale' in which we will discuss the details of the data depends on the viewpoint. The 'glocalization' is not a new phenomenon which is also seen in Victoria's letter. *Pliis*, 'please', which Victoria uses is still widely used, even though it is one of the oldest words of the type where an English word is adopted as such into Finnish but written in accordance with Finnish orthography that is fairly close to the word's phonetic form; another widely used old loaned word is *tänks* for 'thanks'. Also using a term like *tjtn* (*tai jotain* 'or something') which is an unconventional abbreviation is a way to present one's knowledge of the genre. By using the term *äpärä* ('bastard'), Victoria is able to show not only how skilled she is in the genre but also how intimate she is with her friend: mocking is allowed only in cases of total trust (e.g. Rastas, 2005). For Victoria, it has been important to show the researcher that she has this type of skill. Compared to the two writings analysed above, Victoria can be described as consciously resisting the good girl stereotypes in relation to the content and perhaps also the register of the writing. However, also she fulfills the expectations in relation to doing the task – and actually does it in a more authentic way than Siiri and Henna.

Writing the spoken variety of Helsinki is in many ways taken to its extreme in the next case, Ayanna's (a multilingual, Finnish as L2 speaker) letter:

Hey Liza

Liza it is already the Id-party Liza say
to the principal that I am there or come with me
Say to her if you can and
Tell like that we both have I mean that
You too have it come at the twelve break if you can.
Wishes Aya

The feature in which this writing differs from most others in the data is the authenticity of the spoken variety written down. Even though there were a lot of features of this in two previous cases as well, here the text as a whole is as close to the spoken variety as is possible, and some of the solutions go further than is conventionally done even when trying to write in a speech-like style, for example *munka* 'with me' (from the closest vernacular form to the most literal one: *munkaa, minunkaa, mun kanssa, mun kanssani, minun kanssa* and *minun kanssani*)[10], maybe also *sulki* 'you too have' (again from the closest vernacular form to the most literal one: *sullaki, sullakin, sinullaki* and *sinullakin*). Variation in a vernacular can thus manifest itself in more than one feature: the personal pronoun, the word final *–n* and the clitic versus postposition dimension. If Victoria and Siiri's writings were very authentic in how they had written in a spoken variety, Ayanna goes just a bit further

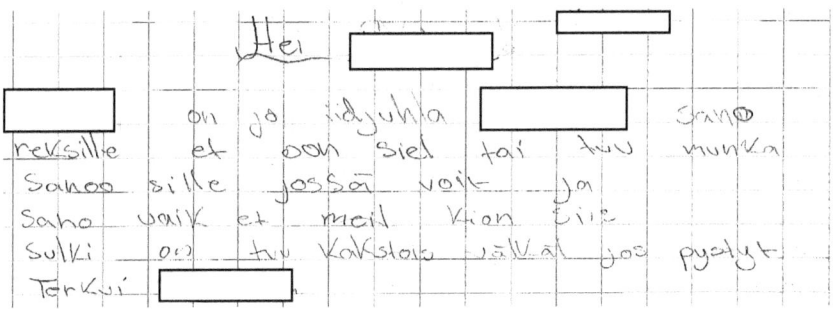

Figure 5.4 Ayanna [56 T114 A]

in speech-like writing. Even though the morphological features are the same as in Victoria and Siiri's writings, the practices of speech are more present in Ayanna's. Some features of this are the combinations of two words such as *jossä* [jos sä] 'if you' and splits of words that have been combined with another word, as in *meil kion* [meilki on] 'we too have'. All these forms that are split up or combined can be pronounced in this way, but not written. One could say that this letter is an ultra-authentic picture of the Helsinki spoken variety, and Ayanna is a very skilled analyst of this particular variety.

Some of the features (*meil kion* vs. *meilki on* 'we too have') seem to result from Ayanna's being a second language Finnish speaker. For example, clitics such as *–ki/-kin* are so familiar to L1 speakers that they would not separate them from the main word or at least not combine them with another word starting with a clitic as Ayanna has done. Second, the recipient is addressed twice by name in the writing (covered by white boxes). This might result from Ayanna' Somali background: pupils of Somali descent often address each other by name in their speech, which is unusual for Finns and in Finnish where direct second person addressing is often avoided, and especially addressing someone by name is very rare. Also, the placement of the second address is very much speech-like.

There are also other possible explanations for Ayanna being so vernacular. One of them is that she shows her appreciation of this register in this genre, and the other her being especially talented in writing 'phonetically', which could also arise from her being a L2 speaker. Thus, Ayanna is more accurate in 'really' hearing instead of being familiar with conventionalized ways of representing speech in writing. There might be other culture-based explanations for this type of writing in a letter to a friend. Based on ethnographic fieldwork and interviews of the pupils, girls (12 years old) of Somali descent rarely have either cell phones or opportunities to use a computer – both of which are media in which youngsters practise the use of a suitable amount of speech-like features in their writing to be taken as serious members in the community of practice of the Finnish social media (Lave & Wenger, 1991). Furthermore, the continuing deep appreciation and use of spoken interaction in the Somali culture that is still prevalent among the young might make children of Somali descent better able to analyse spoken language (Heath, 1983: 196–201; Hirsi Ali, 2007: 3–17). For example in Ayanna's case, it is definitely not a question of her not being skilled enough to write Standard Finnish; she writes, for example, a very appropriate letter to the principal. Rather, as I have argued above, this is a matter of becoming familiar with a particular genre.

A letter to a friend is nowadays kind of an unusual genre: pupils do not normally write letters to their friends anymore. Probably, this is one of the reasons for both the diverse assessments and their justifications and the diverse attitudes towards the task evident in the letters. In the light of the performances of these four girls, it seems that the pupils know perfectly well what they are expected to do in the tasks and that they can also respond to very controversial expectations within one writing. For example, 'writing spoken language', that is writing phonetically the way one speaks, can be used both to show genre awareness and to rebel against doing the task, the whole school or attending the research. Thus, the choices in the pupils' performances are very conscious and really 'done' (see Sacks, 1992 [1970]). If the pupils do write letters, they do not write this type of letters with paper and pencil and about this type of a topic, inviting a person somewhere. This would normally be done through digital devices: texting, chatting, etc. It is also very important for the pupils to show in their answers to the task that they normally write in digital environments. I will next turn to this complex relation between skills and performances of 'real skills'.

Performing Multiple Resources and Genre Awareness: Presenting the 'Real' Writers as Multilingual, Diginative and Independent

Due to the intertwined developments of technologization and globalization, the concept of literacy, the 'skill', has changed. Digital and technology-based environments are nowadays the most familiar written contexts for children and adolescents. At the same time, the older conventionalized writing practices also have a more significant role in societies; pupils in the Nordic countries live a double life between the old and the new world and their requirements. Here, I will take a look at two major devices the pupils constantly used to present their 'real-writer' personality or identity as writers, which I could describe as multilingual and digibased (often) adult-exclusive but 'adult-understandable' practices[11]; youngsters are diginatives, adults digi-immigrants (Leppänen, forthcoming; Prensky, 2001). I will present these practices through a couple of cases, a couple of instances of literacy events (Street, 1995, 2000). Many of the resources draw from outside of 'pure' language: they might make use of the general layout, comments on the margins of the paper, drawings, etc. (see Kress, 2003; Kress & van Leeuwen, 2006 [1996]).

All these devices have their own functions in the complex processes of producing the writings, presenting genre awareness and multiple resources the pupils have either to make use of for getting good assessments or for rebelling against expectations – or often for doing both together ('conflicting expectations', Chapter 4; 'conflicting ideologies of language and literature',

Chapter 7). Genre awareness and either adjusting to the expectations or rebelling against them are means of presenting oneself as one wishes. Three aspects seem to be of special interest to the pupils in presenting themselves: 'doing being' multilingual, diginative (or at least digiwise) and independent in their stances and attitudes towards school and the research.

The picture below gives us a glimpse into various multilingual resources: different languages, pieces of languages, registers, indexes and local varieties.

First, there is the possibility to use some other language instead of or together with Finnish (1; Finnish and Somali); especially the pupils with migrant origins used these 'mobile resources' (Blommaert, 2010) but not exclusively as many foreign languages are studied in Finnish elementary schools. Second, there were hybrid forms and innovations (2). *Siisdaa* (often written as one word) is placed in the margins as a comment marking the task as being stupid. It is a hybrid form of Finnish and English, commonly used by Finnish adolescents, consisting of a Finnish particle *siis* which could be paraphrased as 'like' or 'so' and *daa* originating from English *duh* (conventionally written orthographically as d-u-h). This sign indexes that the previous speaker or the recipient has done or asked something very surprising, either in the sense of the answer having been self-evident or the action very unexpected (English and Finnish Urban Dictionaries; more on this sign, Halonen, forthcoming). Third, there were different types of resources used as indexes for some type of a 'speaker' or an 'attitude' (3–5). The article *da* (3) stands for AAVE pronunciation of 'the', a way of writing which is

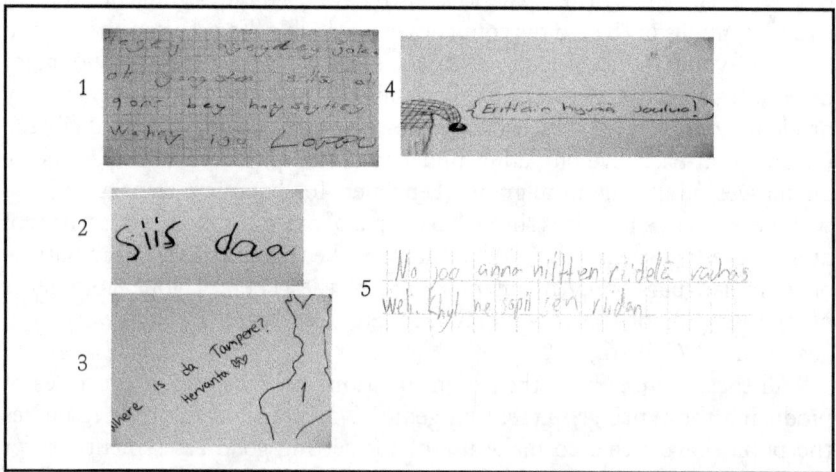

Figure 5.5 Multilingual resource

widely used as an index of rap and hip-hop culture (e.g. Androutsopoulos, 2007; Pennycook, 2007; Sebba, 2003). In all, English and the 'local' use of it was the most typical and in general very frequent resource for different types of actions for the pupils. (About 'world' and 'lingua franca' Englishes, see, e.g. House, 2003; Pennycook, 2007, 2010; truncated repertoires and mobile resources, Blommaert, 2010; crossings, Rampton, 1995.).

In the following two examples, 4 and 5, writers make use of the distinction of Standard written Finnish and the spoken Helsinki variety, that is, multilingualism inside 'a' language (Bailey, 2007). In his answer to a 'chat question' of how to solve a potentially racist fight between friends of Finnish and Turkish origin (5), Tomi writes:

Well ok let them fight in peace brother [*veli* in Finnish; here written *weli*]. Surely [*kyllä* in Finnish; here written *khyl* with the *h* indexing an accent] they will agree.

The answer indexes very much the same things as the *da* in (3): rap and hip-hop phrases and style (Androutsopoulos, 2007; Pennycook, 2007; see also Victoria's letter's analysis above), a genre, here totally in Finnish. But Tomi also constructs other markers of 'foreignness' or at least 'non-Finnishness' by writing the word *veli* 'brother' with a *w* – a letter (and a phoneme if we think of the English pronunciation) that does not belong to the Finnish orthography. The same goes with the combination *kh* in the word *khyl* 'surely' where the phonemes symbolize a foreign accent. With these 'small' choices in a task with the topic of racism, the pupil is doing a very complex presentation of his knowledge of the genre, perhaps his commitment or attitude towards hip-hop culture and 'foreigners' or more accurately towards the topic of racism (about which one cannot interpret what his attitude exactly is, but with the prominent unconventional choices, he still is marking that he has one) – and also, and probably in particular, towards the task. With these devices, he is able to not only fulfill the task requirements but also present his 'real-life' attitudes.

In contrast, the other writer (4) plays with hypercorrection: she wishes 'Merry Christmas' in a very unconventionally hypercorrect way, by using the word *erittäin*, 'extremely', which is never used in the phrase. Just like writing the spoken variety of Helsinki is one way of indexing something, the hypercorrect use of the standard is doing its own indexing. Especially, the strength of the expressions lies in the variation between these two (see, Lappalainen, 1999): normally, this pupil writes in a very vernacular style but here an elf (or some such figure) is 'walking away' in the margin of the paper, saying goodbyes. As Rampton (1995) has pointed out, commenting, greeting and other types of 'rituals', are the ones where 'crossings' often take place. Here, the crossing happens inside a language, the standard probably indexing also – if not the 'upper class' as in Finland the concept of class is not in active use – still something 'too posh', which again indexes, for example, something 'totally unnecessary and vain' (Rampton, 2006 on indexes of classes).

This is just what is happening here when the pupil has fulfilled the task but then comments on the whole task – maybe on the whole set of tasks. These choices (among others) are the tools for the pupils to construct their performances. They play with stereotypes, with iconizations (Irvine & Gal, 2000) of some linguistic features and the stereotypes that grow in the complex system of iconization, repeated use of a feature in some type(s) of context(s), the continuing indexicalization of the features from the first order 'sign' to an X-order index, symbol and stereotype – the metapragmatics of the signs. The processes of indexicalization are complex enough as such but as a 'totally indexical' phenomenon – as the whole language actually is – they are in addition in constant movement (Silverstein, 1998, 2003).[12]

What is of interest with regard to the focus of this chapter is that it appears to be extremely important for the pupils to present themselves as multilingual, language sensitive and analytically skilled diginatives. The picture below shows some examples.

Also, varieties of a language constitute part of these resources: the spoken variety of Helsinki offers the pupils a great writing tool, as the variety is both an index of 'being a Helsinkian' and a cosy variety for writing in the digiworld as words used are very short with lots of different types of disappearance phenomena – apocopes, abbreviations and drops. But there are also other devices for presenting one's familiarity with the digital world which are seen in the next picture. First, very common resources are like and dislike signs (1) drawn from social media, mostly Facebook. From the digital

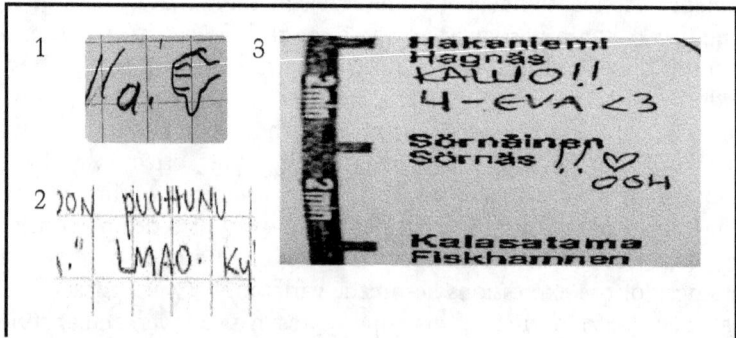

Figure 5.6 Resources adopted from digital world

world (but not exclusively) come also acronyms, the example here being LMAO (2) – 'laughing my ass off' – or hybrid unconventional spellings, 4-eva, and emoticons (3)[13]. (About these digital resources, in digital contexts, see e.g. Bergs, 2009; Jones, 2009; Kataoka, 2003; Quan-Haase, 2009; Rowe, 2009.)

Relating Skills and Performing

In this chapter, I have discussed how the pupils are able to produce, at the same time, in-school and out-of-school practices, present themselves both as compliant with and skilled in the conventionalized literacy practices and as reluctant and resistant participants in doing school tasks – and in general the pen and paper style literacy practices of the school. By their writings as a whole, with the content and commentaries, they can present their skills and also comment on these skills and present their typical, digibased literacy practices.

The writings show an extensive set of resources and repertoires and skills the pupils are able to use in and as performances. They clearly show how the pupils are able to draw on various sources of genres and registers, for example on Standard Finnish taught in school and diverse varieties of Finnish, other languages and digital worlds' devices learned in interaction in spare time. In the light of the performances of all the pupils, it is clear that they know perfectly well what they are expected to do in the tasks and that they also are able to respond to these often controversial expectations within just one writing. For example, by writing phonetically, they are able to show genre awareness and in that way respond to the academic expectations of their writing and at the same time to highlight their identity as proficient writers of genres typically used by writers of their age in their most typical space of writing, internet and other digital spaces. What is of great importance is that performing all these skills and identifications seems to be highly important for the pupils: using that comprehensive language skills they showed to have requires efforts. It could thus be said that writing – even in a task in school – is for the pupils not only to claim skills but also, and probably mostly, for claiming and constructing their identities as writers and persons. It is of great interest that they are also able to show their understanding and belonging to the complex and diverse indexical field of Nordic postmodern society where ways of talking, accents and registers are ways to position oneself – and others – into various places in this field. All the choices in the performances seem to be very conscious and 'done' (Sacks, 1992 [1970]).

Coming back to the general question of skills and performing, what I have tried to argue here is that performances can – and should – be looked at as presentations of pupils' analyses of their own use of language and the expectations they face in fulfilling a task. Thus, the 'products' are complex mixtures of pupils' meta-level representations of some social factors combined with their analyses of what and how they are expected to write. In this frame of presenting and performing, the pupils showed how skilled they were in 'multitasking': fulfilling the task and at the same time showing their attitudes, positioning themselves in the situation, showing different orientations such as school orientation, task orientation and situation orientation. Writing is also to be seen as an action in its own right, as a means to position oneself in the world: pupils can rebel against the expectations not only by writing but also by not writing.

In the beginning, I argued that writing in a school context for a researcher should be looked at only as primarily a performance. The performing pupil

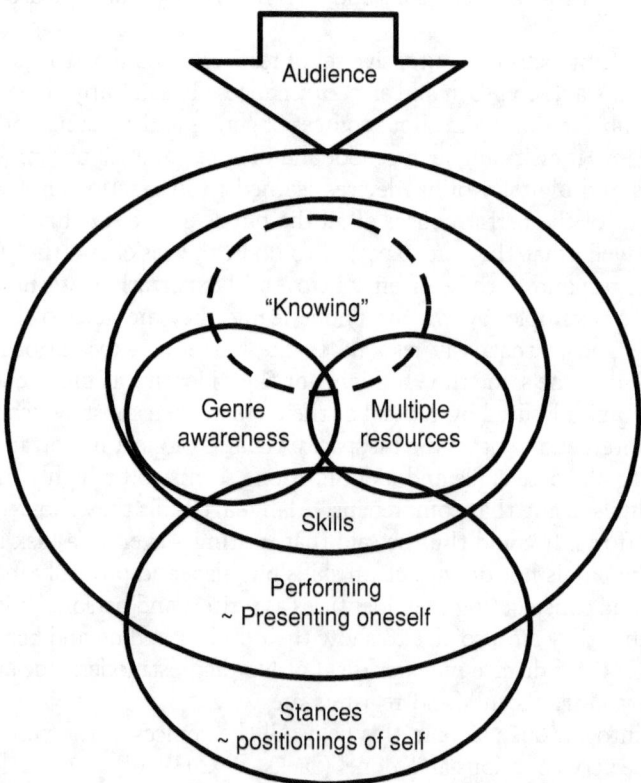

Figure 5.7 Relation between skills and performances

then decides what to perform – and no researcher can 'know' that decision: the presentation contains only the things the pupil wishes to present. This is not to say that there is no such thing as language skills or proficiency but that there is no methodological way of getting to know the skills in, so to speak, 'pure' form – the performance always surrounds the skills. The picture below is an attempt to describe how I see the relation between skills, performances and perceiving them in the light of the analyses of the writings.

In this frame, we can ask more questions. Is being skilled having the ability to perform how one is able to use different genres, registers and resources in general? Or is a skill the ability to choose an 'appropriate' genre? Or is it an ability to impress one's attitudes and opinions on and direct them towards the ongoing situation as a whole – and do it by writing? At least we can say with certainty that performing is a skill and showing a skill is a performance.

Notes

(1) This view is often described as being 'Goffmanian' but I would like to point out that this view on social (inter)action draws on diverse research traditions from (ethnographic) linguistics (e.g. Hymes, 1974; Derrida, 1977), literacy research (e.g. Bahtin, 1984 [1929]), philosophy (e.g. de Certeau, 1984), anthropology (e.g. Bauman, 1977), theatre research (e.g. Scheichner, 1985; Turner, 1982) to sociology (e.g. Schutz, 1964; Garfinkel, 1964).
(2) For an extensive introduction to the tradition, see Carlson (1996).
(3) This chapter is part of the project 'Helsinki Finnish: Diversity, Social Identity and Attitudes in an Urban Context' led by Professor Marja-Leena Sorjonen at the University of Helsinki. In the task design, I combined different types of examples from evaluation research, for example a task collection called Kike 2005, and the work of research projects Cefling and Topling led by Professor Maisa Martin at the University of Jyväskylä.
(4) All the writer names are pseudonyms and possible names in the text have been covered. The handwriting of a 12-year-old is not yet fully developed and does not identify the informant.
(5) I show here the authentic texts or parts of them after which I give a paraphrase of their content. Neither I have made any grammatical glossary of the texts nor have I tried to catch their 'speech-likeness', the Helsinki vernacular or slang in the paraphrase since they actually cannot be translated in any way that would give the same impression: what would be the English variety to choose, how to translate a linguistic feature which does not have a correlate in English etc.? In the analysis, I describe their overall style and pick up some details to discuss – when it is necessary for the argumentation. I have marked in bold the paraphrases of the details I am taking up in the analyses.
(6) *Moi* (with one *m*) is 'hi' in Finnish.
(7) Another way to look at the construction of a friend far away is that this is Siiri means to construct some sense into this nowadays pretty obsolete genre.
(8) Talking about the autumn holiday is common in the texts because at the time of gathering data this holiday was approaching.

(9) One popular word of a similar type or mechanism is *kolea* or *kolee* which is a genuine Finnish word meaning 'cool' or perhaps more accurately 'chilly'. The English orthographic form ('cool') matching the Finnish phonetic form in writing (and speaking), with both matching well in the meaning, seems to fascinate the young.
(10) The postposition *kanssa* 'with' is a feature that has probably at least since the 1970s become grammaticalized in Finnish as a clitic particle *-kaa* both in speech (Laitinen & Lehtinen, 1997: 7–8) and nowadays, as the school data show, also into writing.
(11) This distinction – exclusive but understandable – brings us to the extensive phenomenon of 'signing': how in analyzing signing or writing practices one should take into account not only the results, the sign itself, but also and above all the process and motivation for using the signs in question. Signs reveal for whom they are meant – 'who can "read" the sign" – and how they are intended to be read. (For further views on this, see e.g. Blommaert & Rampton, 2011; Coulmas 2009; Malinowski, 2009; Pennycook, 2009; Spolsky, 2009.)
(12) Furthermore, complexity increases if we take the signing view on the whole picture: who knows, what they know and so on (see also note 12).AQ: Please check for correctness the citation of Footnote 12. In this chapter, I cannot go any further into this complexity of indexicality: the presented pieces of analyses are merely an overview of and scratch the surface of this complex web of linguistic features and the attitudes and images that are for some reason connected to them. (For more, see especially Agha, 2007; Rampton, 2006; Silverstein, 1998, 2003.)
(13) Emoticons in paper and pencil writings are of special interest in the sense that – as in so many others as well – the resource alternate between drawn, hand-written, spoken and typed – and the cycles go on. Here, you can see two types of hearts in the very same paper (3) (where they mark metro stations in Helsinki), one of them being a heart 'typed' in handwriting and the other an 'original' handwritten heart which is imitated in the typed one. What kind of distinctions in affection or stance these diverse signs index, I cannot say for sure (there are possibilities like the *4-eva* also influencing the writing style of the heart, or [maybe a more conscious choice] indexing different types of 'love' in different places. There also seems to be a gender distinction here, boys using more often typed-style hearts, girls varying more in their use (see, Halonen, 2009).

References

Agha, A. (2007) *Language and Social Relations*. Cambridge: Cambridge University Press.
Alim, H.S. and Pennycook, A. (2007) Glocal linguistic flows: Hip-hop cultures, identities, and the politics and language education. *Journal of Language, Identity, and Education* 6 (2), 89–100.
Androutsopoulos, J. (2007) Style online: Doing hip-hop on the German-speaking web. In P. Auer (ed.) *Style and Social Identities* (pp. 279–320). Berlin: Mouton de Gruyter.
Androutsopoulos, J. (2010) Localizing the global on the participatory web. In N. Coupland (ed.) *The Handbook of Language and Globalization* (pp. 203–231). Chichester: Blackwell.
Bahtin, M. (1984) [1929] *Problems of Dostoevsky's Poetics*. Translated by C. Emerson. Minneapolis: Minneapolis University Press.
Bailey, B. (2007) Multilingual forms of talk and identity work. In P. Auer and L. Wei (eds) *Handbook of Multilingualism and Multilingual Communication* (pp. 341–367). Berlin: Mouton de Gruyter.

Barton, D. and Papen, U. (2010) (eds) *The Anthropology of Writing: Understanding Textually Mediated Worlds*. London: Continuum International Publishing Group.
Bauman, R. (1977) *Verbal Act as Performance*. Rowley: Newbury House.
Beauvoir, S. (1964) [1949] *The Second Sex*. Translated and edited by H.M. Parshley. New York: Bantam Books.
Bergs, A. (2009) Just the same old story? The linguistics of text messaging and its cultural repercussions. In C. Rowe and E.L. Wyss (eds) *Language and New Media: Linguistic, Cultural, and Technological Evolutions* (pp. 55–74). Cresskill: Hampton Press.
Blommaert, J. (2010) *The Sociolinguistics of Globalization*. Cambridge: Cambridge University Press.
Blommaert, J. and Rampton, B. (2011) Language and superdiversity. *Diversities* 13. www.unesco.org/shs/diversities/vol13/issue2/art1_
Carlson, M. (1996) *Performance: A Critical Introduction* (2nd edn). London: Routledge.
De Certeau, M. (1984) *The Practice of Everyday Life*. Translated by S.F. Rendall. Berkeley: University of California Press.
Coulmas, F. (2009) Linguistic landscaping and the seed of the public sphere. In E. Shohamy and D. Gorter (eds) *Linguistic Landscape: Expanding the Scenery* (pp. 13–24). New York: Routledge.
Derrida, J. (1977) Signature event context. *Glyph* 1, 172–197.
Ellis, R. (2005) *Planning and Task Performance in a Second Language*. Philadelphia: John Benjamins.
Garfinkel, H. (1964) Studies of the routine grounds of everyday activities. *Social Problems* 11, 225–250.
Goffman, E. (1959) *Presentation of Self in Everyday Life*. Harmondsworth: Penguin.
Goffman, E. (1986) [1974] *Frame Analysis*. With a foreword by Bennett M. Berger. Boston: Northeastern University Press.
Grabrucker, M. (1985) *Typisch Mädchen* [A typical girl]. Frankfurt: Fischer.
Halonen, M. (2009) Puhutun kielen variantit resurssina monikielisten koululaisten kirjoitelmissa [Variants of spoken language as a resource in the writings of multilingual pupils]. *Virittäjä* 113 (3), 329–355.
Halonen, M. (forthcoming) Social media as a linguistic landscape of ambiguous activities: Navigating through with the help of a sign. In M. Laitinen and A. Zabrodskaja (eds) *Dimensions of Linguistic Landscapes in Europe: Materials and Methodological Solutions*. Frankfurt: Peter Lang.
Heath, S.B. (1983) *Ways with Words: Language, Life, and Work in Communities and Classrooms*. Cambridge: Cambridge University Press.
Hirsi Ali, Ayaan (2007) *Infidel*. New York: Free Press.
House, J. (2003) English as a lingua franca: A threat to multilingualism? *Journal of Sociolinguistics* 7(4), 556–578.
Hymes, D. (1974) *Foundations in Sociolinguistics: An Ethnographic Approach*. Philadelphia: University of Pennsylvania Press.
Irvine, J.T. and Gal, S. (2000) Language ideology and linguistic differentiation. In P.V. Kroskrity (ed.) *Regimes of Language: Ideologies, Polities, and Identities* (pp. 35–83). Santa Fe, New Mexico: School of American Research Press.
Ivanič, R. (1998) *Writing and Identity: The Discoursal Construction of Identity in Academic Writing*. Amsterdam: John Benjamins.
Ivanič, R. and Camps, D. (2001) "I am how I sound" – Voice as self-presentation in L2 writing. *Journal of Second Language Writing* 10(1–2), 3–4.

Jones, R.H. (2009) Inter-activity: How new media can help us to understand old media. In C. Rowe and E.L. Wyss (eds) *Language and New Media: Linguistic, Cultural, and Technological Evolutions* (pp. 13–32). Cresskill: Hampton Press.
Kataoka, K. (2003) Emotion and youth identities in personal writing: An analysis of pictorial signs and unconventional punctuation. In J.K. Androutsopoulos and A. Georgakopoulou (eds) *Discourse Constructions of Youth Identities* (pp. 121–149). Amsterdam: John Benjamins Publishing.
Kress, G. (2003) *Literacy in the New Media Age*. London: Routledge.
Kress, G. and van Leeuwen, T. (2006) [1996] *Reading Images: The Grammar of Visual Design* (2nd edn). London: Routledge.
Laitinen, L. and Lehtinen, T. (1997) Johdanto [Introduction]. In T. Lehtinen and L. Laitinen (eds) *Kieliopillistuminen: Tapaustutkimuksia suomesta* [Grammaticalization: Case studies in Finnish] *Kieli* 12 (pp. 6–9). Helsinki: The Department of Finnish Language in the University of Helsinki.
Lappalainen, H. (1999) Young adults and the functions of the standard. *SKY* 12, 63–86.
Lave, J. and Wenger, E. (1991) *Situated Learning: Legitimate Peripheral Participation*. Cambridge: Cambridge University Press.
Leppänen, S. (forthcoming) Linguistic and discursive heteroglossia on the translocal internet: The case of web writing. In M. Sebba, S. Mahootian and C. Jonsson (eds) *Language Mixing and Code-Switching in Writing: Approaches to Mixed-Language Written Discourse*. London: Routledge.
Malinowski, D. (2009) Authorship in the linguistic landscape: A multimodal-performative view. In E. Shohamy and D. Gorter (eds) *Linguistic Landscape: Expanding the Scenery* (pp. 107–125). New York: Routledge.
Marcus, G. E. (1995) Ethnography in/of the world system: The emergence of multi-sited ethnography. *Annual Review of Anthropology* 24, 95–117.
Paunonen, H. (1995) [1982] *Suomen Kieli Helsingissä: Huomioita Helsingin Puhekielen Historiallisesta Taustasta ja Nykyvariaatiosta* [Finnish language in Helsinki: Observations of historical background and present variation]. Helsinki: The Department of Finnish language in University of Helsinki.
Pennycook, A. (2007) *Global Englishes and Transcultural Flows*. London: Routledge.
Pennycook, A. (2009) Linguistic landscapes and the transgressive semiotics of graffiti. In E. Shohamy and D. Gorter (eds) *Linguistic Landscape: Expanding the Scenery* (pp. 302–312). New York: Routledge.
Pennycook, A. (2010) *Language as a Local Practice*. Oxford: Routledge.
Prensky, M. (2001) Digital natives, digital immigrants. *On the Horizon* 9(5), 1–6.
Preston, D.R. (1999) *Handbook of Perceptual Dialectology* (Vol. I). Amsterdam: John Benjamins.
Quan-Haase, A. (2009) Text-based conversations over instant messaging: Linguistic changes and young people's sociability. In C. Rowe and E.L. Wyss (eds) *Language and New Media: Linguistic, Cultural, and Technological Evolutions* (pp. 33–54). Cresskill: Hampton Press.
Rampton, B. (1995) *Crossing: Language and Ethnicity Among Adolescents*. London: Longman.
Rampton, B. (2006) *Language in Late Modernity: Interaction in an Urban School*. Cambridge: Cambridge University Press.
Rastas, A. (2005) Racializing categories among young people in Finland. *Young* 13(2), 147–166.
Robertson, R. (1995) Glocalization: Time–space and homogeneity–heterogeneity. In M. Featherstone, S. Lash and R. Robertson (eds) *Global Modernities* (pp. 25–44). London: Sage.

Rowe, C. (2009) E-mail play and accelerated change. In C. Rowe and E.L. Wyss (eds) *Language and New Media: Linguistic, Cultural, and Technological Evolutions* (pp. 75–98). Cresskill: Hampton Press.
Sacks, H. (1992) [1970] Doing being ordinary. In G. Jefferson (ed.) *Lectures on Conversation II*. Oxford: Blackwell Publishing.
Scheichner, R. (1985) *Between Theater and Anthropology*. Philadelphia: University of Pennsylvania Press.
Schutz, A. (1964) *The Problem of Rationality in the Social World: Collected Papers*. Haag: Marinus Nijhoff.
Scollon, R. and Scollon, S.W. (2004) *Nexus Analysis: Discourse and the Emerging Internet*. London: Routledge.
Sebba, M. (2003) Spelling rebellion. In J.K. Androutsopoulos and A. Georgakopoulou (eds) *Discourse Constructions of Youth Identities* (pp. 150–172). Amsterdam: John Benjamins.
Silverstein, M. (1998) Contemporary transformations of local linguistic communities. *Annual Review of Anthropology* 27, 401–426.
Silverstein, M. (2003) Indexical order and the dialectics of sociolinguistic life. *Language and Communication* 23, 193–229.
Spolsky, B. (2009) Prolegomena to a sociolinguistic theory of public signage. In E. Shohamy and D. Gorter (eds) *Linguistic Landscape: Expanding the Scenery* (pp. 25–39). New York: Routledge.
Street, B. V. (1995) *Social Literacies: Critical Approaches to Literacy Development, Ethnography, and Education*. London: Longman.
Street, B.V. (2000) Literacy events and literacy practices: Theory and practice in the New Literacy Studies. In M. Martin-Jones and K. Jones (eds) *Multilingual Literacies: Reading and Writing Different Worlds* (pp. 17–29). Amsterdam: John Benjamins.
Taalas, P., Tarnanen, M., Kauppinen, M. and Pöyhönen, S. (2008) Media landscapes in school and in free time – two parallel realities? *Digital Kompetanse* 3, 240–256.
Turner, V. (1982) *From Ritual to Theatre*. New York: Performing Arts Journal Publications.
Vaattovaara, J. (2004) On language attitudes and behaviour in the light of local identity: Controlling the self-reported dialect use. In B. Gunnarsson *et al.* (eds) *Language Variation in Europe* (pp. 418–431). Uppsala: Uppsala University.
Wertsch, J.V. (1991) *Voices of the Mind: A Sociocultural Approach to Mediated Action*. Cambridge, MA: Harvard University Press.

6 Multimodality in the Science Classroom

Monica Axelsson and
Kristina Danielsson

Introduction

The development of the field of scientific literacy has been described by Klein and Kirkpatrick (2010) and Waldrip et al. (2010) as appearing in three waves. The first wave during the 1970s and 1980s leaned heavily on writing across the curriculum with a starting point in personal narrative writing (Zinsser, 1988). During the second wave in the 1980s and 1990s, the concept 'scientific literacy' was introduced (Halliday & Martin, 1993) and expanded further to reading, writing and the context in which it occurred, recognizing the specific ways of expressing the scientific content. The third wave, starting in the 1990s, drew attention to the role of graphics and other representations central to science and science education (e.g. Lemke, 1990). From then on, and with Kress and van Leuween's (2001) theory of multimodality making a significant contribution, we have seen an increasing interest in the ways in which different modes such as language, print, image, movement, graphics, gestures, animation and sound create meaning (Simpson & Walsh, 2010). Today, multimodality is considered central to science with the science classroom being a particularly multimodal learning environment, where a variety of semiotic resources in various modes are used for meaning-making purposes. Consequently, some researchers consider learning science more as a way of 'learning to think with representation' (Klein & Kirkpatrick, 2010: 88) than of acquiring resolved scientific concepts. This further indicates that the simple dichotomy of everyday language as opposed to academic language has more layers in science, not least since a vital aspect of meaning making within science involves re-semiotization (Iedema, 2001), that is transforming or transducting (e.g. Kress, 2003, 2010) 'knowledge from one representation into another' (Klein & Kirkpatrick, 2010: 89).

In Chapter 4, Daugaard and Laursen discuss valued literacy practices in the school context. As regards literacy practices in natural sciences, the valued practices to a great extent draw upon multiple modes. In this chapter, using a social-semiotic multimodal perspective, our aim is to examine and make visible the various meaning-making resources in different modes used in grade 2 and grade 8/9 science classrooms focusing on different content areas. The chapter examines the ways in which various modes for meaning making are used, for example as regards what modes are foregrounded and how they are combined in two different age groups. By doing this, we can provide a view of the highlighted modes used to express various meanings and make evident any differences in use and function in relation to both students' ages and subject content.

The Social-Semiotic Theory of Multimodality

A key concept within the social-semiotic theory of multimodality (e.g. Kress, 2010) is the semiotic resource, which, in a broad sense, can be defined as everything we do or use to communicate. The ways in which semiotic resources are used for meaning making in social environments can be grouped into different modes, such as writing, speech, action, body movements (e.g. gestures) and so on, and the ways in which these various modes interplay within texts form the core aspect of multimodal analyses. However, it is worth stressing that *all* communication is multimodal, that is in all communicative situations we simultaneously draw upon a number of modes. In spoken communication, along with the spoken words, we use gestures, tone pitch, facial expressions, etc. In writing, apart from choosing verbal expressions, we always have to make choices about where on the page/screen to write the text, what styles to use (in handwriting whether to use block letters, connected writing, etc.), if any words should be highlighted, etc. As Kress puts it in his recent book, we should take multimodality as 'the normal state of human communication' (Kress, 2010: 1).

Within the social-semiotic framework, communication is viewed as sign making, and anyone who wants to communicate something makes a number of choices about what semiotic resource (in what mode) to use for sign making in the communicative situation at hand. This choice is never arbitrary. Instead, it is linked to the social situation in which the sign-maker makes her/his choices, which can be based on, for example, the participants or modes and media at hand. As regards participants, the sign-maker possibly will try to choose the most apt representations for communicating with eight-year-olds around the formation of soil, or with high school students around the atomic model. As regards modes and media, in a science classroom the choice of semiotic resource can be based on what tools for sign making are available, such as computers, smart-boards, flipcharts, three-dimensional models of molecules, etc., each tool carrying with it different possibilities and limitations for representation.

Closely linked to choice in sign making is the concept of affordance (Gibson, 1986), that is the possibilities and limitations of a particular mode or semiotic resource (e.g. Kress, 2003; Kress et al., 2001). Since verbal language is temporal in itself, it is often perceived as an effective way of meaning making around sequential aspects, such as what happens when organic material decomposes. To explain spatial information, such as what particles the atom consists of and how these are spatially related to one another, the choice of image could be more suitable (Kress, 2003; Lemke, 1998). However, the choice of mode is more complex than that. For example, there are a number of more or less conventionalized ways of representing temporal order visually (e.g. by using arrows or by placing images in a conventionalized reading order). Also, a specific semiotic resource used for representation is never represented in one sole mode. To take a two-dimensional image of the atom in a textbook as an example, apart from choosing to represent the atom as a visual image, the sign-maker makes choices about spatiality (e.g. where to place the image on the book page or where to place the electrons in relation to the nucleus in the image) and color. Yet another choice is whether to combine the visual image with verbal text integrated into the image or as a caption. Furthermore, especially in pedagogical situations like the science lesson, various semiotic resources in different modes are often used in parallel and a major question is what mode to choose for what purpose (Kress et al., 2001).

A natural consequence of the theory of multimodality is that 'scientific literacy' (like any specific literacy) always involves multiple modes. Also, learning about particular scientific phenomena cannot be separated from learning how to represent them (e.g. Hubber et al., 2010; Klein & Kirkpatrick, 2010). Using the wordings of Tang and Moje (2010: 83), we view 'science literacy /.../ as the cultural practices that encompass specific ways of talking, writing, viewing, drawing, graphing, and acting, within a specialized discourse community'. Since experimental work is a central aspect of scientific work, the action mode is particularly important in the science classroom (Kress et al., 2001).

Multimodality in Science Learning

Lemke (1990) has stressed that it is important not only to talk science but also to 'juggle and combine in canonical ways verbal discourse, mathematical expression, graphical-visual representations, and motor operations in the natural world' (Lemke, 1998: 90). The work of scientists has also shown the reliance on and need for a variety of representations (Kozma *et al.*, 2000; Roth & McGinn, 1998) and multimodal representations in science communication have been considered the most effective (Yore & Hand, 2010: 93).

From a learning point of view, students appear to have difficulty in understanding both how multimodal representations are used and how to select, combine and use different semiotic resources in representing their own science knowledge (Kozma, 2003). In short, students have to learn how to 'maximize representational opportunities' (Waldrip *et al.*, 2010: 65) and to understand that one single representation cannot cover all aspects of a topic (diSessa, 2004) or that different representations treat the same content from different perspectives (Knain & Hugo, 2007). Furthermore, the competence to express conceptual knowledge and understanding with different representations is seen as a criterion for learning (Knain & Hugo, 2007).

Those students who have representational competence use multiple modal representations to explain phenomena and support their results and claims (Kozma & Russell, 2005). As for chemistry, it has been argued that mental manipulation of symbolic representations is central to learning (Wu & Shah, 2004). Hand and Choi (2010) report on a study comprising 111 American university students developing their argumentative capacity by using the Science Writing Heuristic (SWH) approach (Keys *et al.*, 1999). The SWH template relates questions to six phases to encourage students to articulate themselves about a topic.

Table 6.1 The SWH template for students (from Hand & Choi, 2010: 32)

Phase	Questions related to phase
Beginning ideas	What are my questions?
Tests	What did I do?
Observations	What did I see?
Claims	What can I claim?
Evidence	How do I know? Why am I making these claims?
Reading/Reflection	How do my ideas compare with others? How have my ideas changed?

By using the SWH approach, it is argued that students develop three modal forms: a verbal, a symbolic (chemical symbols) and a visual (graphs, diagrams and drawings). The results reported by Hand and Choi (2010) indicate a strong connection between a high score for embedded multiple modal representations in students' written reports and high-quality arguments. But since not all students used multimodal representations, the conclusion is that students, also at university level, need pedagogical support to understand the role and function of multiple modal representations in science, something which appears to be unusual according to a number of empirical studies investigating text practices in science classrooms, regardless of age group studied (e.g. Danielsson, 2011a; Lemke, 2000; Liu, 2011; Løvland, 2010; Nygård Larsson, 2011; Skjelbred & Aamotsbakken, 2010). The SWH approach (Keys et al., 1999) and the study performed by Hand and Choi (2010) deals with writing in connection to laboratory work in science classrooms. In this chapter, we examine other modes as well, and as mentioned above, concerning investigations and experimental work, action is highly relevant.

In our grade 2 and grade 8/9 classrooms, few instances of explicit instructions or discussions about how to use different modes were noted (e.g. Axelsson & Jakobson, 2010; Danielsson, 2011a). Nevertheless, in different subject contexts, the students encounter a variety of modes with different functions. The ways in which various modes for meaning making are used, and what modes are foregrounded (i.e. what is made salient or emphasized in the various classrooms in different contexts [Kress et al., 2001]) and combined as a consequence of the affordance of mode or semiotic resource, can shed light on the possibilities students are offered to gradually become part of the multimodal discourse of science. By using the concept of foregrounding in the analyses, we can focus on how teachers move between modes to vary what is brought to the attention of the students (Kress et al., 2001).

Overview of Data

Data from the grade 2 classroom derive from a study on young L2 students' (around eight years old) meaning making in natural science when engaging with the components of soil, and the processes in which soil is formed (Axelsson & Jakobson, 2010). The subject content in this classroom was dealt with within the frame of a Swedish version of Science and Technology for Children (STC). A special focus of the project was to study the relation between learning the subject and using the content-specific language. The data comprise about 100 hours of transcribed audio recordings from classroom work on the topic and collected student texts and digital images of flipcharts, whiteboard notes and hands-on activities. The data collection during the first year was financed by the City of Stockholm.

Data from grade 8/9 classrooms (students around 14/15 years of age) were collected within the interdisciplinary project 'Chemistry Texts as Tools for Scientific Learning: A Comparative Study of Teaching Practices in Swedish and Finland–Swedish Classrooms' (e.g. Danielsson, 2010, 2011a; Eriksson, 2011), financed by the Swedish Research Council. The project followed a number of lessons in four Finland–Swedish (in Finland) and three Swedish (in Sweden) chemistry classrooms during the teaching periods that dealt with the atomic model, the periodic chart, acids, bases and chemical bonds. The data consist of video and audio recordings as well as collected texts and digital images from all literacy events (Barton, 2007; Heath, 1983) around a number of focus students in each classroom. In summary, over 100 lessons were filmed, and during these, thousands of digital images around literacy events were taken. Examples used in this chapter are taken from both Finland–Swedish and Swedish classrooms.[1]

The subject content areas in the two age groups, with the concrete soil theme in grade 2 and the highly abstract theme around the atom and chemical bonds in grade 8/9 might have consequences for the use of different modes used in meaning making. Possibly, semiotic resources that can make visible and demonstrate the components of soil differ from those suitable for explaining abstract phenomena that have to be imagined, such as the ways in which an ionic bond is formed (cf. affordance).

A typical lesson in both age groups starts with the teacher initiating a conversation about what was done during the last session, going through homework or giving an overview of a new topic of the theme studied during the teaching period. In grade 2 all lessons started with a revision of last session's content, while in grade 8/9 the pattern varied between revision, run-through of homework and overview of new content.

Often some kind of experimental work was done after the introductory phase. This was the routine in grade 2, while the pattern varied between the classrooms in grade 8/9. Quite a few, but not all, lessons in grade 8/9 involved experimental work, though to what extent this was the case varied both between countries and classrooms (Eriksson, 2011). The experimental work was commonly followed up in a group discussion in grade 2, while there was variation between classrooms in this aspect in grade 8/9 (in Swedish – but not Finland–Swedish classrooms – the teachers sometimes did no follow-up after experimental work).

In grade 2, the lessons commonly finished after the follow-up while in grade 8/9 new theoretical content could be introduced (sometimes including working with questions in the textbook), new homework could be given or the school bell rang and the students just left the classroom.

Multimodal Communication in the Science Classrooms

In the following section, we first give an overview of the two age groups concerning foregrounded modes in the classroom practices; second, we describe the variation of modes. In both sections, we complete the overview with examples from both age groups.

Foregrounded modes

In the grade 2 classroom, spoken language is the overall foregrounded mode for creating meaning with the focus on making sense of new knowledge, and it does not appear to function as a bridge to written language (Wells, 1992). Teacher and students perform a dialogic speech, either when recounting last session, connecting everyday knowledge with scientific knowledge, or when discussing the current investigation. In grade 8/9 classrooms, spoken language is generally also foregrounded. However, the typical pattern in these classrooms is a teacher monologue accompanied by blackboard notes, more or less copied by the students into their notebooks. Thus, the written mode appears to be almost as important as the spoken mode in these classrooms. (However, as reported in Danielsson, 2010, 2011a, extended texts in the written mode are almost non-existent in the actual classroom practices, even though all classrooms but one visited have a final test based on a textbook, and on a weekly basis students are supposed to read sections from the textbook as their homework).

At the beginning of a typical science lesson in grade 2, the teacher through speech invites the students to make a verbal narrative of what they have done during the preceding science lesson. After a short dialogue, the teacher amplifies student meaning making by generating the core message from the students' narrative, and writes it down on the whiteboard (Figure 6.1). In this classroom, text written on the whiteboard or on flipcharts is typically generated from teacher–student dialogue. In Figure 6.1, we can see how the teacher graphically and in written words indicates the content of each test tube that was used during the previous lesson (and afterwards placed in mugs). At this specific moment, it is the choice of the graphic mode (here, drawn lines going from the words 'three test tubes' to 'sand', 'clay', 'humus') that carries the meaning, illustrating the three components, sand, clay and humus, as parts of a whole, that is the three test tubes placed in a mug (Figure 6.6).

Multimodality in the Science Classroom 147

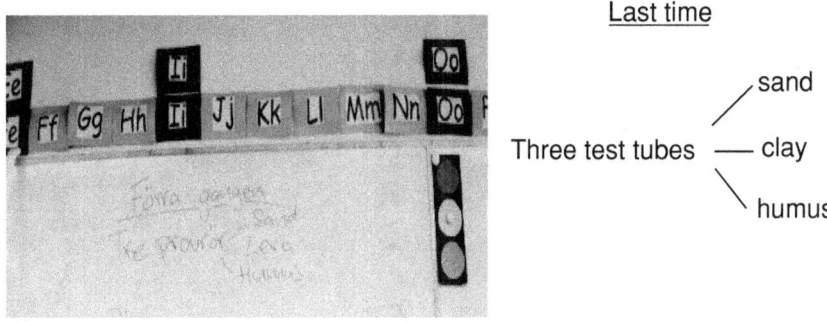

Figure 6.1 Teacher whiteboard notes in grade 2

After this initial dialogue, the speech mode continues to be foregrounded and the teacher asks a student to give a summary of the work on soil so far to update two teacher students visiting the class, thus using this opportunity for authentic revision. The narrative, the teacher's whiteboard notes and the repetition of the topic all work together to create coherence. Furthermore, these recounts present recurrent opportunities for the second language speakers of Swedish to produce extended speech.

During the teacher reviews or run-throughs that open the lessons in grade 8/9 classrooms, the students typically contribute by giving short answers to the teachers' questions (however, especially in one Swedish classroom, students sometimes initiate topics that the teacher then takes up, see e.g. Eriksson *et al.*, 2011). Thus, the spoken mode is foregrounded, but in general it is the teacher who is doing the talking. As was mentioned above, the written mode is also foregrounded in these classrooms. This is to a great extent due to the teachers' extensive use of the blackboard or whiteboard, and especially in one classroom when students read and answer questions on the content (see below). Blackboard notes in 8/9 grade classrooms are with few exceptions both written by the teacher and generated by the teacher monologue. Commonly, the teacher 'chalk talks' and makes blackboard notes in parallel with the spoken exposition (Figure 6.2). These notes commonly consist of a combination of verbal texts, chemical symbols and images (e.g. Figures 6.2, 6.7 and 6.11).

A striking difference between the grade 2 and grade 8/9 classrooms is that only rarely do the teachers in grade 8/9 classrooms use students' wordings or comments in the blackboard notes, and if so, these can be considered 'fill-ins' in the teacher's notes, and they would probably have been added by the

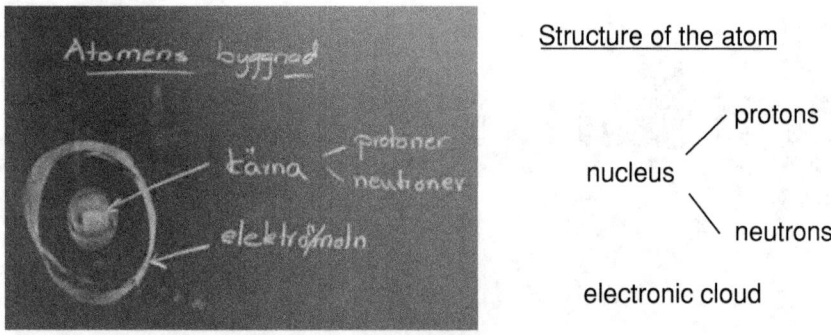

Figure 6.2 Blackboard note during theoretical overview, grade 8 (Fred's classroom, Lesson 1)

teacher even if the students had not given them. In the grade 2 classroom, no parallel note taking is done by the young students while this is almost always the case in grade 8/9 classrooms; in grade 8/9 classrooms, this commonly results in students having more or less exact copies of the teacher's notes in their own notebooks (Danielsson, 2010, 2011a). However, close comparisons between teacher and student notes sometimes reveal small differences (this is further discussed in Danielsson, 2011a, 2011b). One such example is in Figure 6.8, where the student mistakenly has drawn two electrons around the hydrogen nucleus. Another is the student note in Figure 6.3, where the student both has redesigned the circle around the nucleus in the teacher note (Figure 6.2) into a well-defined circle and has added the word 'elektroner'

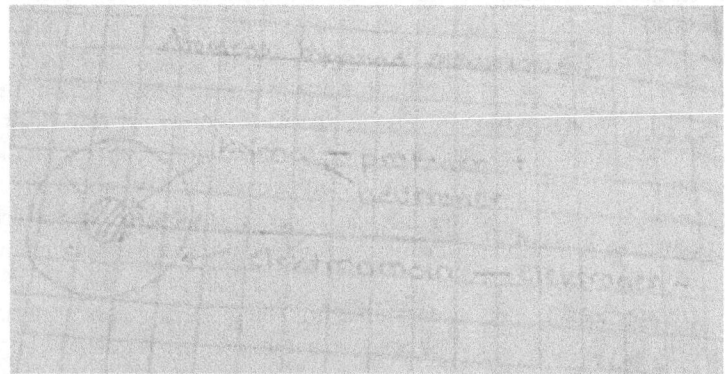

Figure 6.3 Blackboard note transformed into student notebook in grade 8 classroom (Fred's classroom, Lesson 1)

(*electrons*) beside 'elektronmoln' (*electronic cloud*), in parallel with 'protoner' (*protons*) and 'neutroner' (*neutrons*) (see also next section).

Variation of modes

The usage and variation in modes in grade 2 can be connected to a compiled and implicit[2] 'scientific cycle' whose stages to some extent correspond to the SWH template (Keys *et al.*, 1999). This structure guides the discourse throughout the topic and is, apart from the recurring repetitions at the beginning of lessons, at the core of how STC topics are structured. The stages in the scientific cycle comprise (1) finding out what we already know, (2) raising questions, (3) making predictions, (4) doing investigations, (5) recording the findings and (6) comparing predictions and findings, and within every stage a variety of modes (speech, notes on paper, whiteboard notes, action and worksheet writing and/or drawing) are used in the classroom. Every stage in the cycle is not performed in every lesson, but a minimum of two or three stages are at play in each lesson and all can be realized.

During the first recording of the topic, the focus is on finding out what the students already know about soil (stage 1) starting off with joint teacher–student speech. After a short whole-class discussion, students are grouped in pairs for closer interaction and written documentation of their previous knowledge of the content. Next, the students are told to share their ideas with the whole class while the teacher writes down their sentences on a flipchart. All student contributions are accepted by the teacher and written under headings and in bullet form on a flipchart (Figure 6.4).

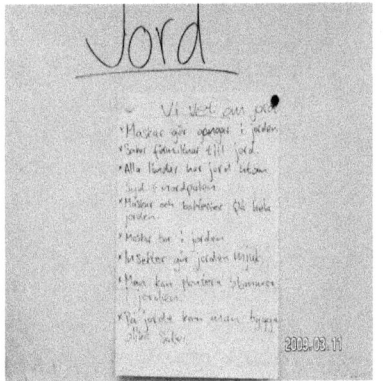

Soil

We know about soil

- Worms make tunnels in the soil.
- Things decompose to soil.
- All countries have soil except the South- and Northpole.
- Worms and bacteria on the whole earth.
- Worms live in the soil.
- Insects make the soil soft.
- You can plant flowers in soil.
- On soil you can build different things.

Figure 6.4 Student pre-knowledge on flipchart, grade 2

After four filled flipcharts, the teacher wants to get on and signals reorganization into small groups with the instruction to discuss the questions students want to raise about soil (stage 2). Each group is asked to generate their two most important questions through discussion and voluntary writing. As before, the teacher writes down the students' questions in bullets on a flipchart.

What has happened to the soil samples?			
Humus	Clay	Sand	Water
*Stays at the bottom (almost everything)	Hard as stone	*As before with sand at the bottom	Steam
*Less black	*Darker	Soft	Less water
*Finer pieces	Poo		
	*Stays at the bottom		
	Hard		
	On the edge,		
	at the top and down		
	Muddy down		
	Water at the top		

Figure 6.5 Student predictions about last week's investigation written on the whiteboard, grade 2

After that, the students make predictions about what could have happened to the soil samples after one week (stage 3). Again, students are invited to give voice to their ideas and there is a combination of teacher and student speech with the teacher writing notes on the whiteboard (see Figure 6.5). The teacher accepts the students' wordings when writing them on the whiteboard without valuing or changing them. A core characteristic in the development of scientific knowledge is to transform everyday language into scientific language. In this class, the teacher is more reluctant than the students to perform this transformation. When a student says 'things can decompose into soil' the teacher says 'into soil. Can I write that things **become** soil?' For a moment the teacher hesitates, but then continues: 'No, we should include decompose.'

After discussing and documenting the predictions, it is time for action (stage 4). Students in groups of three are told to carefully fetch the glass with the three test tubes filled with humus, sand or clay. They discuss the results in small groups while the teacher walks around the classroom participating in the discussions. The individual task is to write down the results on worksheet 5A (stage 5) (Figure 6.6).

Multimodality in the Science Classroom 151

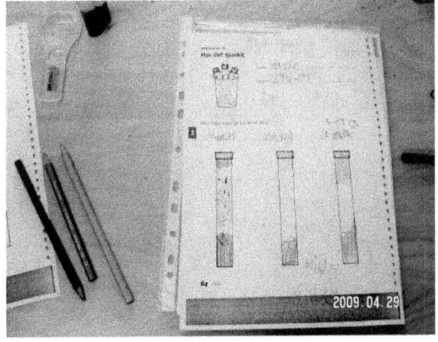

Worksheet 5A

How it has sunk

Name: ....

Date: ....

After a few days the samples look like this

...Humus...   ...Sand...   ...Clay...

Figure 6.6 Worksheet 5A, grade 2

The preprinted worksheet coordinates written language with images to form a coherent text. The headline 'How it has sunk' is followed by a naturalistic image of a glass with three filled test tubes. Below, a verbal written text says 'After a few days the samples look like this' followed by abstract images of three test tubes. The students' task is to discuss the appearance of the samples and write the names of the three components of soil and illustrate through coloring in the preprinted test tubes. Hence, this activity combines action, speech, written language and drawing, thus coordinating the meaning making in each mode into one whole.

The final stage in the scientific cycle (stage 6) is to compare predictions and findings. This is done in the same lesson in whole class speech and the result is further emphasized by the teacher drawing green stars in front of the predictions that came true (see Figure 6.5).

In this instance of a scientific cycle, we can see a connection between the questions put forward by grade 2 students and the first question in the SWH template (What are my questions?) (Keys *et al.*, 1999). In Figure 6.6, the naturalistic image of the glass with three filled test tubes acts as a representation of the second question in the SWH template (What did we do?). Then follows a report equivalent to the third question in the SWH template (What did I see?) through the students' colouring of the three abstract test tubes containing different substances. In this worksheet, written and visual representations are pre-printed as well as demanded from the students. As concerns the variation of modes, the above survey of the scientific cycle reveals that these students are engaged in the verbal (both written and spoken), the visual (images) and the action mode, but they do not encounter a symbolic mode, which is expected both as regards the content area and the grade level.[3] With few exceptions, images used in grade

2 are found in worksheets illustrating concrete objects like test tubes or a bag filled with soil (e.g. Figure 6.6) or actions (how to perform an investigation, e.g. by looking through a magnifying glass, or smear the three components sand, clay and humus onto a piece of paper). However, the images can in the same worksheet be depicted naturalistically or slightly more abstractly, the latter a step towards a higher degree of 'scientificness' (e.g. Figure 6.6).

In grade 8/9 classrooms, a great variety of semiotic resources in different modes – often used in parallel – were noted. However, even though experimental work does take place in most classrooms, no instance of a full scientific cycle was noted.[4] Instead, the use of various modes is better described through a number of recurring classroom activities, including theoretical overviews, experimental work and working with textbook questions (for a more complete description of text use during classroom activities, see Danielsson, 2011a).

During theoretical overviews, a combination of speech, writing, drawing and gesturing was noted in the classrooms, with some instances of action. The teachers typically 'chalk talk', with students contributing short answers to teacher questions and making notes; commonly by transferring the blackboard notes into their notebooks. The notes are highly multimodal, containing symbolic and verbal language as well as drawings of scientific phenomena such as the atomic model (e.g. Figures 6.2 and 6.7a), or the process of ion formation. During the overviews, teachers often combine the foregrounded spoken and written modes with a simultaneous use of body movements (gestures with hands/arms, e.g. Figure 6.7b). The following examples of how two teachers introduce the atom in their respective classrooms give an image of the ways in which the teachers make use of multiple modes in parallel (Figures 6.2 and 6.7a and b). Both teachers talk about the different parts of the atom and combine the spoken explanation with a drawing of a two-dimensional model of the atom on the blackboard. In the drawing, they both indicate the various parts of the atom (a nucleus containing protons and neutrons, surrounded by electrons) by writing verbal labels close to the drawing, using arrows or repeating symbols from the drawing. In connection to the labels, both teachers write plus and minus signs to indicate the negative and the positive charge of the particles.[5] Thus, both blackboard notes are highly multimodal, consisting of verbal language, schematic drawings and symbolic language (in this case well-known symbols from mathematics, though when concerning electrical charges in atoms they depict something quite different).

One of the teachers (Fred, Figure 6.2) has drawn the electrons as an 'electronic cloud' to point out the fact that electrons do not move in clearly separated shells. He uses the broad side of the chalk to make the shell more 'cloudy'. When in spoken language telling the students that the electrons

Multimodality in the Science Classroom 153

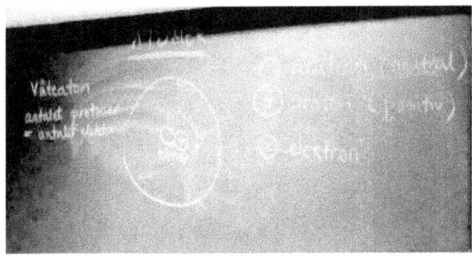

Figure 6.7 (a) and (b) Teacher note and teacher gestures during introduction of the atomic model, grade 8 (Fia's classroom, Lesson 1)[6]

move 'around and around, not in well-defined circles' he moves his hands back and forth around an imagined sphere between his hands. The other teacher (Fia, Figure 6.7a) has drawn a clear circle around the nucleus with the electron indicated as a small circle. Fia uses the spoken mode to point out that the electrons are not static, and while giving the spoken explanation she makes clear circular gestures with her forearms towards the class (Figure 6.7b).

Thus, the students in these two classrooms get approximately the same information about the structure of the atom and the nature of the particles, by ways of a combination of speech, writing and gestures. Both teachers highlight the 'blurriness' of the electronic shells using oral wordings and gestures. Fred draws an 'electronic cloud', thus giving the same information through all three modes, while Fia's clearly defined circle in the drawing contradicts the blurriness of the electrons that she highlights through speech and gestures. For students in this classroom who copy Fia's blackboard note without transducting the information given in speech or gestures into the written mode, an essential aspect of the atom will be missed (Figure 6.8). However, even though Fred makes the choice to draw an electronic cloud and the students in his class transfer the blackboard note into their notebooks, one of the focus students ends up with an image of the atom containing contradicting information. This student has redesigned the teacher note slightly, and as opposed to Fred's 'cloudy' circle around the nucleus (Figure 6.2), the word 'elektronmoln' (*electronic cloud*) besides the drawing in the student note points towards a well-defined circle (Figure 6.3).

The above examples are representative of the choice of modes during theoretical overviews, though a few instances of action were also noted. This was when teachers introduced the process of ion formation, a process in which the number of valence electrons (i.e. electrons in the outermost shell) in the atom is crucial. One teacher arranged students in groups around tables representing different substances, where each student acted as a valence electron. The

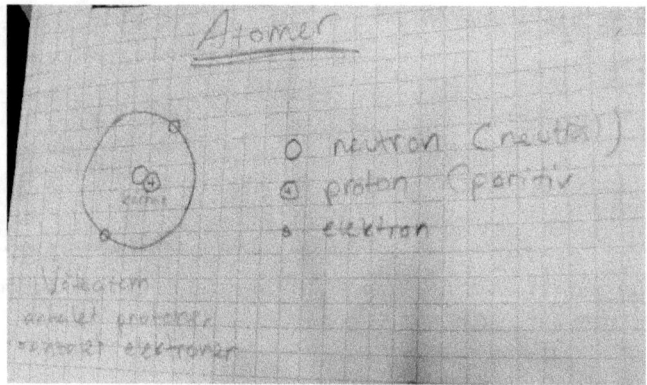

Figure 6.8 Student note transformed into student notebook in grade 8 (Fia's classroom, Lesson 1)

students were then supposed to decide whether to leave the atom (which then became a positive ion with a full outermost shell) to form a negative ion with another group, or to welcome other students to get a full outermost shell.

Experimental work is typically introduced by the teacher 'chalk talking' what the students are supposed to do, with blackboard notes often depicting concrete experimental equipment present in the classroom, such as test tubes in combination of written words (Figure 6.9). From time to time, chalk talking is combined with gestures (Figure 6.10), and during this activity, too,

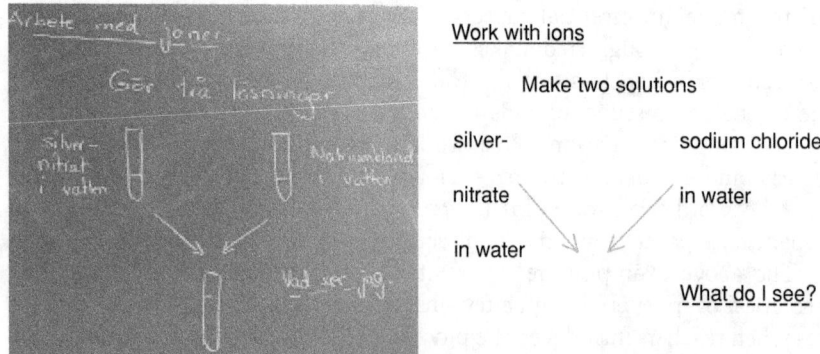

Figure 6.9 Blackboard instruction before experimental work, grade 8 (Fred's classroom, Lesson 8)

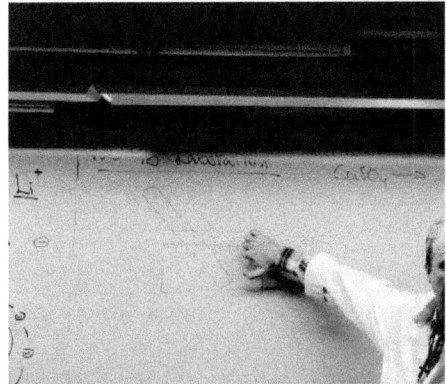

Sc 9b Experimental work

Figure 6.10 Whiteboard instruction and gesture before experimental work, grade 9 (Sören's classroom, Lesson 7)

students (especially in Finland–Swedish classrooms) transfer the blackboard notes into their notebooks.

After the introduction, students carry out the experiment in groups of two. In particular at the beginning of the teaching period, the teachers point out the importance of wearing protective glasses and coats, as well as handling the equipment in an appropriate and safe way.[7] During the experiments, students handle experimental equipment and chemical substances, often discussing what to do and how. When carrying out the experiments, as well as when writing down results afterwards, the students appear to be occupied with exactness. This is, for example, seen as meticulousness around measuring, or a tendency to 'correct' observations of flame color if they do not coincide with the teacher's answer (e.g. Danielsson, 2011a). While the students carry out their experiments, the teacher walks around the classroom, checking that students handle the equipment in the appropriate way or discussing the results that students come up with. Sometimes, but not always, the students are supposed to make written notes around the results (as when carrying through the experiment introduced in Figure 6.9).

After the experiment, the teacher sometimes has a run-through (this is routine in Finland–Swedish classrooms, but not in the Swedish ones), again often 'chalk talking', with students sometimes being prompted to fill in with their observations from the experimental work. The written notes typically contain chemical symbols and written words, sometimes presented in tables. In Figure 6.11, we can see an instance of the use of parallel semiotic resources (verbal and symbolic respectively) for representing the process in which silver ions and chloride ions form the ionic compound silver chloride.

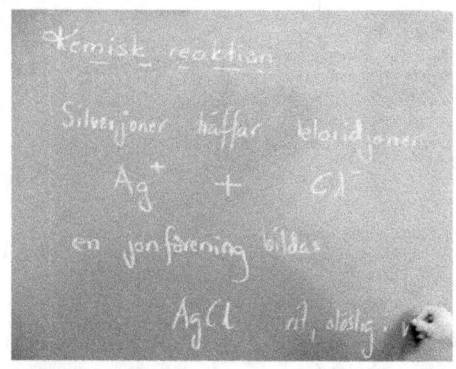

Chemical reaction

Silverions   meet   chloride ions

Ag^+ + Cl^-

an ionic compound is formed

AgCl   white, undissolvable, ...

Figure 6.11 Teacher note during follow-up after experimental work, grade 8 (Fred's classroom, Lesson 8)

Another recurring activity in most grade 8/9 classrooms is when students work in pairs or small groups with written questions. During this activity, the spoken and the written modes are used in parallel. The students discuss the questions in the small groups; they search for answers in textbooks, and then write down the answers in their notebooks (from time to time copying key sentences from the textbook [Danielsson, 2011a]). The written answers contain verbal writing, chemical symbols and drawings (usually models of chemical substances, ions or molecules). If a follow-up is done after this activity (which is not always the case), this is also typically done by 'chalk talk', with students being prompted for answers and sometimes correcting their written notes.

To sum up, a great variety of semiotic resources in different modes are used in the 8/9 classrooms, such as verbal writing and speech, gestures, images, symbolic language and action. These are often used in parallel, such as when the teachers introduce the atomic model, then using images showing the various particles and their spatial relation to each other, while using gestures and speech to highlight the ways in which electrons move around the nucleus. The action mode was mainly noted in connection to experimental work, an exception being when action was used to focus on the role of valence electrons in ionic formation. When dealing with a concept using both chemical symbols and verbal language, the teacher highlights the importance of *how* to write symbols in the correct way (e.g. that the symbol for a chemical substance always begins with a capital letter) but seldom *why* these symbols are used or, for instance, that AgCl involves a process in itself (i.e. an attraction between positive and negative charges).

Figurative language

A central meaning making resource in natural sciences is the use of figurative language, like metaphors and analogies. The figurative language in science is used for theory building, with metaphors like magnetic fields and electronic clouds. However, more occasionally analogies and metaphors are also used, not least for pedagogic reasons (see e.g. Roth & Lawless, 2002; Rundgren, 2006; Wickman & Jakobson, 2009 for overviews). These verbal expressions can be viewed as multimodal representations, since they can be seen as a combination of language with, for example image (electronic cloud), concrete objects (the atom seen as an apple) or action (humus in water compared to 'snot' going up and down).

During whole-class talk, the teacher in grade 2 brings everyday objects into the communication as meaning-making resources in the form of analogies and comparisons. Wet clay is compared with batter and dry clay is compared with flour. Humus in a test tube with water is described in analogy with a lava lamp and furthermore to nasal congestion going up and down. A close investigation of a leaf leads to an analogy with human blood vessels due to both appearance and function. Similarly, the roots of a flower are described in analogy with a tree. The vegetable parsnip is unfamiliar to the students and the teacher draws an analogy with 'a white carrot'. Most analogical connections are made to a visible everyday world and this might be a way of 'asserting the realism of scientific truth' (Kress et al., 2001: 67).

The ways of using analogies in the grade 2 classroom are similar to the extensive use of metaphoric language in grade 8/9 classrooms, for example around ions and the atomic model (e.g. Danielsson, 2011a, 2011b). In the chemistry classrooms, the teachers bring everyday objects (like apples or bicycle wheels) into the classroom in their oral expositions when describing the atom as consisting of a nucleus with surrounding electrons moving extremely rapidly in different orbits (or electronic shells). In addition, when explaining various chemical substances' disposition for reacting with other chemical substances, metaphoric language is used, especially in the teachers' oral expositions, and also in textbooks. The atoms are sometimes described as having human desires; chemical substances 'want' to 'give away' or 'take' electrons depending on their electronic structure, and noble gases are 'content'. Metaphors such as these are used extensively in all classrooms, but in one of the Swedish classrooms, the teacher uses 'his own' metaphors in a humorous way, talking about substances that react easily as 'mean', while noble gases and ions have 'reached their Nirvana' or they are 'drunk and happy' (Danielsson, 2011b). Thus, everyday objects and well-known processes and human desires are used to explain (abstract) scientific phenomena. Here, it is worth noting that the analogies and metaphors used to a great extent are restricted by the actual language spoken. Noble gases being 'drunk and happy' is a word play, using the homophone Sw. *full,* which can mean both *full* and *drunk.* Other examples are Sw. *skal,* which can mean both fruit *peel* and atomic *shell,* and Sw. *kärna* which can be used both for a fruit *seed* and for the atomic *nucleus.* Therefore, the apple is a possible analogy in a Swedish context, while this might not be the case in, for instance, an English context.

Discussion: Acting Like a Scientist

In this chapter, scientific literacy is defined as incorporating all possible means and modes for making meaning in science, and the aim has been to examine and make visible the various meaning-making resources in different modes used in two age groups working with different content areas in science classrooms. In each grade, the various modes used for meaning making have been studied, and special focus has been directed on what modes are foregrounded and how they are combined, to make evident any differences in use and function due to students' ages and subject content.

In grade 2 the work on the topic 'Soil' follows a 'scientific cycle' whose six stages to some extent correspond to the SWH template (Keys *et al.,* 1999). This cycle guides and influences the discourse and meaning making throughout the topic, and within every stage a variety of modes (speech, writing, action and images) are used in the classroom. Here, acting as a scientist means to, through speech, discuss present knowledge in the group and through speech and writing find out what questions to raise and make predictions before the action takes place. The teacher's flipchart or whiteboard texts are always in bullet form, making students familiar with this common 'scientific' way of presenting meaning. In addition, simple whiteboard drawings are used by the teacher as summaries (e.g. Figure 6.1). However, the foregrounded mode in grade 2 is speech. During the investigations, acting as a scientist means to work together in small groups and to be meticulous when handling the equipment and the substances (everyday objects like mugs and soil and science equipment like pipettes and test tubes). Reporting the findings is done individually in writing (on worksheets) and in speech through whole-class narratives. As for images, students encounter both naturalistic and slightly abstract images in the worksheets (see Figure 6.6) and are likewise expected to write or draw images as a result of their investigations. This makes the worksheets typical examples of integrated verbal and visual realizations (cf. Lemke, 1998). This way of using writing for real cognitive purposes differs greatly from the often reported picture of writing as a de-contextualized activity within the mother tongue subject (e.g. Halonen, Chapter 5). Neither textbooks as resources for meaning making nor graphic taxonomies to illustrate the soil processes are used in the grade 2 classroom. Instead, the teacher narrates central processes in the ongoing whole-class dialogue. As for individual extended writing, this is only done once, at the suggestion of the researcher. Thus, we can conclude that in grade 2 the integration of modes for meaning making is somewhat limited and instead there is a preference for using one mode at a time.

In grade 8/9 during a teaching period focusing on the atomic model and chemical bonds, students' meaning making takes place in a number of recurring classroom activities: theoretical overviews, experimental work and working with textbook questions. Within each of these activities, a variety of modes are used (written and spoken verbal language, symbolic language, images, gestures and action), often combined and used in parallel. During theoretical overviews and when introducing or having run-throughs after experimental work, teachers commonly 'chalk talk', producing multimodal written texts on the whiteboard/blackboard. The texts combine verbal and symbolic language (e.g. chemical formulas) and images (often depicting, abstract phenomena or, around experimental work, concrete objects). In parallel, the teachers highlight important aspects of the content through gesturing (e.g. when talking about the ways in which electrons move around the nucleus of the atom) or metaphoric language (e.g. when talking about ion formation or noble gases). During the teacher's expositions and run-throughs, students commonly give short spoken answers to teacher questions, and they transfer the teacher's multimodal notes into their notebooks, commonly as more or less direct copies of the teacher notes. The teachers' spoken words or gestures seldom get transducted into writing or images. Working with textbook questions involves more student–student and teacher–student dialogues, and students are also engaged in search reading for answers and (sometimes) copying key sentences from the textbook. During experimental work, students handle chemical substances and experimental equipment with care (Bunsen burners, evaporation bowls, etc. which in the spoken discourse are always called by their accurate names) and they are careful about acting out things in a correct manner (involving exact measuring, noting the correct results, etc.). Altogether, acting like a scientist in grade 8/9 classrooms involves meticulousness around both experimental work and engaging with the written mode.[8] Also, students in these classrooms appear to engage in 'right and wrong', something that could be connected to the nature of science. For example, there is an expected correct result of experiments, and theoretical overviews and written teaching material deal with classifications and descriptions, in which the combinations of modes for meaning making has the same function: to help explaining 'the truth' about chemical bonds, atoms, etc. The use of metaphors and analogy appears to have the same function. As opposed to the relatively limited integration of modes for meaning making in the grade 2 classroom, meaning making in grade 8/9 classrooms involves a high level of multimodality, where the combination of modes is more or less the rule. The ways in which these teachers combine various modes in meaning making around the atomic model is a good example of mode choice in relation to affordance (e.g. Gibson, 1986; Kress, 2003). Here, spatial relations are represented in the visual mode, while the spoken mode and gesturing are used to highlight movement and the fact that there is relativeness as to where electrons can be found in relation to the atomic nucleus.

Thus, a variety of modes can be seen in both age groups, though the variation is greater in grade 8/9 classrooms, and a number of modes are used in parallel. The differences regarding the use of various modes in the two age groups can also be linked to the subject content areas. Working with soil means dealing with a concrete substance, thus giving various opportunities to work with hands-on activities. Atoms, electrons, ionic processes on the other hand cannot be seen or touched. Instead they have to be imagined. A way of supporting students' meaning making around these abstract phenomena is using various modes; the choice of semiotic resource being linked to the affordances of the resource in question. Thus, a comparison between our two sets of data implies a link between increased abstraction and an increasing use of a variety of modes.

As regards a development concerning multimodality in science classrooms, some interesting patterns were noted in our two sets of data. In the written mode, already in grade 2, the students are presented with texts combining words and drawings connected to the scientific field (like test tubes), and the teacher also uses bullets in his whiteboard notes and on flipcharts. However, the drawings typically depict concrete objects and processes, and text presented in bullets is generated from the students' wordings. In grade 8/9, written texts also combine words with drawings and bullets/tables and sometimes the drawings depict concrete objects like test tubes in these classrooms, too, but more commonly the drawings are abstract, depicting chemical phenomena and processes. Furthermore, the drawings in the 8/9 grade classrooms are multimodal in themselves, integrating words and symbolic language. In grade 2, the teacher takes up students' exact wordings from the teacher–student dialogue and transfers these into written texts while in grade 8/9, teachers 'chalk talks', presenting scientific facts. Apparently, there is a shift from concrete matters grounded in the students' experiences to complex scientific matters.

Even though students in the higher grades engage with multiple modes, there is little evidence of students using resemiotization of 'knowledge from one representation into another' (Klein & Kirkpatrick, 2010: 89). Instead, these students mainly reproduce teachers' blackboard notes into their notebooks, without transducting spoken words or gestures into writing (see Danielsson, 2011a for rare examples of exceptions to this). Furthermore, in our data, teachers do not talk about why to choose a particular mode for representation or what, for instance, the difference between verbalizing and using symbols in meaning making around chemical bonding. This result is similar to the one reported by Liu (2011) from a chemistry classroom in secondary school.

To conclude, even though our data was collected in different groups, from this comparison between classroom practices in two age groups, it appears as if there is a development in which learners in later grades engage with a greater variety of modes. This development can be explained both by the age of the participants and the content areas. However, it appears that the ways in which various modes and representations can be used for meaning making is supposed to be learned implicitly. For students to develop a high level of thinking with representation (Klein & Kirkpatrick, 2010: 88), we might need a more structured and explicit teaching focusing, for example the affordances of various semiotic resources (e.g. Danielsson, 2011b; Hand & Choi, 2010; Lemke, 2000; Liu, 2011).

Notes

(1) All names are assumed (with Finland–Swedish teacher names beginning with F and Swedish teacher names beginning with S) so as not to reveal the identity of the subjects.
(2) The scientific cycle is considered 'implicit' in the respect that the teacher works along this cycle during the topic, referring to each stage, but without mentioning the scientific cycle as a whole or as a concept.
(3) In higher school grades, the symbolic mode could be more prominent, also when dealing with this content (e.g. as regards pH value).
(4) Typically, the experimental work is (a) introduced by the teacher (b) carried out in pairs by students and sometimes, but not always, followed by (c) teacher follow-up (see e.g. Danielsson, 2011a). As compared to the SWH template (Keys *et al.*, 1999) in connection to experimental work, if the students produce texts (spoken or written), these can be related to the two questions 'What did I do?' and 'What did I see?'.
(5) In Fred's drawing, the plus and minus signs beside 'proton' and 'electron' were added after the picture was taken.
(6) Apart from indicating the names of the various particles, a verbal text to the left of the drawing says 'Hydrogen atom – number of protons = number of electrons'.

(7) In interviews, some teachers assert that the actual outcome of the experiments is of minor importance compared to working according to safety regulations, using experimental equipment in the correct manner, etc. (Eriksson *et al.*, 2011).
(8) Danielsson (2011a) describes the ways in which students engage with texts in these classrooms as reading and writing 'with tweezers'.

References

Axelsson, M. and Jakobson, B. (2010) Yngre andraspråkselevers meningsskapande i naturvetenskap genom tre analysverktyg [Young second language learners' meaning making in science through three tools for analysis]. *Nordand* 5 (2), 9–34.

Barton, D. (2007) *Literacy: An introduction to the Ecology of Written Language* (2nd edn). Malden, MA: Blackwell.

Danielsson, K. (2010) Chemistry learning: Text use and text talk in one Finland–Swedish chemistry classroom. *IARTEM e-journal* 3(2), 1–28.

Danielsson, K. (2011a) Att närma sig en naturvetenskaplig diskurs. Text och textanvändning i svenska och finlandssvenska klassrum. In I. Eriksson (ed.) *Kemiundervisning, text och textbruk i finlandssvenska och svenska skolor – en komparativ tvärvetenskaplig studie* [To approach a scientific discourse: Texts and text use in Swedish and Finland–Swedish classrooms] (pp. 161–237). Stockholm: Stockholms Universitets Förlag.

Danielsson, K. (2011b) Då blir de fulla och glada. Multimodala representationer av atommodellen i kemiklassrum [Then they become drunk and happy. Multimodal representations of the atomic model in chemistry classrooms]. In B. Aamotsbakken, J. Smidt and E.S. Tønnesen (eds) *Tekst og tegn.* [Texts and signs] (pp. 121–144). Trondheim: Tapir Forlag.

diSessa, A. (2004) Metarepresentation: Native competence and targets for instruction. *Cognition and Instruction* 22, 293–331.

Eriksson, I. (ed.) (2011) *Kemiundervisning, text och textbruk i finlandssvenska och svenska skolor – en komparativ tvärvetenskaplig studie* [Chemistry education, texts and text use in Finland–Swedish and Swedish schools – A comparative, multidisciplinary study]. Stockholm: Stockholms Universitets Förlag.

Eriksson, I., Lindberg, V. and Ståhle, Y. (2011) Kemikemi eller samhällskemi – skilda betoningar i finlandssvenska och svenska kemiklassrum [Chemistry–chemistry or chemistry in society – different emphases in Finland–Swedish and Swedish chemistry classrooms]. In I. Eriksson (ed.) *Kemiundervisning, text och textbruk i finlandssvenska och svenska skolor – en komparativ tvärvetenskaplig studie* (pp. 76–113). Stockholm: Stockholms Universitets Förlag.

Gibson, J.J. (1986) *The ecological approach to visual perception.* Hillsdale, NJ: Erlbaum.

Halliday, M.A.K. and Martin, J.R. (1993) *Writing Science: Literacy and Discursive Power.* Pennsylvania: University of Pittsburgh Press.

Hand, B. and Choi, A. (2010) Examining the impact of student use of multiple modal representations in constructing arguments in organic chemistry laboratory classes. *Research in Science Education* 40, 29–44.

Heath, S.B. (1983) *Ways with Words: Language, Life, and Work in Communities and Classrooms.* Cambridge: Cambridge University Press.

Hubber, P., Tytler, R. and Haslam, F. (2010) Teaching and learning about force with a representational focus: Pedagogy and teacher change. *Research in Science Education* 40, 5–28.

Iedema, R.A. (2001) Resemiotization. *Semiotica: Journal of the International Association for Semiotic Studies* 137 (1), 23–39.
Keys, C.W., Hand, B., Prain, V. and Collins, S. (1999) Using the Science Writing Heuristic as a tool for learning from laboratory investigations in secondary science. *Journal of Research in Science Teaching* 36, 1065–1084.
Klein, P.D. and Kirkpatrick, L.C. (2010) Multimodal literacies in science: currency, coherence and focus. *Research in Science Education* 40, 87–92.
Knain, E. and Hugo, A. (2007) Pendelen mellom erfaring og representasjon: en fagdidaktisk modell for 'scientific literacy' [The pendulum between experience and representation: An educational model for scientific literacy]. In S. Matre and T.L. Hoel (eds) *Skrive for nåtid og framtid: Skriving i arbeidsliv og skole* [Writing for the Presence and the Future: Writing at the Workplace and in School] (pp. 333–347). Trondheim: Tapir Akademisk Forlag.
Kozma, R. (2003) The material features of multiple representations and their cognitive and social affordances for science understanding. *Learning and Instruction* 13, 205–226.
Kozma, R., Chin, E., Russell, J., and Marx, N. (2000) The role of representations and tools in the chemistry laboratory and their implications for chemistry learning. *Journal of the Learning Sciences* 9(2), 105–143.
Kozma, R. and Russell, J. (2005) Students becoming chemists: Developing representational competence In J. Gilbert (ed.) *Visualization in Science Education* (pp. 121–146). London: Kluwer.
Kress, G. (2003) *Literacy in the New Media Age*. London: Routledge.
Kress, G. (2010) *Muldimodality: A Social Semiotic Approach to Contemporary Communication*. London: Routledge.
Kress, G., Jewitt, C., Ogborn, J. and Tsatsarelis, C. (2001) *Multimodal Teaching and Learning: The Rhetorics of the Science Classroom*. London: Continuum.
Kress, G. and van Leuween, T. (2001) *Multimodal Discourse: The Modes and Media of Contemporary Communication*. London: Edward Arnold.
Lemke, J.L. (1990) *Talking Science: Language, Learning and Values*. Norwood: Ablex.
Lemke, J.L. (1998) Multiplying meaning: Visual and verbal semiotics in scientific text. In J.R. Martin and R. Veel (eds) *Reading Science* (pp. 87–112). London: Routledge.
Lemke, J.L. (2000) Multimedia literacy demands of the scientific curriculum. *Linguistics and Education* 10(3), 247–271.
Liu, Y. (2011) Scientific literacy in secondary school chemistry: A multimodal perspective. Unpublished PhD Thesis, National University of Singapore.
Løvland, A.M. (2010) *På jakt etter svar og forståing: Sammensette faktekstar i skulen* [Chasing answers and understanding]. Bergen: Fagbokforlaget.
Nygård Larsson, P. (2011) *Biologiämnets texter. Text, språk och lärande i en språkligt heterogen gymnasieklass* [Texts in the subject of biology. Text, language and learning in a linguistically heterogeneous class in secondary school]. Malmo Studies in Educational Sciences No 62. Lund: Lunds Universitet.
Roth, W.-M. and Lawless, D. (2002) Scientific investigations, metaphorical gestures, and the emergence of abstract scientific concepts. *Learning and Instruction* 12, 285–304.
Roth, W.M. and McGinn, M.K. (1998) Inscription: Toward a theory of representing as a social practice. *Review of Educational Research* 68, 35–59.
Rundgren, C-J. (2006) Att börja tala 'biokemiska' – betydelsen av metaforer och hjälpord för meningsskapande kring proteiner [Beginning to talk 'biochemistry' – the role of

metaphors and supporting words for meaning making around proteins]. *NorDiNa* 5, 30–42.
Simpson, A. and Walsh, M. (2010) Multiple literacies: Implications for changed pedagogy. In F. Christie and A. Simpson (eds) *Literacy and Social Responsibility: Multiple Perspectives* (pp. 24–39). London: Equinox.
Skjelbred, D. and Aamotsbakken, B. (2010) *Lesing av fagtekster som grunnleggende ferdighet* [The reading of subject texts as a basic skill]. Oslo: Novus Forlag.
Tang, K-S. and Moje E.B. (2010) Relating multimodal representations to the literacies of science. *Research in Science Education* 40(1), 81–85.
Waldrip, B., Prain, V. and Carolan, J. (2010) Using multimodal representations to improve learning in junior secondary science. *Research in Science Education* 40 (1), 65–80.
Wells, G. (1992) The centrality of talk in education. In K. Norman (ed.) *Thinking Voices: The Work of the National Oracy Project* (pp. 283–310). London: Hodder and Stoughton.
Wickman, P.-O. and Jakobson, B. (2009) Estetiska processer i naturvetenskap – att behandla en förgiftning [Aesthetic processes in natural sciences: Treating a poisoning]. In F. Lindstrand and S. Selander (eds) *Estetiska lärprocesser: upplevelser, praktiker och kunskapsformer* [Aesthetic Learning Processes: Experience, Practices and Forms of Knowledge] (pp. 127–152). Lund: Studentlitteratur.
Wu, H. and Shah, P. (2004) Exploring visuospatial thinking in chemistry learning. *Science Education* 88 (3), 465–492.
Yore, L.D. and Hand, B. (2010) Epilogue: Plotting a research agenda for multiple representations, multiple modality, and multimodal representational competency. *Research in Science Education* 40 (1), 93–101.
Zinsser, W.K. (1988) *Writing to Learn: How to Write and Think Clearly About any Subject at All*. New York: Harper Collins.

7 Discourses of Literacy on an International Master's Programme: Examining Students' Academic Writing Norms

Laura McCambridge and Anne Pitkänen-Huhta

Introduction

English has long been the dominant *lingua franca* in international scientific communities. Hamel (2007: 53) estimates that in international periodical publications 75% of articles within the humanities and social sciences, and over 90% within natural sciences, are published in English. This dominance is in turn reflected in higher education worldwide: students are increasingly expected to be able to read course material written in English and, particularly in Nordic countries, are expected to be proficient in academic English before graduating. A more recent development in this trend is the growing number of degree programmes conducted entirely through English in EFL countries. Finland is a prime example; all Finnish universities now offer at least one higher education programme through English (Maiworm & Wächter, 2002), with most offering many more. These 'international' programmes attract students and teachers both from within Finland and from around the world, forming remarkably multicultural, multilingual discourse communities where English is used both for participation and learning and for instruction and assessment. Literacy in particular typically plays a central role on these programmes, with students' learning and assessment culminating in the completion of a thesis.

Most research into students' English writing in non-English speaking countries has thus far been from an EAP (English for Academic Purposes) perspective with the aim of determining how students can best improve their language and acquire the academic writing norms of an apparently monolithic English-speaking world. Fewer studies have yet looked at this context from a sociolinguistic perspective, with the aim of understanding the norms of English use within these programmes as discourse communities in their own right and how they reflect the social world in which they exist. With this agenda in mind, we take an 'Academic Literacies' approach to investigate students' expressed norms of academic writing on an International Master's programme at a medium-sized university in Finland, perceiving these norms to be ideological, contextual and interwoven with the purposes, values and power structures of the society that shapes them. English-medium higher education, in contexts where English is used as a *lingua-franca*, is particularly interesting from this viewpoint, as an intersection between local and global social scales. These contexts offer a valuable opportunity to explore the tensions and conflicts brought about by the globalization of English in academia.

Barton and Hamilton (2000: 7) define literacy practices as including discourses of literacy, that is 'how people talk about and make sense of literacy'. In this chapter, we focus on students' ideological discourse on academic writing upon beginning an English-medium master's programme, looking particularly at the norms they express of 'good' academic English and the authorities they orient to in explaining these norms. Blommaert (2010: 39–40) refers to these 'centers of authority' as being 'the places where good discourse about this topic is made.' Uncovering these centres can improve our understanding of global academic English trends and in turn the present power relations within international academia.

Approaches to Academic Writing Practices

Lea and Street (1998) identify three main theoretical approaches to investigate students' academic literacy practices, namely 'Study Skills', 'Academic Socialization' and 'Academic Literacies'. The skill-based approach is where writing is taken as an individual cognitive skill with objective standards that are universally applicable. In ESL and EFL literature, this approach has been particularly prevalent, with the standard being that of the apparently universal native speaker or native speaking ability. For example, Silva (1993) summarizes research findings on the differences between native writers and non-native writers of academic English. Although he states that he is not aiming to portray non-native writers in a negative light, he nevertheless describes their norms in terms of deficiencies not only regarding their language choices and textual conventions but also regarding their writing process. For example, they are described as doing less planning, goal-setting, reviewing and even reflecting on their writing compared to the gold standard of the native speaker (Silva, 1993: 661–662).

The second approach, Academic Socialization, acknowledges the idea that writing practices are contextual to discourse communities. These communities, however, tend to be viewed as rather unique, homogeneous entities into which the novice writer must be acculturated. In ESL and EFL literature, this view can be seen in much of the genre-based research on writing, where the English norms of an academic discipline are first identified and then taught to non-native speakers (e.g. Hyland, 2006; Swales, 1990). It can also be seen in early Contrastive Rhetoric research, where the norms of academic discourse are contrasted between English and other languages or cultures, in order to create greater understanding of cultural difference in writing and again ultimately teach non-native students the appropriate way to write in English (e.g. Connor, 1996).

Although the Academic Socialization approach has certainly improved our knowledge of socially situated literacy practices, it tends to oversimplify the context by ignoring the variation, conflicts and overlap brought about through interaction and often competition with other discourse systems on both local and global scales. Discourse communities are often demarcated rather broadly, with academics within a discipline all agreeing to and adhering to the same literacy practices and norms unproblematically. Moreover, the suggestion seems to be that these practices rarely change and that all new scholars or non-English-speaking scholars can and should adopt them.

Stemming from New Literacy Studies, the Academic Literacies approach, however, views these practices as being rather more dynamic, conflicted and ideological. Discourse communities, as Blanton (1994: 221) puts it, are 'constantly in the making'. Their practices change depending on the individuals who constitute them, the purposes they serve and the social power structures that govern their use. Both students and teachers bring their social backgrounds, language backgrounds, literacy histories, pedagogical philosophies and content approaches with them to class. These are just some of the factors that can influence their ideologies of writing and in turn their academic writing norms. Moreover, academic writing norms cannot be seen simply as vehicles for universal ideals of good thinking, but are rather in themselves a means of producing, structuring and limiting thought. As Canagarajah (2002: 79) puts it, 'the medium is also the message' – pragmatic and discursive expectations for academic writing shape what we regard as acceptable content.

Previous studies taking and developing this approach have been primarily concerned with exploring new contexts that have arisen in UK higher education and the conflicts of literacy practices that result. They have focused particularly on the literacy practices of non-traditional students – that is students with social backgrounds that have previously had very limited access to higher education. Ivanič (1998), for example, highlights the role of these students' social identities in their language choices and how they subtly conflict with the identities they are expected to evoke as academic writers in UK universities. In a similar case study, Lillis (2001) also highlights the role of students' identities in their writing practices, while exposing the confusion non-traditional students face in understanding the expectations of teachers who perceive writing norms to be autonomous and transparent intellectual ideals.

Similar work has been carried out from an EFL perspective on a global scale, for example by Canagarajah (2002) and by Lillis and Curry (2010). Both projects emphasize the close relationship between concepts of valid academic literacy and valid knowledge production. In doing so, they demonstrate the struggles that periphery or simply non-Anglophone scholars face in contributing to scientific knowledge production worldwide as a result of their varying language and literacy norms. The gates of prestigious 'global' journals are often kept by Anglo-American editors, reviewers and proofreaders who review articles for an imagined Anglo-American readership. Lillis and Curry (2010: 150–153) give one example of a Southern European scholar being told that her article was 'too Latin', with 'pretentious' word choices, to be received well by Anglo-American readers. Another non-Anglophone scholar's paper came under fire for use of 'weasel words', such as 'phenomena' and 'approach'. This was presented not as a socially developed language preference but as a transparent intellectual truth. In this way, valid knowledge production globally is limited to those who are able and willing to satisfy the discourse expectations and connotations of a perceived Anglo-American authority. In this way, 'global' in scientific communication becomes 'a place called the "US"' (Lillis & Curry, 2010: 135).

The majority of academic literacy studies have focused on writing in the United Kingdom or on scholars in non-Anglophone countries writing for international publications. A context in which both students and teachers from varying cultural and social backgrounds come together to form a discourse community in which English is used as a *lingua franca* is rather different. The potential for variation in language and literacy practices is clearly greater and the need to negotiate conflicting ideologies is heightened. Moreover, many earlier studies on transnational literacies have focused on immigration: situations where people move to a new place and face new practices both in everyday life and in education (e.g. Blommaert, 2008). However, in the case of the master's programmes which we focus on in this chapter, we are facing a situation of temporary migration, with people shifting localities in search of global education, and thus practices are constantly on the move and in flux, merging and transforming. As the title 'International Master's Degree Programme', adopted by most Finnish universities, suggests, these programmes are orientated towards an imagined global community and the perceived practices of that community, while still being clearly situated in a local Finnish context.

The Global and Local in English Literacy Practices

In recent years, the emphasis in literacy studies has been heavily on local practices, as an opposition to autonomous views of literacy as a neutral transferrable skill, which is unaffected by individual, contextual or societal factors. Focus on the locality of practices has resulted in an extensive body of research showing that literacy is indeed multiple, varying and ideologically loaded (e.g. Barton & Hamilton, 1998; Prinsloo & Breier, 1996; Scribner & Cole, 1981; Street, 1984). At the same time, however, it seems that not enough attention is paid to the transnational literacies and global flows prevalent in present-day societies (Warriner, 2009). Brandt and Clinton (2002), for example, call for Literacy Studies scholars to focus on the dialectical relationship between the local and the global, and to examine local literacy events and practices in the light of the global. Similarly, Baynham (2004) calls for more attention to issues of schooling, with a particular emphasis on transnational movement. This focus would help shed light on the interaction between the global flows and the local contexts, as Warriner (2009: 167) argues. These calls do not undermine the significance of the local, but there is a need for studies that look at the intersections of local practices and global flows, and the historically and culturally formed social patterns and structures.

There have been claims that globalization makes the world smaller; it unites people and ideas and turns the world into a global village (e.g. Modiano, 1999). It has also been claimed that the English language has a significant role in this process as an international *lingua franca*. The present sociolinguistic situation is, however, a lot more complex than this idealized picture of a world united. The world has not, as Blommaert (2010: 1) says, 'become a village, but rather a tremendously complex web of villages, towns, neighbourhoods, settlements connected by material and symbolic ties in often unpredictable ways.' Movement of people cannot be described merely in terms of emigration and immigration. Instead, people are constantly on the move in unpredictable ways, forming new communities that are not stable but emergent and expanding; they mix and transform, and then perhaps die out and remerge elsewhere. This kind of movement has recently been called 'superdiversity' (Blommaert, 2010; Vertovec, 2007). Present-day international higher education is a good example of such communities: students seek educational possibilities globally and thus they come together with different cultural and linguistic backgrounds for a limited period of time, 'resulting in changing practices in the new "educational contact zones"' (Pennycook, 2007a: 25). Eventually, they again disperse in different directions.

This kind of haphazard movement creates a new kind of sociolinguistic situation and calls for new kinds of conceptualizations. Blommaert (2010: 5) talks about a sociolinguistics of mobility, where the focus is not on 'language-in-place', but on 'language-in-motion'. People move across spaces and their linguistic resources move with them, taking new shape in new places. However, this movement is not unproblematic, as Blommaert (2010: 6) notes:

> Movement of people across space is therefore never a move across empty spaces. The spaces are always someone's space, and they are filled with norms, expectations, conceptions of what counts as proper and normal (indexical) language use and what does not count as such. Mobility, sociolinguistically speaking, is therefore a trajectory through different stratified, controlled and monitored spaces in which language 'gives you away'.

To understand the complexities of the temporarily created space, we need to consider the role of English as a global language as we cannot deny the fact that English has a significant role in the processes of globalization. English is the language of opportunities and imagined communities (see Anderson, 1983; Norton, 2001; Pitkänen-Huhta & Nikula, 2012; Yashima, 2012). As Pennycook (2007b: 101–102) says, we need to examine more closely what role English plays in global flows and how people use English and appropriate it to meet their own needs. In the case of English-medium higher education, the students come together with their own resources of English, which they have acquired through participation in their respective previous spaces where they have come across academic literacy practices. In this new multilingual and multicultural community, conflicting ideologies of language and literacy (that is beliefs about the value of various language and literacy practices (McGroarty, 2010)) are bound to meet. In particular, the ownership of the new space becomes extremely complex. Whose space is it, in fact? Whose norms are at play? What expectations are there for the use of English and where do those expectations come from?

The World Englishes perspective has been quite influential in examining the role of English in communities and societies where it does not have an official status. The three circles of English speakers by Kachru (1985) have been used to explain the spread of English in the world. The circles are the inner circle (native speakers of English), the outer circle (ESL) and the expanding circle (EFL). Pennycook (2007a, 2007b), among others, has criticized the World Englishes view, however, and has proposed that instead of understanding 'English' as different forms or varieties of the core native English, we should see it as a phenomenon that moves across spaces and communities, and is at the same time both fluid and fixed (Pennycook, 2007a: 8). This take on language and language use allows us to look beyond the distinction of the global and the local, and enables us to understand the complex connection between current sociolinguistic spaces and the use of English as a shared linguistic resource in new emergent and fluid communities. In the same vein, Blommaert (2010) uses the terms *scales* and *indexicality* to tackle the connection between the global and the local, the macro and the micro. He points out that the spaces in which mobile people operate are not only horizontal spaces but also vertical spaces, which are layered and stratified. In these spaces, there are various kinds of social and cultural distinctions, and these distinctions are indexical of broader social and cultural patterns (Blommaert, 2010: 5). These 'orders of indexicality' (Blommaert, 2005: 69) 'organize distinctions between, on the one hand, "good", "normal", "appropriate", and "acceptable" language use and, on the other, "deviant", "abnormal", etc. language use' (Blommaert, 2010: 6).

What is important in the context under scrutiny in this chapter is that these patterns of indexicality also involve control and evaluation: some forms of language use are made acceptable by real or imagined sources of authority and are therefore valued and useful (Blommaert, 2010: 38). In traditional or popular belief, the owners of a language (and in turn its discursive genres) are usually viewed as its native speakers or, to be more exact, its socially powerful native speakers. With English and its global use, the situation is naturally more complex. English has now been called 'pluricentric', meaning that there is more than one 'norm producing' centre of authority in its use (Lillis & Curry, 2010) both on local and on global levels – or indeed across both horizontal and vertical spaces. The perceived norms of British or American 'standard English' can no longer be assumed to suit the purposes of the entire globe, let alone the purposes of every local community in which English is used.

In this study, we explore the issue of normativity in global English academic literacy practices by analysing students' ideological discourse on academic writing. This discourse reveals how students make sense of academic writing practices and attach value to particular writing norms in

English over others. Moreover, analysing students' discourse on writing will also help to identify the authorities they draw from in articulating English academic writing norms – or in other words, the sources from which the correct ways to write originate in their perceptions. This discourse is gathered through interviews with the students shortly after beginning the master's programme in Finland. In this way, we aim to catch students in transition, that is having left one local context and upon facing a new local context, which is, as the programme's title suggests, internationally orientated. The students are therefore situated in a fascinating space in which their resources from one local community, their expectations for another local community and their understanding of global community norms meet. Specifically, the study aims to answer the following questions: (1) What norms of academic writing in English do students express upon beginning the programme? What common or conflicting discourse patterns can be found in how they express these norms? (2) What authorities do students orient to or draw from in explaining these norms?

Data and Methods

The data consist of extensive semi-structured interviews with six students upon beginning their studies on an English-medium master's programme in the Faculty of Humanities at a medium-sized university in Finland. The interviews were conducted by Laura McCambridge as part of her doctoral study. Below are brief profiles of the students, along with important features of their cultural and educational backgrounds (see Figure 7.1). They have all been given pseudonyms.

The students were asked to talk about their previous experiences with English academic writing, their ideas about good versus bad English academic writing and their strengths and weaknesses in English academic writing. They were also asked more specifically about their experiences with writing for evaluation in English – that is the purpose of written assignments and their thoughts about feedback they have received on their texts. Finally, they were asked how they thought good academic writing practice in English is best learnt. Although these questions made up the framework for the interviews, the students were encouraged to talk freely about any issues that came to their mind when thinking about academic writing in English.

Each interview was first transcribed and then analysed to identify the norms that students express in their discourse as well as the authorities they use in order to justify these norms. Comparisons were then made across

Amir	A 33-year-old man from Iran whose first language is Persian. Completed his Bachelor's in Computer Engineering in Iran through Persian and English.
Mei	A 29-year-old woman from China whose first language is Chinese. Completed her Bachelor's in English Translation in China through Chinese and English.
Stephanie	A 26-year-old woman from Germany whose first language is German. Completed her Bachelor's in British and American Studies in Germany through English. Has spent 6 months in Finland previously as an exchange student. Has also lived in Ireland for 2 years.
Tommi	A 26-year-old man from Finland whose first language is Finnish. Completed his Bachelor's in Media Design from a University of Applied Sciences in Finland through Finnish.
Julia	A 36-year-old woman from Brazil whose first language is Portuguese. Completed her Bachelor's in Linguistics in Brazil through Portuguese. As a child, she attended an English-medium school both in Brazil and, for 2 years, in Germany.
Kimiko	A 30-year-old woman from Japan whose first language is Japanese. Completed her Bachelor's in Fine Art in the United States through English. Has also studied for 1 year in Turkey through Turkish.

Figure 7.1 The participants

all six interviews to identify similar patterns or conflicts in the students' discourse. These patterns and conflicts were in turn analysed to understand how their ideologies of English writing practice are drawn from local and global indexical scales (Blommaert, 2010)

When talking about discourse, we take as our starting point the idea of language as social action and as a resource for creating social realities (Blommaert, 2005; Pietikäinen & Mäntynen, 2009; Scollon & Scollon, 2004). When the students talk about academic literacy, they make sense of the phenomenon and the social reality it is related to, thus creating their discourse of academic literacy in that particular space and time. At the same time, they draw upon socially available discourses, using, sometimes in contradictory ways, patterns of talking about writing that are familiar to them in their social worlds (Ivanič, 2004).

The interview extracts are displayed here using the following symbols:

w::ord   = stretched sound
(.)   = a pause
wo-   = word or sentence cut-off
?   = rising intonation
hhh = laughter
$word$ = speech while laughing

Unclear speech and minimal responses were removed from an example if they were not important to the analysis. This removal is marked by '...'.

Findings: Global Norms

Throughout the interviews, the students tended to discuss good or bad academic writing on a general, global scale and the discourses created imply that they perceive there to be a typical global norm. Kimiko, for example, implied that the structure of academic writing is universal, something that *'everybody should know'* regardless of their local environment. Upon moving to the United States from Japan and beginning her studies at a community college, she was surprised by the need to teach these norms:

> Kimiko   It seemed in the beginning it was kind of easy for me because they are teaching like there should be like a proposing sent – paragraph in the beginning and then develop and then closing and it's everybody should know that but some people had no clue

In discussing good academic writing in English, the ideas and the language used to express these ideas were remarkably similar between the students, despite their differing cultural, linguistic and even disciplinary backgrounds. The first striking feature in the interviews was the students' familiarity with the essay and thesis writing genres. When asked about the texts they had been required to write in their previous studies, they put forward essays or theses as genres that required very little explanation or elaboration. This can be seen especially in the following extract from Tommi's interview:

> Laura   So did you write a lot like academic writing or how were the courses assessed

> Tommi   Usually like to pass this like essay or some kind of like a diary type of thingy (.) usually essays

For Tommi, the 'essay' is offered as a straightforward answer to the question. The 'diary' on the other hand, is hedged with *'some kind of like'* and *'type of thingy'* and therefore seems to be a rather vague genre to Tommi. Several of the students seemed, in fact, to understand the essay or thesis formats as being the definition of academic writing.

As essay and thesis text types therefore seemed to represent the students' understanding of academic writing, these genres became the focus of the interviews. In discussing what constitutes good essay and thesis writing, the students stressed two features in particular: the importance of one's own point of view and the importance of structure.

For all of the students, the idea that academic writing should express a personal opinion was very important. The phrase *'point of view'* was repeated throughout the interviews, the following extracts being just two examples:

Mei   I think it's like (.) first you have your own point of view and it's like you can just take the reference from others but it's not all from others you have your own point of view

Julia   I am a very critical think – thinker so it helps me when I'm writing … and I always have a point of view it might be good or it might be really bad I always have a very strong point of view about things and I can um not promote myself but I can uh defend myself … for this kind of um for most subjects there isn't any wrong or right there is points of view so if you can defend your own point of view you're good

In both examples, the students emphasize that this *'point of view'* ought to be personal (*'you have your own point of view'*), unique (*'it's not all from others'*) and firmly held (*'I always have a very strong point of view'*). Moreover, Julia's comments suggest that this *'own'* viewpoint is somehow in conflict or debate with the viewpoints of others. Julia uses the phrase *'I am a very critical thinker'* – a familiar educational ideal – and talks about her ability to *'defend'* her views as her strength. Several other students, using almost the same phrasing, echoed this idea.

Overall, we would describe this as an individualistic discourse on writing, where writing is perceived to be ideally a personal and individual endeavor with the aim of expressing one's own perceptions and setting oneself apart from the perceptions of others. The individuality of one's ideas was, in fact, deemed by the students to be more important than the validity of those ideas. Julia claimed, *'there isn't any wrong or right there is points of view'* and Mei similarly stated, *'there has to be some point of view anyway'*, implying that the existence of the point of view is the priority in writing, regardless of the actual points expressed.

The second aspect of academic writing that all the students stressed was the importance of having an effective structure. There was a sense in all their answers that academic writing is 'structured writing' and that this structure is difficult to achieve. When asked what his weaknesses in academic writing were, Tommi replied:

> Tommi   Weaknesses hh I think most likely I guess I write too much like uh well like in a flow because uh I should more structure from the grammar and the ideas because I if I write in a flow I have to go back and just s- structure again and again ... yeah more like uh I guess the flow way it's not structured in a good way

From his answer, it is clear that for Tommi academic writing requires a structure into which his natural way of thinking, his *'flow'* of thoughts, must be forced through hard effort, *'again and again'*. *'The flow way'*, as Tommi puts it, is not *'a good way'* in academic writing. Stephanie, likewise, describes the structure of academic writing as being a 'problem'.

> Stephanie   I s:ometimes really have problems to like really structure to I don't know but I think that my biggest problem is to put everything into proper paragraphs that are like somehow that is (.) connected

For Stephanie, the *'problem'* is achieving *'proper paragraphs'* – again giving the sense that in academic writing there is a strict way in which the writing must be formed in order to be correct. This correct structure is linear or as Stephanie puts it *'connected'*, where you do not deviate from the line of thought you have begun. This notion was repeated continually in all of the interviews, for example with Mei stating that a weak essay is one in which *'you start the point but go in a different direction'*. When asked why this linear structure should be adhered to, all the students emphasized the importance of clarity and simplicity in academic writing. Academic writing in their view should not be *'complicated'* (Mei), *'blurry'* (Kimiko), *'mixed up'* (Stephanie), *'dubious'* (Amir) or *'confusing'* (Julia).

As with *'point of view'*, the students stressed the importance of structure and clarity over the validity of the ideas themselves. Julia commented that *'the main point would be do I understand... it doesn't matter if I agree or not but does it all make sense because the arguments are well put and they are well organized'*.

When asked to explain more specifically what a correct structure is, all of the students gave the format as introduction, main body and conclusion. In fact, this structure was apparently so obvious to the students that it was difficult to induce them to explain it in detail. The following is an example of this:

Stephanie	Well introduction main part conclusion hh to make it
Laura	Yup okay that's the short version
Stephanie	To make it easier
Laura	Any other points perhaps or
Stephanie	Well you have your argument that you want to prove and like I don't know some kind of opening question and then try to in the main part try to prove your argument and develop it

In this extract, Stephanie gave her initial answer *'introduction main part conclusion'* very quickly in one breath and then laughed, as though acknowledging that she is repeating a clichéd phrase. And again, the students used very similar discourse to describe the essay sections and their functions. For example, in regards to the introduction, Stephanie stated *'you have your argument that you want to prove'*, whereas Mei said *'you give the thing you want to talk'* and Julia explained *'you present what you are talking about'*, and all three stated that the main body should then *'develop it'*

Findings: Authority

On the basis of the above, the students seemed to create a fairly uniform, global discourse around good academic writing in English. On a local level, however, the students clearly perceived teachers or professors as local authorities. There was a sense in all the students' answers that their writing is subject to teachers' expectations. The following extract from Mei's interviews sums up this perception nicely:

Mei	So sometimes you just write it in the way you think it should be but sometimes it's like it should be just like teachers think it should be like the sentences should be maybe more like shorter but uh to the uh to the

Laura   To the point yeah

Mei   Yeah but sometimes you will just forget and use the way you write in day

Here, Mei clearly positions her writing as being incorrect, contrasting the way she *'thinks it should be'* with the way *'teachers think it should be'* and clearly giving the latter the final verdict. She also makes an interesting contrast between her normal way of writing – implied by the phrase *'the way you write in day'* – and academic writing, which is the domain of the teachers.

As local authorities, however, teachers' academic writing norms were perceived by most of the students as being variable and often contestable. Kimiko, for example, repeated several times when asked what she thought constitutes a *'good'* essay that *'it depends on the teacher'*. Several of the students explicitly contested the authority of local teachers in evaluating their writing. In doing so, they tended to draw on ideals or authorities that they perceived to be more global or higher ranking than teachers' opinions. In particular, the ideal they expressed of writing being an individualistic practice seemed to conflict with the notion that they should care about a teacher's opinion of their work. When asked directly about his experience of grading, Tommi expressed these sentiments quite clearly:

Laura   Do you usually know what kind of grade you're going to get

Tommi   I didn't actually care hhh just because usually if I'm doing something I'm interested in I usually (.) at that point I don't care what's the grade

He went on to explain:

Tommi   Sometimes like I find some kind of teachers they can be professional in some way but if you give them like a new point of view or something that is entirely different from theirs even if it's good writing or good research and they don't like it they don't give you the good grade

Here, Tommi reiterates that the important thing in academic writing is to have a *'new point of view'* and to be *'doing something I'm interested in'*. He, in fact, seems to see his teachers as often transgressing this important global yet individual purpose of writing. His disclaimer, *'they can be professional in some way but'*, clearly suggests in his view that failing to accept new opinions is in some way failing to be professional teachers or academics.

This ideological conflict was also referred to by several students as a conflict between teachers themselves, where some teachers understood the importance of having an original point of view and some teachers did not. Kimiko even commented that she could tell already from the teacher's course description *'which side'* the teacher is on, defining the sides as follows:

> Kimiko   Some professors um they weigh quite heavily on academic writing to good academic writing so they just care about the styles … how well you write and use of language it's quite important for them more than perhaps what's written in the I mean like the idea … um some professors preferred to see something um some um personal thing ideas and opinions

This also seems to be a conflict between the two norms that students described earlier, namely to have *'personal ideas'* and to conform to strict structural and linguistic conventions, where *'good academic writing'* is a question of *'styles'*.

Amir also expressed some uncertainty about which side the teachers on the master's programme in Finland would take in this apparently global conflict. He explained that he would like to try to be more creative in structuring his writing and use more of what he termed a *'way of narrating'* in essays, but that he was not sure whether teachers would accept it. In his words, he was not sure *'how much they (professors) believe that every student is coming here to make a unique identity for himself'*. In this comment, the ideal of students' individuality or *'unique identity'* is framed as a global creed to which a professor or community of professors may or may not ascribe.

Beside this individualistic creed, students drew from two other apparently global authorities in challenging a teacher's right to judge their writing. The first we would summarize as the authority of 'professional writers' – particularly within literary or journalistic fields. When Amir is asked directly about his perceptions of teachers' grades, he – like Tommi in the earlier example – dismisses the question:

> Laura   So you knew if you were going to get a bad mark from it or if you were going to get a good one
>
> Amir   Yes yes
>
> Laura   Okay

Amir   But you know (.) after the university writing was my profession in a way I was a $writer$ I wrote so many so many journals in uh so many places (the) books that I have fourteen books in my language

In this extract, the question received a quick *'yes yes'* response with a descending intonation, indicating irritation. This is followed by the conjunction *'but'*, implying that the details he gives are rather in dismissal of the question. The basis of this dismissal can be summarised by the statements *'writing was my profession'* and *'I was a writer'*. Claiming an identity as a professional writer somehow contradicts the notion implied by the question – that is that he should be concerned with good or bad marks from teachers. Moreover, Amir went on to place literary writing at the top of an ideological hierarchy of writing practices. He explained that *'as a poet'*, academic writing conventions are simply *'not correct'* and in fact *'primitive'*.

Julia also claimed the authority to challenge her teachers' expectations due to her identity as a journalistic writer (albeit unpaid):

Julia   I'm always writing for uh journals and magazines every chance I have I write text as freelancer I never get anything like paid for that but well it's fun but it's a different terminology it's different level especially if you're working with public it's supposed to be a light reading and interesting and appealing it's different from academic although I have one thing that my teachers here they are kind of scared of me because I still think that I can do although it's academic writing I still think I can do the thesis in a way that is interesting and appealing and easy to read I don't want to this heavy academic writing

Like Amir, she sees her experience in and enthusiasm for journalism, *'always writing for journals and magazines'*, as giving her the ability to go against her teachers by insisting on writing in a way that is *'interesting'* and *'appealing'*. The teachers, presumably the bastions of uninteresting and unappealing, *'heavy academic writing'*, are *'scared of her'* as a result.

The final centre of authority in English academic writing practice seemed to override local teachers' authorities, students' universal right to individuality and professional writer's identity. On a global hierarchy, the viewpoints and practices of native English speakers – especially native speakers from the United Kingdom or the United States – seemed to rank the highest in the students' perceptions ('norm-providing inner circle' in Pennycook, 2007a).

Non-nativeness and lack of experience in English-speaking communities were repeatedly referred to as a *'problem'* in being able to write well – both in regards to language and in regards to structure. The following extract is from Stephanie's description of her experience with teachers' grading in Germany (in an English department):

Stephanie   It was quite funny and after a while I stopped wondering I wrote two essays for two of my two major classes and a friend from Ireland corrected them for me and for those two essays and for $those$ two essays I got the comment that I should seriously work on my English so $hhheh$

Laura   From the teachers or from the friend

Stephanie   From the teachers no from the teachers but the problem is like none of teachers was a real native English speaker they were all Germans well they've been living abroad and everything but anyway

Here, the fact that her teachers were not *'real native English speakers'*, but had only spent time abroad, clearly decreases their authority in Stephanie's perception. In this scenario, she positions her Irish friend's opinion of her essay as correct and her German teachers' opinion as incorrect – with her teachers as having a *'problem'*. Her belief in her Irish friend's authority was, in fact, so emphatic that its contradiction by her teachers is intended to be humorous, as suggested by her laughter. No further qualifications are given for her friend's authority other than being *'from Ireland'*.

Amir, whose own authority as a professional writer was stressed emphatically throughout the interview, nevertheless also seemed to view the lack of nativeness as a *'problem'*. In explaining his weaknesses in English academic writing, he stated:

Amir   I've translated so many difficult poets into my language and uh my reading I'm sure about it and my way of writing I could communicate all the time but my problem in English is that I was not in English an English society

Despite having translated *'so many difficult poets'* and despite being able to *'communicate all the time'*, he nevertheless sees himself as lacking due to not being in *'an English society'*. What he lacks and how his writing is affected by this *'problem'* was not explained.

Moreover, both Amir and Julia in supporting their teachers' right to use English as a medium during their university studies in Iran and Brazil, respectively, explained that they had been educated in America and England.

Amir   … completely were in English and even the physics the mathematics all of them were in English

Laura   Okay yeah and did you write in English there or was it in Persian

Amir   Writing in English yes because the professors you know in my university most of the professors came as educated in USA

Julia   No for the English school we had Brazilians and we had English people we had both but the Brazilian teachers of course they lived in England for some time and they did uh mostly their master's and PhD in England and then they came back to teach

In Julia's answer especially, she seems to justify the fact that her English-medium school used Brazilian teachers by explaining their experience in England, adding the information with the conjunction '*but*' as though worried that the school might be devalued. Also, the words '*of course*' suggest that she considers this experience with English society to be an obvious necessity for teaching through English.

It was also interesting in the interviews that, although native speakers were authorities in general, the real centre seemed to be British or American academics. For Julia, in fact, a blending of British and American English was the globalization of English. To her, the blend of British and American academic writing styles is the creation of a global style that everyone can understand:

Julia   most books I re- uh most books people here has to read they are not only American they are not only British they are American authors too and what I see in the books in the thesis is that there are like semantic differences but not as much as the structural differences as I used to see before I kind of feel globalization of this area too that the texts are getting to a new common level so everybody can understand doesn't matter where you live

Here, the research in English that she reads is explicitly determined to be British or American and their combination is creating global English, '*a common level so everyone can understand*' regardless of their local communities. She later recommended that in order to learn to be a better academic writer in English, everyone should read these 'original' texts. The clear global centre for English writing, for Julia, is therefore British and American.

Discussion

In an emergent transnational community of mobile academic writers such as those in this study, literacy is indeed in transition. The global and local meet in students' discourse on good, normal and correct academic literacy in English. On a global level, students readily and easily resort to seemingly universal norms of what counts as good academic writing. The analysis found surprising similarity in this discourse, despite the students' differing cultural and linguistic backgrounds. As Strässler (2008: 218–299) also demonstrates, the academic world seems to be subscribing not only to the use of English as a *lingua franca* but also to a common set of discourse practices which it seems to involve.

Specifically, academic writing was characterized by the students as essay and thesis writing, which entail strict, linear structures as well as individualistic, critical 'points of view'. The individualistic discourse on writing is particularly remarkable considering the students' cultural backgrounds. Much contrastive rhetoric research into academic writing carried out in the 1990s took up in particular the expectation of a personal viewpoint in academic writing as being a major difference between cultures. It was claimed that especially Asian students avoided expressing their own ideas, aiming for harmonious writing that is obedient to rather than critical of authority (e.g. Ballard & Clancy, 1991; Connor, 1996; Ramanathan & Atkinson, 1999). The students interviewed for this study, however, from Asia and Western Europe alike, seemed to be very well versed in discourse on writing as individual and critical. While this does not necessarily mean that they will adopt similar strategies for expressing their viewpoints in practice, it does suggest that this ideology of academic writing as individualistic is now widespread, at least for 'transmobile' students such as these.

On a local level, however, these norms seemed to clash with their personal experiences of writing in various contexts. When describing their experiences with writing at university, teachers were clearly authorities for the students. The students challenged this authority, however, with their perceptions of universal writing ideals, and teachers' professionalism was even measured by their understanding of academic writing as an individualistic endeavour. Moreover, several students challenged both their local teachers' authority and their understanding of global academic writing norms through their experiences with other writing genres. They claimed authority for themselves as good writers by drawing from norms in genres that they considered to be better than academic writing—particularly literary and journalistic. Their ways of expressing this superiority was close to what Ivanič (2004: 329) describes as a 'discourse of creativity', where writing is creative self-expression, with the goal of entertaining or intriguing the reader. Their discourse clearly illustrates that ideological conflict in literacy practices occurs not only between different language varieties or between different cultural norms (e.g. a British versus a Finnish context) but also between different genres of writing.

Most frequently, however, ownership of English academic writing on both local and global levels was ascribed by the students to native English speakers, and among native English speakers, mostly to British and American academics. Students evaluated both their own and their local teachers' authority in English writing based on their proximity to native speaker identity. They also felt that good academic writing practices were best learnt by studying 'original' texts produced by native English speakers and, in one case, the globalization of English was specifically described as a blending of British and American writing norms. This reiterates Lillis and Curry's (2010: 135) observation that for many academic writers in English, 'global is a place called the "US"' – or rather, in this case, an international domain of the United States and the United Kingdom.

With these fluctuating norms of academic literacy, the students begin the English-medium master's programme within Finland and start to adapt their literacy practices to the emerging context. Despite acknowledging their lack of native ability as a 'problem', however, students expressed very little apprehension at the thought of writing essays or even a master's thesis in English on the programme. It was as though upon travelling between local communities where English is not the native language, native authority need not be feared and one's own understanding of global practices might be trusted. The use of English therefore seemed to represent for students the ability to travel unproblematically between ELF contexts, while studying to become part of an imagined global community of academics within their field.

References

Anderson, B. (1983) *Imagined Communities: Reflections on the Origin and Spread of Nationalism*. London: Verso.
Ballard, B. and Clanchy J. (1991) *Teaching Students from Overseas*. Melbourne: Longman Cheshire.
Baynham, M. (2004) Ethnographies of literacy: Introduction. *Language and Education* 16 (4), 285–290.

Barton, D. and Hamilton M. (1998) *Local Literacies: Reading and Writing in One Community*. London: Routledge.
Barton, D. and Hamilton, M. (2000) Literacy practices. In D. Barton, M. Hamilton and R. Ivanič (eds) *Situated Literacies: Reading and Writing in Context* (pp. 7–15). New York: Routledge.
Blanton, L.L. (1994) Discourse, artifacts and the Ozarks: Understanding academic literacy. In V. Zamel and R. Spack (eds) *Negotiating Academic Literacies: Teaching and Learning Across Languages and Cultures* (pp. 219–236). Mahwah, NJ: Lawrence Erlbaum Associates.
Blommaert, J. (2005) *Discourse: A Critical Introduction*. Cambridge: Cambridge University Press.
Blommaert, J. (2008) *Grassroots Literacy: Writing, Identity and Voice in Africa*. London: Routledge.
Blommaert, J. (2010) *The Sociolinguistics of Globalization*. Cambridge: Cambridge University Press.
Brandt, D. and Clinton, K. (2002) Limits of the local: Expanding perspectives on literacy as a social practice. *Journal of Literacy Research* 34(3), 337–356.
Canagarajah, A.S. (2002) *A Geopolitics of Academic Writing*. Pittsburgh: University of Pittsburgh Press.
Connor, U. (1996) *Contrastive Rhetoric: Cross-Cultural Aspects of Second-Language Writing*. Cambridge: Cambridge University Press.
Hamel, R.E. (2007) The dominance of English in the international scientific periodical literature and the future of language use in science. In A. Carli and U. Ammon (eds) *Linguistic Inequality in Scientific Communication Today*, AILA Review 20, 53–71.
Hyland, K. (2006) *English for Academic Purposes: An Advanced Resource Book*. London and New York: Routledge.
Ivanič, R. (1998) *Writing and Identity: The Discoursal Construction of Identity in Academic Writing*. Amsterdam: John Benjamins.
Ivanič, R. (2004) *Discourses of writing and learning to write*. Language and Education 18(3), 220–245.
Kachru, B.B. (1985) Standards, codification and sociolinguistic realism: The English language in the outer circle. In R. Quirk and H. Widdowson (eds) *English in the World: Teaching and Learning the Language and Literatures* (pp 11–36). Cambridge: Cambridge University Press.
Lea, M. and Street, B. (1998) Student writing in higher education: An academic literacies approach. *Studies in Higher Education* 23 (2), 157–172.
Lillis, T.M. (2001) *Student Writing: Access, Regulation, Desire*. London and New York: Routledge.
Lillis, T.M. and Curry, M.J. (2010) *Academic Writing in a Global Context: The Politics and Practices of Publishing in English*. London: Routledge.
Maiworm, F. and Wächter, B. (2002) *English-Language-Taught Degree Programmes in European Higher Education: Trends and Success Factors*. Bonn: Lemmens.
McGroarty, M. (2010) Language and ideologies. In N. Hornberger and S. McKay (eds) *Sociolinguistics and Language Education* (pp. 3–39). Bristol: Multilingual Matters.
Modiano, M. (1999) International English in the global village. *English Today* 58(15), 22–58.
Norton, B. (2001) Non-participation, imagined communities and the language classroom. In M. Breen (ed.) *Learner Contribution to Language Learning: New Directions in Research* (pp. 159–171). Harlow: Pearson Education.
Pennycook, A. (2007a) *Global Englishes and Transcultural Flows*. London: Routledge.

Pennycook, A. (2007b) The myth of English as an international language. In S. Makoni and A. Pennycook (eds) *Disinventing and Reconstituting Languages* (pp. 90–115). Clevedon: Multilingual Matters.
Pietikäinen S. and Mäntynen A. (2009) *Kurssi Kohti Diskurssia* [Taking a course towards discourse]. Tampere: Vastapaino
Pitkänen-Huhta, A. and Nikula, T. (2012) Teenagers making sense of their foreign language practices: individual accounts indexing social discourses. In P. Benson and L. Cooker (eds) *The Applied Linguistic Individual: Sociocultural Approaches to Autonomy, Agency and Identity*. London: Equinox.
Prinsloo, M. and Breier, M. (eds) (1996) *The Social Uses of Literacy*. Cape Town/Amsterdam: Sached/John Benjamins.
Ramanathan, V. and Atkinson, D. (1999) Individualism, academic writing, and ESL writers. *Journal of Second Language Writing* 8 (1), 45–75.
Scribner, S. and Cole, M. (1981) *The Psychology of Literacy*. Cambridge, MA: Harward University Press.
Scollon, R. and Wong Scollon, S. (2004) *Nexus Analysis: Discourse and the Emerging Internet*. London: Routledge.
Silva, T. (1993) Toward an understanding of the distinct nature of L2 writing: The ESL research and its implications. *TESOL Quarterly* 27 (4), 657–677.
Street, B.V. (1984) *Literacy in Theory and Practice*. Cambridge: Cambridge University Press.
Strässler, J. (2008) Can academic writing style be taught? In M. Locher and J. Strässler (eds) *Contributions to the Sociology of Language: Standards and Norms in the English Language* (pp. 281–300). Berlin: Mouton de Gruyter.
Swales, J.M. (1990) *Genre Analysis: English in Academic and Research Settings*. Cambridge: Cambridge University Press.
Vertovec, S. (2007) Super-diversity and its implications. *Ethnic and Racial Studies* 29 (6), 1024–1054.
Warriner, D.S. (2009) Transnational literacies: Examining global flows through the lens of social practice. In M. Baynham and M. Prinsloo (eds) *The Future of Literacy Studies* (pp. 160–180). Basingstoke: Palgrave.
Yashima, T. (2012) Individuality, imagination and community in a globalizing world: An Asian EFL perspective. In P. Benson and L. Cooker (eds) *The Applied Linguistic Individual: Sociocultural Approaches to Autonomy, Agency and Identity*. London: Equinox.

Part 3
Policies and Practices in Transition

Introduction

The inherent contradictions created by mobility and globalization in regard to literacy in education might be characterized as the appearance of both a tendency towards increasing standardization and a tendency towards increasing diversity.

The standardization of literacy in the wake of globalization is related to two general, related processes. The first is the growing influence on the conceptualization of language and literacy of supranational agencies such as the EU, the Council of Europe, the OECD and the PISA consortium, to mention just a few. Closely related to the creation of a more open European (and global) market is the need for common conceptualizations and understandings of language and literacy, which has been promoted by different powerful agencies. For the European Council, the motivation for developing language and literacy standards was originally related simply to the perceived need to enable the free movement of labour within the EU, but as Holm and Pöyhonen show in Chapter 8 in this part, the goals of standardization were gradually broadened to embrace language and literacy education in general. These concepts of literacy and language are not imported into each country as a fixed and definitive recipe, but are interpreted and adapted differently in each national educational context. Holm and Pöyhonen trace this process in Denmark and Finland, and point out that what is naturalized and objectified under the rubric of 'literacy' is not only particular understandings of literacy, learning and bilingualism but also specific reasoning practices closely related to the moral and relational order of the culture. The second is the accountability culture of New Management strategies, which has foregrounded documentation, measurement and international comparisons of literacy. When national placement in international comparisons of literacy levels is put high on the educational agenda, it becomes a political necessity to take part in the international contest, which might lead to an increased demand for 'compact institutionalized concepts, tailor-made for bureaucratic administration [and] for measurement' (Freebody & Freiberg, 2008: 18). In Chapter 9, Kulbrandstad and Danbolt reveal how the Norwegian PISA results have impacted education and teachers' practices.

The permanent migration in and out of societies – the permanent movement of people across the globe – has created complex new sociolinguistic landscapes with messy linguistic marketplaces (Blommaert, 2010). The current multilingual complexity is challenging not only monolingual practices and understandings in education but also basic democratic ideas about equality such as the belief that public institutions in a democratic society ought to reflect the cultural, social, linguistic and gender-related differences in society. Rooted in such an understanding, an educational programme has been implemented in Norway to increase the number of bilingual teachers. Based on bilingual teacher-students' experiences with this programme, Hvistendal analyses in Chapter 10 the space for bilingual teachers' bilingualism in education and asks if they make any difference.

References

Blommaert, J. (2010) *The Sociolinguistics of Globalization*. Cambridge: Cambridge University Press.

Freebody, P. and Freiberg, J. (2008) Globalised literacy education. Intercultural trade in textual and cultural practice. In M. Prinsloo and M. Baynham (eds) *Literacies, Local and Global* (pp. 17–34). Amsterdam: John Benjamins.

8 Localizing Supranational Concepts of Literacy in Adult Second Language Teaching

Lars Holm and Sari Pöyhönen

Introduction

Societal super-diversity (Vertovec, 2006; Blommaert, 2010) has generated new and different perceptions and constructions of participation, identity and societal membership. One special marker of super-diversity, according to Blommaert and Rampton (2011) is the presence of complex and stratified distribution patterns that ratifies and recognizes what counts as language and literacy in particular contexts. It is part of this development that literacy is used more often as a political reference, that is in defining qualifications for permanent stay in the host country, for citizenship or for access to education (Extra et al., 2009).

In this chapter, we are analysing how literacy is conceptualized within education – more specifically within adult second language education in Denmark and Finland. Language and literacy are generally described as highly important for societal growth, coherence and democracy in statements from governments and international agencies. However, in our research literacy appears as a more complex and contradictory resource that is increasingly used as a demarcation line for inclusion and exclusion in the ever more globalized nation states.

Researching Localization of Literacy Concepts

According to Blommaert (2003), specific conceptualization of literacy within education might be seen as a variety of language that should be 'read locally as well as translocally'. Such a perspective makes it possible to investigate how conceptualizations of literacy are being both globalized and localized by whom, for whom, when and how (Blommaert, 2003) –

and with what impact on social selection processes. Conceptualizations of literacy in education have often been researched as an interactional construction of literacy in a classroom (see e.g. Holm, 2004; Pitkänen-Huhta, 2003). Brandt and Clinton (2002) criticize this research approach for under-theorizing the material dimension of literacy and its capacity to travel. This critique is highly relevant for literacy research in a European context where supranational agencies such as the OECD, EU and the Council of Europe seem to, in complex ways, increasingly influence education systems and educational conceptualizations. This influence is sometimes through a rather direct regulation as the application of the ECTS system in higher education in Europe demonstrates, but more often it is through discursive forces – through the production of numerous reports, evaluations and documents and through the creation of various committees, funding streams and programs that support specific conceptualizations within education and function as shapers of emerging discourses in educational policy (Holm & Laursen, 2011; Moos, 2006; Saarinen, 2007). Dynamic processes between national and supranational forces are thus shaping literacy in education.

One specific conceptualization of literacy put forward by a supranational agency, the Council of Europe, in a specific document, the CEFR (2001), has become constitutive for the conceptualization of literacy within adult second language teaching in Denmark and Finland as in many other EU countries. For this reason, we would like to give a 'thing-status' to the document in which this conceptualization is formulated and treat it as an artefact, and regard the Council of Europe as an important 'sponsor of literacy' (Brandt & Clinton, 2002). This artefact with its conceptualization of literacy is re-contextualized, re-interpreted and negotiated by local actors in educational arenas within education. Thus, the CEFR (2001)[1] appears as a shared authority in a supranational network that has created within literacy in education a new 'space of flows' as Castells (2010) coins it, and has become a travelling concept that is localized in different educational settings. This complex dynamics between national and supranational forces and the multiple localizing processes of the conceptualization of literacy in the CEFR invites to a research approach that is 'multi-sited', as suggested by Marcus (1995). Multi-sited research in concepts (e.g. Gustafsson, 2003; Martin, 1994) follows the negotiation and construction of a specific concept in different social arenas. These arenas might be within the borders of the same national state (e.g. Gustafsson, 2010). However, in order to research literacy both locally and translocally, we would like to argue for a research approach that follows the concept of literacy through the arena of a supranational agency and different national and local arenas, and thus combines the approach to literacy put forward by Brandt and Clinton (2002) with a multi-sited perspective. The

CEFR appears as an artefact in its materiality, but when it enters a local arena it also becomes an actor. Seen in this perspective, the CEFR conceptualization of literacy might be researched as a local interaction around a concept that has its origin somewhere else and thus represents a relationship between the local and the global. We hope this might reveal and demonstrate central aspects in the complex way in which literacy is in transition.

In the first part of this chapter, we will trace and analyze the values and norms in the conceptualization of literacy in the CEFR. Central documents produced by the European Council and a range of research articles about the development of this supranational agency comprise the data for this part. In the second part, we will focus on how the CEFR concept of literacy is localized in adult second language teaching in two Nordic countries. Our analysis is based on two cases in two different types of arenas within education; an ethnographic classroom research in Denmark and a development project in a national political arena on setting goals for integration training for migrants in Finland. The classroom research in Denmark was a six-month fieldwork-based project directed towards the construction of literacy. The data for the research consisted basically of classroom observations, national curricula and language tests (Holm, 2004). The Finnish development project was implemented by a provisional law included in the Act on the Promotion of Integration of Immigrants in 2010 and launched in order to 'holistically promote the integration of migrants into Finnish society' (Pöyhönen et al., 2010). The data for this section of the chapter are national curricula, interviews with policy makers, administrators and teachers, classroom observations, and language tests and citizenship acts. In the last section of the chapter, we will discuss the implications of the way in which literacy is conceptualized for adult second language education, for social cohesion and for literacy research.

We are thus both analyzing supranational and national sites, and our aim of tracing the CEFR in different arenas and bringing the analysis into the same analytic frame is inspired by the theoretical and methodological standpoints of multi-sited ethnography. However, this does not mean that the two research projects brought together in this chapter reflect exactly similar kinds of research with similar aims. As Marcus (1995: 102) points out, 'in multi-sited ethnography, comparison emerges from putting questions to an emergent object of study whose contours, sites, and relationships are not known beforehand, but are themselves a contribution of making an account that has different, complexly connected real-world sites of investigation'. In our approach, we are also inspired by policy ethnography (see e.g. Gustafsson, 2010) which focuses on multi-layered analysis of policy processes, and the relationship between policy documents (e.g. laws, curricula) and classroom practice. We are aware that a multi-sited approach promotes on the one hand a high degree of methodological freedom and on the other hand raises hard questions about how to define research boundaries (Candea, 2007). We believe that this fluidity in relation to sites and boundaries is a basic condition for literacy research in a multimodal and globalized world and therefore needs to be empirically researched.

CEFR: From Development Projects to Consensus-Based Supranational Standardization

The development of the conceptualization of literacy in the CEFR has a long history that seems valuable to know. Not only because it reveals that literacy is historically situated but also because it reveals different logics and ways of conceptualizing literacy in language education, which might contribute to a more specific understanding of the transitional processes around literacy in education.

From the 1970s to the 1990s: The development period

The history of CEFR is closely related to the political aim of creating an inner market in Western Europe. One part of this process is standardization of commodities, commercial regulations and currencies among the states. Another part is to provide necessary conditions for the free movement of labour force (Long, 2005; Spolsky, 1995). Given the linguistic diversity in Europe, the ambition of the inner market was a substantial linguistic challenge, and a number of European countries met this challenge by an increased cooperation in language teaching. This cooperation was organized within the Council of Europe and had as its first aim to define the so-called threshold level – a common European linguistic minimum level for adult labour force (Holm, 2006) and to develop 'a European unit/credit system for language teaching' (Trim *et al.*, 1973).

Central to the development of the threshold level was Wilkins' (1976) proposal for 'a notional-functional syllabus'. His ideas about a syllabus based on semantic and pragmatic categories were theoretically related to the concept of communicative competence introduced by Hymes and were a unique contribution to the discussion of syllabus design at the time. For Wilkins, language was a universal and not a language-specific system. Accordingly, he saw language as a prototypical realization of communicative functions that could be organized 'in terms of the purposes for which people are learning language and the kinds of language performance that are necessary to meet those purposes' (Wilkins, 1976: 13). Drawing on these theoretical assumptions, Wilkins developed three main categories: (a) semantico-grammatical categories, (b) categories of modal meaning and (c) categories of communicative function (Wilkins, 1976: 25–54). Wilkins termed his approach 'analytical' and contrasted it with a 'synthetic' approach in which 'parts of the language are taught separately and step by step so that acquisition is a process of global accumulation of parts until the whole structure of language has been built up' (Wilkins, 1976: 2), while in the analytic approach 'the learner is exposed to stretches of language and has the job of analyzing the chunks to develop an understanding of how discrete items operate' (Johnson, 2006: 416).

Wilkins (1976: 81) saw his notional syllabus as a 'more complete view of the nature of language' and as a taxonomy that might be used for foreign language curriculum development. This 'new' view of language was in many ways an open-ended contribution to language education that posed a wide range of challenges rather than offering specific solutions. Wilkins introduced a view of language, defined categories and elaborated an index of notional categories, but he did neither elaborate a full syllabus nor produce a large number of concrete language examples to illustrate his ideas. In the last paragraph of his book, Wilkins reflects on testing and his conclusion is that 'we do not know how to establish the communicative proficiency of the learner' (Wilkins, 1976: 82). Clearly, much was left for educationists to do.

It is a noteworthy feature of the founding documents that the description and identification of 'the necessary language performance' and 'communicate functions' were *intuitively* and not *empirically* based (Long, 2005). The point of departure for the functional-notional approach and the threshold-level development was thus a 'need-analysis' based on speculations and presumptions about language learners' linguistic needs.

From a literacy point of view, it is relevant to notice that the threshold level reflects an understanding of language and language use first of all as oral interaction in speech communities. Neither in Wilkins' seminal work nor in the many national threshold level descriptions in, for instance, English, German, Italian, Danish or Swedish are literacy needs defined or specified (Holm, 2006; Jessen, 1983). Wilkins explicitly gives priority to what he terms 'the language of doing' over the 'language of reporting' (Johnson, 2006), and this cannot but place literacy in a somewhat subordinate position. This priority to oral language is also indicated in Wilkins' brief considerations about the implications of a functional-notional syllabus for language teaching, in which he points to role play as a major teaching technique (Johnson, 2006).

From the 1990s to the 2010s: The standardization period

After the widespread implementation of the functional-notional ideas into a range of national threshold descriptions, curricula and textbooks from the 1970s to the 1990s (Alderson, 2005; Johnson, 2006), the threshold-level thinking went through an expanding process from the 1990s onwards.

According to Alderson (2005), the central stakeholders around the CEFR felt a need for a more differentiated definition of language learning objectives that included more than the original general threshold level for adult labour force. This 'need' clearly relates to political processes such as the EU Maastricht Treaty in 1992 that made education a common European interest instead of perceiving it as a national and cultural matter, and generated a wide range of increased harmonizing efforts within education in the EU (Holm, 2006). The need for 'more differentiated definitions' was thus basically a political ambition rooted in issues about standardization and general educational policy and not in theoretical reflections about language or language acquisition.

The rather pragmatic and non-theoretical approach to the development of the CEFR is evident in the statements about the constitutive categories in the framework. The CEFR is based on 'the classic division into basic, intermediate and advanced' (CEFR, 2001: 23), and the reason given for a further division into six sub-levels is that 'it seems that an outline framework of six broad levels gives an adequate coverage of the learning space relevant to European language learners' (CEFR, 2001: 23). The words 'classic' and 'adequate' clearly assume and relate to a consensus about the meaning of these words and appear to have no foundation in theories about learning, education or language.

The overall conceptualization of language education embedded in the CEFR is presented in Figure 8.1.

Within the Council of Europe, the CEFR is seen as an elaboration of Wilkins' ideas (CEFR, 2001). However, seen from a theoretical linguistic perspective, it would be more precise to talk about a quite radical conceptual reorientation. The differentiation of language levels is one important part of this process of change. The second is the replacement of Wilkins' basic categories with the 'traditional' language teaching sub-skills: listening, speaking, reading and writing (Figueras et al., 2005) which meant that literacy gained an important and visible position. The third important change, compared to Wilkins, is that the framework now is operating with a clear progression – or learning path – through different categories of sub-skills as demonstrated in Figure 8.2 – the scale for 'Overall written production'.

A			B			C	
Basic User			Independent User			Proficient User	
A1	A2		B1		B2	C1	C2
	A2.1	A2.2	B1.1	B1.2	B2.1 B2.2	C1.1	C1.2

Figure 8.1 The levels in the framework (CEFR, 2001: 23)

	OVERALL WRITTEN PRODUCTION
C2	Can write clear, smoothly flowing, complex texts in an appropriate and effective style and a logical structure which helps the reader to find significant points.
C1	Can write clear, well-structured texts of complex subjects, underlining the relevant salient issues, expanding and supporting points of view at some length and with subsidiary points, reasons and relevant examples, and rounding off with an appropriate conclusion.
B2	Can write clear, detailed texts on a variety of subjects related to his/her field of interest, synthesising and evaluating information and arguments from a number of sources.
B1	Can write straightforward connected texts on a range of familiar subjects within his field of interest, by linking a series of shorter discrete elements into a linear sequence.
A2	Can write a series of simple phrases and sentences linked with simple connectors like 'and', 'but' and 'because'.
A1	Can write simple isolated phrases and sentences.

Figure 8.2 General scale for written production (CEFR, 2001: 61)

What is a fundamental feature in the CEFR is that the scales, the description, and the progression in the six levels are neither a theoretical construction nor an empirical construction based on evidence taken from L2 learner data. The empirical base of the CEFR consists of judgements of language teachers and other experts with respect to the scaling and descriptors (Hulstijn, 2007). Thus, the CEFR basically reflects what could be agreed on among the many different national interests and stakeholders in the Council of Europe and thus appears as an expression of consensus (Risager, 2004; Holm, 2004, 2007).

Tracing Wilkins' ideas and the development of CEFR reveals different approaches to how literacy might be conceptualized in language and literacy education and opens a window into the logic of these processes. The CEFR made literacy visible through a consensus process in which literacy was conceptualized as a scaled skill (Figueras *et al.*, 2005).

On the following pages, we will analyse how the conceptualization in the CEFR is localized in adult education planning and discourse in Denmark and

Finland, how the CEFR conceptualization of literacy is localized in classroom practices and how the scales of the CEFR are used in the regulation of access to citizenship.

Localizing the CEFR

Generally speaking, adult migrants' second language teaching has gone through rather similar processes of change in the Nordic countries, even though these processes have been characterized by a certain asynchrony and national differences in the way legislation is implemented and administration organized within education. In all Nordic countries, the CEFR has been adopted as the constitutive conceptualization of language and literacy within adult migrants' second language teaching, and the aim of this adoption has been – among other things – to provide shared nationwide objectives for adult migrants' second language teaching and to unify the educational system and pedagogical practices in the country. Other reasons provided by the policy arena for adopting the CEFR have been related to arguments about improving and making education more effective (Bron, 2003; Holm, 2004; Pöyhönen et al., 2010; Uddannelsestyrelsen, 1999: 3).

Uses and interpretations of the CEFR in and around the curricula

The organizational framework for the education of adult migrants in Denmark has been closely and explicitly related to the CEFR since 1999 (1998 and 2001) (Uddannelsestyrelsen, 1999). In Finland, the CEFR was adopted some years later in 2007.

In Denmark, the students are sorted into three categories based on two criteria. The first is whether the student is able to read and write the Latin alphabet and has attended school. If this is not the case, the student is classified as illiterate and placed in 'Danskuddannelse 1' (Danish Education 1) where the educational aim is to reach the A1 and A2 level. If the student has a short formal schooling, she/he is placed in 'Danskuddannelse 2' (Danish Education 2) where the educational aim is B1+, and if the student has attended school for 12 years or more, she/he is placed in 'Danskuddanelses 3' (Danish Education 3) where the educational aim is B2 or C1. When the student is placed in one of the three courses (Danish Education 1, 2 or 3) she/he is expected to stay in the track and not to move to another course. The impact of this is that adult migrants who arrive in Denmark without any formal education, with a short educational background or as illiterate as regards the Latin alphabet are in a curriculum track with rather low educational ambitions and aims that do not, for example give access to general citizenship. The argument for this categorization is an expected difference in students' language acquisition related to their experience with formal schooling. Students are expected to progress slowly if they have not attended school or if they are Latin illiterates, quicker if they have attended some formal schooling and fast if they have attended formal schooling for a longer period (Holm, 2004). Thus, in the Danish case, literacy has become a central tool for social selection in a way that basically is reproducing global inequalities in education (Holm, 2004).

In Finland, the objective in the national core curriculum for integration training for adult migrants is to 'achieve functional basic proficiency in the Finnish or Swedish language', which in Finnish application of the CEFR means the target level B1.1 (FNBE, 2012a). The overall aim of the integration training is to promote and support 'students' opportunities to participate in Finnish society as active members'. There is also a national curriculum for literacy training, where the objective is 'to learn elementary Finnish or Swedish language skills and the basics of reading and writing skills' (FNBE, 2012b). In the Finnish provisional law project, migrants have been identified according to three paths: adult migrants seeking employment, adult migrants who need special support (including illiterates) and children and adolescents. This type of sorting has been made in order to better support individual learning paths and aims (Pöyhönen *et al.*, 2010). In the public debate, the three-paths model has been mostly welcomed by teachers, but it has also been criticized – quite accurately – for being a political tool in order to create new categories for social selection (e.g. Saarinen & Jäppinen, 2011). In this case, the CEFR is used to discriminate functionally between different perceived language needs related to different future jobs or education. To sum up, both in Denmark and in Finland the use of the CEFR has created new categories of individual through new distinctions and classifications of people.

The conceptualization and scales in the CEFR have thus clearly become *the* structural grid for adult second language educational planning in both Denmark and Finland. The detailed conceptualizations and descriptions of skills and levels in the CEFR are, however, also embedded in a specific rhetoric with specific signposts or mobilizing metaphors that relate to Wilkins' ideas. The most predominant of these concepts is the concept of 'functional language proficiency'.

Finnish curricula on all educational levels emphasize functional language proficiency which is defined as the ability to use a language in a meaningful way in a communicative situation (Tarnanen & Huhta, 2008). The functional view of language proficiency is also strongly present among the Finnish teachers: what is regarded as good teaching is characterized by an emphasis on language proficiency rather than on language knowledge. There are, however, varying views on language in the pedagogic communities, and those teachers who are drawing on the language view prominent in the CEFR criticize the professional competence of those with the language knowledge view in designing local curricula. Although the language teacher in the example below does not explicitly say so, her criticism is focused on the fact that her interpretation of the view of language advocated in the CEFR has not been sufficiently well applied.

> I myself am really disappointed that all the teachers with us don't understand what language proficiency is and what is language knowledge, that language proficiency means that I can speak, answer questions, understand when the bus driver says something and language knowledge is that the partitive case ends in a or ä [---] the goals (of the local curriculum) set by some people concentrate excessively on language knowledge though they should concern language proficiency. (Finnish second language teacher)

The same language teacher described later in the same interview the difference between a CEFR-based and a not-CEFR based approach to language teaching in the following way:

> ...they [the other teachers] always look at me in a funny way when we go somewhere like the chemist's to run errands – 'what are you going there for?' or anything else except sitting and studying with a paper under your nose. There is this awful psychological threshold to do anything (laughs) but it's really that you don't get any support from anybody for that. (Finnish second language teacher)

Thus, the adoption of the CEFR in Finland has in this case created, in a way, new antagonisms. The proponents of the CEFR are clearly using their own interpretation of the CEFR in an authoritative manner to define what is good or bad, right or wrong, in language teaching.

Not only the central keywords but also the scales of the CEFR seem to have a great impact on the discourses about adult second language teaching. The scales and levels also produce the categories and logic that are used in the discourse about language proficiency levels and employment, as the following two examples show:

> Well it [B1] is the absolute minimum, but even if you pass the test you can ask if this level of language proficiency is useful, but on the other hand I've been raised (laughs) to accept this minimum. (Finnish as a second language teacher)

Well for those who have no real chance of getting a job in the labour market this level [B1] is enough, you cope with this kind of language proficiency in banks and shops and wherever you have to get along, but we have only a few jobs where you can manage with this proficiency, well there's still some industry and construction work left. (Finnish official in a ministry)

What is interesting about these two examples from interviews conducted in relation to the revision of the development of the Finnish integration training for adult migrants is that the CEFR levels frame the discussion as naturalized and taken-for-given categories that are not questioned.

The adoption of the CEFR in Denmark and Finland had a profound influence on the development of curricula by defining specific categories and levels for language teaching and by setting the conceptual scene for discourses about adult second language education. In addition to this, the adoption of the CEFR had another and quite often overlooked impact. It moved the power over the general conceptualization of language and literacy from a national (or local) level to a consensus-based supranational level. Although the rhetoric of the CEFR implies that the framework is a reference and not a prescription, the basic conceptualizations and scales of language and literacy are stated as given and are not open to redefinition or re-conceptualization, but basically only to application and adoption. Both the Danish and the Finnish cases clearly reveal that the CEFR is regarded as an authoritative and constitutive instrument for organizing language teaching with concepts and scales that are beyond discussion.

In Finland and Denmark, the CEFR has become a norm with a very strong influence on the political discourse on adult second language learning. It involves various kinds of people who are in gate-keeping positions in everyday language assessment, for example administrators in employment services (who try to place people on right courses), tenders (who provide training) and language teachers (who report on the learning progress). In general, there seems to be a firm, shared belief that the CEFR is based on solid research evidence even though this is not the case (Holm, 2007; Hulstijn, 2007). Moreover, the adoption of the CEFR has strongly contributed to establishing a perspective on the adult migrant where his or her progression through the predefined levels of the CEFR is the only way to demonstrate the ability and willingness to be a 'good' migrant. Actual 'integration' into or contributions to different local contexts outside classrooms are overlooked or at least not valued (Baynham & Simpson, 2010; Pöyhönen & Saario, 2009).

CEFR in the classroom

After having shown how the CEFR has impacted educational planning and discourses, we now turn to classroom practices and examine how the conceptualization of literacy in the CEFR has been localized in the literacy practices in adult second language teaching. Based on ethnographic classroom data, Holm (2004) points out that the texts produced in the adult second language classroom represents a narrow range of genres that reflects those genres defined by ALTE, a supranational language testing agency working within the CEFR conceptualization of language and literacy. Consequently, a considerable 'washback-intensity' from the CEFR (Cheng *et al.*, 2004) is evident in the classroom.

The texts produced within the given genres in the classroom are in general based on the reading of different types of texts related to issues in contemporary Danish society. The texts are read as authoritative and as revealing objective knowledge. Seen from a classroom perspective, this practice gives a teacher the role of an authority, not only because of her/his superior command of the language or because of the structural authority built in the role of a teacher but also because being Danish her/himself (the teachers are usually Danes with very few exceptions) gives authoritative power as regards the interpretation of Danish issues. The production of mostly individually produced and handwritten texts in the classroom is closely monitored by the teacher and students are given both oral and written feedback. The aim of the interaction is to eliminate linguistic mistakes and to make sure that the texts come up to the norms of the testing system concerning writing tasks, including the required number of words, rhetoric structure, headings and appropriateness.

This condensed description of the construction of literacy in second language teaching clearly reveals how the understanding of predefined 'needs' in relation to literacy creates a specific relation between teacher and students. Teachers are placed in an expert role and as providers of the 'needed' language, and students are placed as receivers of some 'needs' predefined for them. Furthermore, it is quite evident that the adoption of the CEFR has led to an understanding of second language literacy as a predefined step-by-step progression, or as a 'lock-step-march' to literacy, to quote Graff (1994). Such an approach tends not to be sensitive to an individual's former experience, present needs and future aims. It also appears infantilizing because it implies that adults have to, once again, learn many aspects of language and literacy right from the start and in a given order.

The following example from a language test was used (together with many other similar examples) in the classroom to prepare students with 12 or more years of schooling for the test in Danish Education 3. It demonstrates the localization of the CEFR conceptualization of literacy in a Danish context.

Letter to a friend

Situation: You have received this letter from your girlfriend Marie. In the letter she talks about some problems she has with her daughter at 13 years.

Dear ...

Thank you for last. It was very cozy.

I actually write to you because I want to hear your opinion about a problem I have. This is Louise. She has of late become so preoccupied with how she looks and what clothes she walks in. She talks constantly about buying some specific clothes that cost a fortune. As you know, we have not so much money at the moment, so even if I wanted, I cannot buy something for her, and not the expensive clothes she wants. She will or cannot understand that we are not able to afford it, so either she's mad at me or she cries. What should I do? Can you give me some advice, likely as soon as possible. I look forward to hearing from you. Greet everyone for me.

Love
Marie

Task
Write a letter to Marie.

You must:

- thank her for the letter
- comment on Marie's problem
- propose something she can do

You must initiate and complete the letter in an appropriate manner.

This example reveals how literacy in adult second language teaching is conceptualized as production of a predefined and given genre with specific content demands and requirements for writing according to the norms for appropriateness. Furthermore, the conceptualization of literacy in this case requires the students to put on a writer's identity as a Dane with interest in and experience of bringing up a child, and leaves no door open either for critical comments to the letter and the whole issue or for introducing other issues which the writer might find relevant.

CEFR and citizenship

In their analysis of testing regimes in Europe, Hogan-Brun et al. (2009) point out that in the past decade linguistic proficiency has emerged as one of the key conditions for granting a residence permit and for naturalization in an increasing number of European countries. They also argue that institutional systems for 'immigration and citizenship can only be developed at state level since there are no Europe-wide frameworks for citizenship legislation that could bind states to a code of practice in determining regulations and procedures for granting residence rights and citizenship' (Hogan-Brun et al., 2009: 4). From a formal legislative perspective they are right, but if the EU is seen as a network state with travelling concepts (such as the CEFR) that are localized in different ways the situation appears to be quite different (Extra et al., 2009). The CEFR is clearly an EU-wide framework with a great impact on the way proficiency Europe-wide in a particular language is used as a criterion for granting residency rights or citizenship. Extra et al. (2009) argue that even though the CEFR is not a prescriptive model and its main aim is to offer a frame of reference, many European countries use it in language courses and tests for migrants. The CEFR has thus become a safe basis, an unchallenged and unquestioned norm, for choosing a particular level of language proficiency in setting a language policy for citizenship, for example. Extra et al. (2009: 18) conclude that the CEFR which was primarily meant for promoting plurilingualism 'is used by some policy makers as a scientific justification to promote monolingualism in official state languages and to focus more on what newcomers lack than on what they might be able to contribute.'

In both Finland and Denmark, it is a precondition for citizenship to prove one's language proficiency. This means, as Simons and Masschelein (2008: 391) argue, that 'citizenship is not just perceived as a legal matter that is related to rights and obligations, but as a performance based upon particular competencies'. The language competences needed for citizenship in Finland and Denmark, as in many other European countries, are based on the language proficiency levels developed in the CEFR.

The CEFR is thus used as a normative standpoint not only for adult migrants' second language teaching but also in granting or denying citizenship. The CEFR thus forms a basis for the attempts to prevent social segregation or for promoting social inclusion of migrants. Yet, at the same time, the CEFR and the accompanying discourse on literacy and language proficiency is a powerful device in doing the opposite: to widen the gap between social groups through mechanisms that Blackledge (2006) refers to as 'the double language of political discourse'. The increasing demands on language and literacy skills for acquiring citizenship in many European countries based on the CEFR (2001) might function as a considerable threat to social cohesion because more and more adult migrants seem to be denied the possibility of becoming EU citizens. This clearly contradicts the aim of the CERF as being a contribution to 'the democratization of language teaching' that is presented as a central impetus for its groundwork.[2]

Discussion

The development from the comparatively open-ended functional-notional suggestions by Wilkins for curriculum development to the detailed framework found in the CEFR represents a shift from a presentation of a linguistic *idea* for curriculum development and language teaching to a general supranational and predefined conceptualization of skills, levels and scales in language teaching. This change in educational planning from *development* of curricula to the *application* of supranational conceptualization and standards to language teaching has to a large extent established the CEFR as something authoritative and objective beyond critical scrutiny. This naturalization of a specific view of language, literacy and learning might lead to a situation in which many conceptual and pedagogical discussions about literacy in adult second language teaching might seem to be irrelevant.

The localization of the CEFR in Denmark and Finland did not take place at the same time and the conceptual framework was not used for the same purposes and in the same way. However, our analysis shows how consensus-based concepts developed by supranational agencies function as a discursive force that frames what count as legitimate conceptualizations of language and literacy, and how the conceptualizations and levels of the CEFR have been firmly established in education as a general instrument for educational planning and practice and for regulation of access to citizenship. As a result, the CEFR has become a political tool, which has consequences for adult migrants' second language teaching. It can also lead to high stakes decisions for migrants themselves and to a situation in which different actors (migrants, teachers and policy makers) change their behaviours according to the demands of the tests (Shohamy, 2001).

Literacy in the EU is in transition and quite strongly related to supranational concepts and supranational agencies and networks. Understanding the CEFR as an artefact and analysing the localization of this conceptualization of literacy through a multi-sited ethnographic approach have made it possible to read literacy both locally and translocally. The different interpretations and uses of the CEFR in Denmark and Finland are thus a perfect example of the fluidity that appears when a shared authority is naturalized in a supranational network.

To sum up, a basic criticism of the CEFR is that it contains very detailed descriptions of literacy. Literacy is seen as something already given and not as a multiple and negotiable phenomenon – as literacies that are created, developed and shaped under changing social conditions (Levine, 1994). Moreover, the CEFR represents a very narrow understanding of language and literacy with a predefined understanding of the progression of language and literacy learning. This does not give much room for challenging genres or for constructing new ones. It also gives little room for autonomy, subjectivity and negotiation in relation to content, form and genre. As a consequence, the CEFR does not seem to be a suitable point of departure for educational planning if priority is given to an approach that is sensitive to an individual student's experiences, wishes and needs, and to the development of creativity and aesthetics. If the CEFR understanding of language and literacy progression is the starting point in language teaching programmes, it might create a situation in which all students, no matter what their educational background and their already existing experiences with language and literacy are, are placed in a position where they have to learn a new language from scratch (Blackledge, 2000; Holm, 2004).

Modern society is often characterized as a learning society in which literacy skills are in a vital position. Membership in society such as being employed and keeping one's job requires from an individual the ability and desire to learn and keep up and develop his/her competence. Consequently, social problems such as unemployment might be perceived as problems in learning that are to be solved through education (Simons & Masschelein, 2008). An example of this type of thinking is the debate on the sufficiency of migrants' language skills for their integration and employment for which the central solution from society's point of view appears to be offering them more language education. This type of social selection for education is quite often hidden, but it can be traced by examining normative assumptions about the roles and interplay of migrants' language skills, education and employment (Forsander, 2004; Tarnanen & Pöyhönen, 2011).

If the development within the EU is seen as a process towards a learning society, this has considerable implications for pedagogies. A learning society seems to imply a growing need for literacies and uses of texts. Technological development offers new possibilities for combining text, picture and sound in the creation of meaning, and globalization processes mean that the construction of meaning increasingly takes place between persons who communicate in a second or foreign language or in combinations of languages. This might lead to a more frequent need for negotiations of meaning, for code-switching and for a creative use of multimodality. All this indicates that new types of multimodal and multilingual literacies – not reflected in the CEFR – might play an important role in the learning society of the future (Holm, 2004, 2007; Taalas et al., 2008).

In our view, literacy is a complex, changing and dynamic social practice of great importance in identity construction and for the understanding of knowledge, and therefore it is difficult for us to see the need for European standardization. On the contrary, it becomes important to direct attention to the multiple ways literacy is used and to relate knowledge about this to the ongoing development of literacy education. Literacy in language education has potential for contributing to personal and societal development. There are three preconditions for this. First, literacy is understood as a multiple, multilingual, multimodal and negotiable phenomenon. Second, the writer – or actually the author – is seen as a subject and a co-producer of literacy. Third, the curricula are sensitive towards the learner's experiences, aims and wishes.

Notes

(1) In the rest of the chapter CEFR (2001) is referred as 'the CEFR'.
(2) http://www.coe.int/t/dg4/linguistic/historique

References

Alderson, J.C. (2005) *Diagnosing Foreign Language Proficiency: The Interface between Learning and Assessment*. London: Continuum.

Baynham, M. and Simpson, J. (2010) Onwards and upwards: Space, placement, and liminality in adult ESOL classes. *TESOL Quarterly* 44 (3), 420–440.

Blackledge, A. (2000) Power relations and the social construction of 'literacy' and 'illiteracy': The experience of Bangladeshi women in Birmingham. In M. Martin-Jones and K. Jones (eds) *Multilingual Literacies: Reading and Writing Different Worlds* (pp. 55–69). Amsterdam: John Benjamins.

Blackledge, A. (2006) "The men say 'They don't need it.'" Gender and the extension of language testing for British citizenship. *Studies in Language & Capitalism* 1, 143–161.

Blommaert, J. (2003) Commentary: A sociolinguistics of globalization. *Journal of Sociolinguistics* 7 (4), 607–623.

Blommaert, J. (2010) *The Sociolinguistics of Globalization*. Cambridge: Cambridge University Press.

Blommaert, J. and Rampton, B. (2011) Language and superdiversity. *Diversities* 13(2), 1–21.

Brandt, D. and Clinton, K. (2002) Limits of the local: Expanding perspectives on literacy as a social practice. *Journal of Literacy Research* 34 (3), 337–356.

Bron, A. (2003) From an immigrant to a citizen: Language as a hindrance or a key to citizenship. *International Journal of Lifelong Education* 22 (6), 606–619.
Candea, M. (2007) Arbitrary locations: In defense of the bounded field-site. *Journal of the Royal Anthropological Institute* 13, 167–184.
Castells, M. (2010) Grassrooting the space of flows. *Urban Geography* 20(4), 294–302.
CEFR (1998) *Modern Languages: Learning, Teaching, Assessment: A Common European Framework of Reference.* Strasbourg: Council of Europe.
CEFR (2001) *Common European Framework of Reference for Languages: Learning, Teaching, Assessment.* Cambridge: Cambridge University Press.
Cheng, L., Watanabe, Y. and Curtis, A. (eds) (2004) *Washback in Language Testing. Research Contexts and Methods.* Mahwah, NJ: Lawrence Erlbaum Associates.
Extra, G., Spotti, M. and Van Avermaet, P. (2009) Testing regimes for newcomers. In G. Extra, M. Spotti and P. Van Avermaet (eds) *Language Testing, Migration and Citizenship* (pp. 3–33). London: Continuum.
Figueras, N., North, B., Takala, S., Verhelst, N. and Van Avermaet, P. (2005) Relating examinations to Common European Framework: A manual. *Language Testing* 22, 261–279.
FNBE (Finnish National Board of Education) (2012a) *National Core Curriculum for Integration Training for Adult Migrants 2012.* Helsinki: Finnish National Board of Education. Publications 2012:6.
FNBE (Finnish National Board of Education) (2012b) *National Core Curriculum for Literacy Training for Adult Migrants 2012.* Helsinki: Finnish National Board of Education. Publications 2012:7.
Forsander, A. (2004) Social capital in the context of immigration and diversity: Economic participation in the Nordic welfare states. *Journal of International Migration and Integration* 5 (2), 207–227.
Graff, H.J. (1994) Literacy, myths and legacies: Lessons from the history of literacy. In L. Verhoeven (ed.) *Functional Literacy* (pp. 37–60). Amsterdam: John Benjamins.
Gustafsson, J. (2003) *Integration som Text, Diskursiv och Social Praktik* [Integration as a text, discursive and social practice]. Göteborg: Acta Universitatis Gothoburgensis.
Gustafsson, J. (2010) Pedagogical integration and regionalization. *Nordisk Barnehageforskning* 3 (3), 105–114.
Hogan-Brun, G., Mar-Molinero, C. and Stevenson, P. (2009) Testing regimes: Introducing cross-national perspectives on language, integration and citizenship. In G. Hogan-Brun, C. Mar-Molinero and P. Stevenson (eds) *Discourses on Language and Integration: Critical Perspectives on Language Testing Regimes in Europe* (pp. 1–12). Amsterdam: John Benjamins.
Holm, L. (2004) *Hvilken vej ind i hvilken skriftlighed? Et studie af undervisning i skriftlighed i dansk som andetsprog for voksne* [Which way into which kind of literacy? A study of adult second language literacy teaching]. København: Danmarks Pædagogiske Universitet.
Holm, L. (2006) Sprogtests i et andetsprogsperspektiv – med særligt henblik på literacy [Language tests from a second language perspective – with specific focus on literacy]. *Nordand – Nordisk Tidsskrift for andrespråksforskning* 1 (2), 57–77.
Holm, L. (2007) Konstruktionen af en fælles europæisk skriftlighed. En kritisk diskussion [The construction of common European literacy]. In S. Matre (ed.) *Skrive for nåtid og framtid* (pp. 52–62). Trondheim: Tapir Akademisk Forlag.
Holm, L. and Laursen H.P. (2011) Migrants and literacy crises. *APPLES: Journal of Applied Language Studies* 5(2), 3–16.

Hulstijn, J.H. (2007) The shaky ground beneath the CEFR: Quantitative and qualitative dimensions of language proficiency. *The Modern Language Journal* 91, 663–667.
Jessen, J. (1983) *Et taerskelniveau for dansk* [A threshold level for Danish]. Strasbourg: Council of Europe.
Johnson, K. (2006) Revisiting Wilkins' Notional Syllabuses. *International Journal of Applied Linguistics* 16(3), 414–418.
Levine, K. (1994) Functional literacy in a changing world. In L. Verhoeven (ed.) *Functional literacy: Theoretical Issues and Educational Implications* (pp. 113–131). Amsterdam: John Benjamins.
Long, M.H. (2005) A rationale for needs analysis and needs analysis research. In M.H. Long (ed.) *Second Language Needs Analysis* (pp. 1–18). Cambridge: Cambridge University Press.
Marcus, G.E. (1995) Ethnography in/of the world system: The emergence of multi-sited ethnography. *Annual Review of Anthropology* 24, 95–117.
Martin, E. (1994) *Flexible Bodies: The Role of Immunity in American Culture from the Days of Polio to the Days of AIDS*. Boston: Beacon Press.
Moos, L. (2006) What kinds of democracy in education are facilitated by supra- and transnational agencies? *European Educational Research Journal* 5(3–4), 160–168.
Pitkänen-Huhta, A. (2003) *Texts and interaction: Literacy practices in the EFL classroom. Jyväskylä Studies in Languages* 55. Jyväskylä: University of Jyväskylä.
Pöyhönen, S. and Saario, J. (2009) In the land of paper: Migrant pupils and adolescents learning literacies in Finland. In S. May (ed.) *LED2007: Refereed Conference Proceedings of the 2nd International Conference on Language, Education and Diversity*. Hamilton, New Zealand: Wilf Malcolm Institute of Educational Research (WMIER), University of Waikato.
Pöyhönen, S., Tarnanen, M., Vehviläinen, E-M., Virtanen, A. and Pihlaja, L. (2010) Osallisena Suomessa. Kehittämissuunnitelma maahanmuuttajien kotoutumisen edistämiseksi [Participative integration in Finland: A development plan]. University of Jyväskylä: Centre for Applied Language Studies, Finnish Cultural Foundation. CD Rom.
Risager, K. (2004) A social and cultural view to language. In H.L. Hansen (ed.) *Disciplines and Interdisciplinarity in Foreign Language Studies* (pp. 21–34). University of Copenhagen: Museum Tusculanum Press.
Saarinen, T. (2007) *Quality on the move: Discursive construction of higher education policy from the perspective of quality*. Jyväskylä Studies in Humanities 83. Jyväskylä: University of Jyväskylä.
Saarinen, A. and Jäppinen M. (2011) Political inclusion of migrants in Finland: The five policy phases in 1990s–2010s. Paper presented at a conference on Migrant Labour: Contested Integration, Prospects for Citizenship, September 15–16, 2011. Peace Institute and City University (London), Ljubljana.
Shohamy, E. (2001) *The Power of Tests: A Perspective of the Uses of Language Tests*. London: Longman.
Simons, M. and Masschelein, J. (2008) The governmentalization of learning and the assemblage of a learning apparatus. *Educational Theory* 58(4), 391–415.
Spolsky, B. (1995) *Measured Words: The Development of Objective Language Testing*. Oxford: Oxford University Press.
Taalas, P., Kauppinen, M., Tarnanen, M. and Pöyhönen, S. (2008) Media landscapes in school and in free time – two parallel realities? *Digital Kompetanse - Nordic Journal of Digital Literacy* 3 (4), 240–256.

Tarnanen, M. and Huhta, A. (2008) Interaction of language policy and assessment in Finland. *Current Issues in Language Planning* 9(3), 262–281.
Tarnanen, M. and Pöyhönen, S. (2011) Maahanmuuttajien suomen kielen taidon riittävyys ja työllistymisen mahdollisuudet [Adequacy of migrants' Finnish proficiency and employment opportunities]. *Puhe ja kieli* 4, 139–152.
Trim, J.L.M., Richterich, R., van Ek, J. and Wilkins, D. (1973) *Systems Development in Adult Second Learning.* Strasbourg: Council of Europe.
Uddannelsestyrelsen (1999) *Spor 3. Undervisningsvejledning* [Track 3. Teaching guide]. København: Undervisningsministeriet.
Vertovec, S. (2006) *The emergence of super-diversity in Britain.* Centre on Migration, Policy and Society. Working Paper No 25, University of Oxford.
Wilkins, D. (1976) *Notional Syllabuses.* Oxford: Oxford University Press.

9 Teacher Reflections Under Changing Conditions for Literacy Learning in Multicultural Schools in Oslo

Anne Marit Vesteraas Danbolt and Lise Iversen Kulbrandstad

Introduction

Global trends like migration and international pupil assessment are rapidly changing the daily lives of teachers in Norway. Thirty years ago few teachers met pupils with multicultural backgrounds. Today, linguistic minority pupils make up 9% in compulsory school in the country as a whole and 38% in the capital, Oslo. At the same time, as diversity increases, emphasis on mainstreaming and the teaching of Norwegian has replaced the official school policy of the 1980s which aimed at bilingual competence for minority pupils. This shift is not typical for Norway; it can be seen in several other countries as well (Blommaert, 2010; Mohan et al., 2001).

Another change which affects the teaching profession is testing (see also Holm & Pöyhönen, Chapter 8, in this volume). Thirty years ago, there was hardly any testing in Norwegian schools. The first time Norway took part in an international comparison of reading competence was in the early 1990s with the IEA study of reading literacy (Elley, 1992). The first compulsory reading tests were introduced as recently as in 2000. Today, there are national tests in reading, mathematics and English. Reading is tested in the 5th, 8th and 9th grades, and screening of reading is mandatory in the 1st, 2nd and 3rd grades. In addition several municipalities have made other tests and assessments obligatory as well. In a recently published survey, 64% of teachers agreed that the focus on tests and results now controls too much of their and the schools' priorities (Union of Education Norway, 2011).

The strong international trend of comparing learning outcome across countries not only results in international, national and local rankings but also calls for action in countries which aim at higher rankings in future studies. These ambitions lead to the transition of ideas and teaching and testing practices from high scoring countries to lower scoring countries. The international studies themselves contribute to this transition by analysing the reading results in light of several background factors, presented in publications like *Effective Schools in Reading: Implication for Educational Planners* (Postlethwaite & Ross, 1992), *Northern Lights on PISA 2003: A Reflection from the Nordic Countries* (Mejding & Roe, 2006) and *PISA 2009 Results: What Makes a School Successful* (OECD, 2010). In the Norwegian context, changing governments have introduced a lot of initiatives to strengthen reading results the last 10 years following up on the so-called PISA-shock in 2001 when Norway was ranked 13th of 31 countries (see Kulbrandstad, 2010).

How do teachers react when the politicians suddenly make great changes in the curriculum in an effort to improve reading results? What do the teachers think, and what do they do? These questions were a start for an action research project called 'Classroom Cultures for Language Learning' (Danbolt & Kulbrandstad, 2008). We worked together with teachers in multicultural schools in Oslo who tried to change their teaching practices. Working in teacher education ourselves, we wanted to gain knowledge on how an action research approach could be used to support and understand the ways teachers adapt their teaching practices of literacy under changing circumstances and to analyse the teachers' reflections on conditions for literacy learning. In this chapter, we concentrate on the part of the action research project which focused on the study of teacher reflections.

The School Context

Our research project was situated in five multicultural schools in Oslo in the school year 2005–2006. Between 40 and 60% of the pupils had family background other than Norwegian. In the local ranking of schools according to reading results, they were all ranked above average. Still all the schools reported that they worked hard on improving their reading results. The strong focus on tests and on mainstreaming as a way to improve reading results was a new challenge facing the teachers the school year we met them. The school politicians in Oslo had decided to put away the curriculum guidelines for Norwegian as a second language and replace it with Norwegian, the subject developed for pupils with mother tongue knowledge of Norwegian. To adapt the teaching of Norwegian, the politicians introduced a project called 'Strengthened, Adapted Teaching of Norwegian'. This project also involved competence development of teachers and school leaders and a research group following the project. The decision made by the politicians in Oslo was the result of a growing concern since the publishing of alarming test results in 2002. A reading survey in 2003 was, for example, later commented on in the following way:

> It is worrying that many minority language pupils with Norwegian as a second language need special follow-up in reading. This is true for all grades where the mapping of reading abilities has been conducted. A particular challenge is to what extent teachers have adequate competence to follow up these pupils. (Municipality of Oslo, 2004, p.7, our translation)

The local project 'Strengthened, Adapted Teaching of Norwegian' marked the start of a long-lasting effort to strengthen the schools' competence in reading, writing and language education in order to improve the pupils' test results and learning outcome. Hedmark University College was engaged in the years 2005–2008 to contribute to the competence development and for the research project. An action research approach was chosen for the first phase. We designed a way to link the competence raising and the action research through a series of courses, and to participation in a network of schools. Two central concepts in our study were *innovations and reflections*. Small-scale innovations in different aspects of literacy teaching were carried out in four situations (see Danbolt, 2007; Danbolt & Kulbrandstad, 2008; Kulbrandstad, 2008). The teacher reflections occurred in three contexts: in connection with the innovations, in the network of five schools as part of the competence building and as part of retrospective interviews the following school year.

In the innovation part of the project, the teachers were challenged to make changes in their practices of teaching literacy and to try out new practices. While trying out new practices of course can be considered part of the teaching profession, seeking research-based knowledge as a way to improve teaching practices has no long tradition among Norwegian teachers in primary school. The action research approach was chosen because it offers a way of combining research-based and experience-based knowledge to conduct small-scale innovations.

Broadening the Concept of Reading

Brian Street (2008) points to the conflicting views on literacy among policy makers and researchers, which in essence can be described as embodying the distinction between autonomous and ideological models of literacy. This distinction can be illustrated by the situation surrounding our research project. In Norway, the new school policies both at national and local levels are concerned with schools providing documentation of their work. Pupils' learning outcomes are an important part of this and since reading tests are frequently used as a measure for learning outcomes, improvement of reading very often is discussed among politicians. These discussions are often in danger of using a too narrow concept of reading, viewing reading as a stable, context-free, isolated skill that can easily be measured, reflecting Street's (1984, 2008) characterization of an autonomous view on reading.

In all four innovations in our research project, the teaching of Norwegian in mainstream classrooms was the starting point. The national curriculum *Knowledge Promotion* (Ministry of Education and Research, 2006) defines Norwegian as a subject which has a particular following-up responsibility regarding four of the five basic skills which are highlighted in the curriculum. The four skills are expressing oneself orally, expressing oneself in the written language, reading and using digital aids. In the curriculum, each skill is described as part of the content in all subject areas. As teacher educators, we have experienced that this way of structuring the guidelines together with the strong emphasis on tests primarily in reading, and also with efforts of making tests in writing, easily promotes work with skills in isolation. Therefore, we were concerned with emphasizing a broader view of reading in the competence development and in the action research project. In this context, broadening the view meant moving from a narrow focus on reading results to building classroom cultures for literacy learning. We leaned on the research body of New Literacy Studies with their ideological models of literacy, providing culture- and context-sensitive approaches with focus on use and practice.

All the four skills as expressed in the Norwegian curriculum guidelines are touched upon through the projects we have worked with. In daily use the skills often are integrated, as pointed out, for example, by Heath (1983: 195) in her ethnographic study *Ways with Words,* 'For most of these [Tracton children interpreting print], oral communication surrounded the print', and by Barton and Hamilton (1998: 9) in their ethnographic study of literacy practices in working class communities in Lancaster, 'in many literacy events there is a mixture of written and spoken language'. Through the title of our project, Classroom Cultures for Language Learning, we have wished to signal that working with Norwegian and with reading have to be put in a larger context. In the innovation projects, teachers both worked with reading as language practice (i.e. to build classroom cultures for listening, speaking, reading and writing in interaction) and with reading as a functional and cultural practice (i.e. to build classroom cultures for reading in order to learn, for identity development and for education in a multicultural society).

Methodological Approach

In the field of educational science, action research was first used in connection with the implementation of curricula aiming at narrowing the gap between knowledge gained from research and knowledge gained from practice (Zeichner, 2001). Contributions to both practice and theoretical development are considered the dual objectives of this research approach, and this possibility of a dual aim was the main reason for our choice of research approach. Zuber-Skerrit (1996: 83) suggests that the 'aims of any action research project or program are to bring about practical improvement, innovation, change or development of social practice, and the practitioners' better understanding of their practices'. The emphasis on practical innovations ties action research to particular situations which can be said to be in line with the context sensitivity promoted by the New Literacy Studies. Zuber-Skerrit stresses not only innovations but also the practitioner's reflections (their 'better understanding of their practices') as aims of action research. In our study, the teacher reflections are as important as the innovations. And here we can argue for another parallel to key concepts from New Literacy Studies where literacy practices are defined in a way that includes thinking. As Street (2000: 22) writes: 'Literacy practices refer to this broader cultural conception of particular ways of thinking about and doing reading and writing in cultural contexts'. The focus of our study is not on literacy practices but on the practices of teaching literacy. Nevertheless, Street's reflections on research methods in studying literacy practices are relevant for our purpose as well:

> You can photograph literacy events but you cannot photograph literacy practices. There is an ethnographic issue here: we have to start talking to people, listening to them and linking their immediate experience of reading and writing out to other things that they do as well. (Street, 2000: 21)

Our action research approach builds on four principles: the principle of double objectives (see Zeichner, 2001), the principle of cooperation between compulsory school and a research institution, the principle of linking action research to competence raising (courses and network meetings) and the principle of making the teachers' experiences visible. The network and the cooperation between the researchers and the practice field set the frames for the teachers and the school administrators' self-reflection. Consequently, self-reflection is the basis for the realization of our fourth principle.

The preparation phase was introduced with a get-to-know phase in the two schools where we conducted the action research[1]. The aim was to get a first impression. Gaining confidence and listening to the teachers' descriptions of their challenges were vital. Through observations in the classroom, the researchers visualized their own picture of the challenges. In light of this, reflective conversations were conducted to find which innovative efforts teachers might be interested in trying out through the practice period. The researchers responded and suggested ideas and were responsible for giving the teachers relevant contributions from the knowledge base which lies in theory and prior research. We call the innovation small-scale because it was an important principle that it should be possible to carry out the changes in teaching practices without extra resources in forms of, for example, more teachers or heavy investments in artefacts. In the implementation phase, the teachers were responsible for the practical teaching plan, while the researchers observed and collected data. In the reflection phase, the teachers and researchers reflected upon their experiences and what could be learnt from them.

When the attention is directed towards changes in dialogue with practitioners, the role of the researchers gets a new dimension. The researchers cannot place themselves as someone standing on the outside and looking inside; on the contrary, the researchers must contribute to the changes that are to be investigated. The school is not solely an object for the research; the research is done within the school and in close cooperation with it. In situations like these, the researchers have to be aware of the problem of reflexivity. The explicit definition of roles and responsibilities was one way to try to keep a critical distance in our dealing with the practitioners throughout the research process. Nevertheless, as in most qualitative research, the researchers not only use themselves in the interpretation of the data but also take part in creating the data because of their interaction with the informants.

The research data is divided in two parts. To study the innovations we have 13 hours of video recording from four innovations conducted by four teachers at two schools, the researcher's observation notes and logs, photos and written material from the pupils and the teachers. Data to study reflections was collected to shed light on the four innovations and on literacy learning and teaching in general. We have four hours of taped in-depth retrospective semi-structured interviews with the four teachers, the researcher's notes from discussions based on observations and audio-taped presentations and Power Points by two of the teachers at a conference. We also collected data at the network meetings where around 50 teachers and the school leaders from the five schools[2] met once a month. At the end of each day, the participants were challenged to write a reflection log on a given topic. The reflection logs were linked to the series of courses in the way that teachers wrote their reflections on the next theme of the course. This gave the course-holders a unique opportunity to see which thoughts the teachers had about the specific theme, and what they were preoccupied with. We have written logs from five different literacy-related themes. For each theme, between eight and 25 teachers chose to write a log. From the network meetings, we also have the researcher's summaries after each meeting.

Both the video- and the audio-recorded material were transcribed. In analyzing the data, we worked bottom-up by reading and re-reading the material keeping close to the raw data and looking for themes and patterns that emerge from the texts. We also worked top-down by applying theories and earlier research results in interpreting the data. In searching for patterns, our approach is in accordance with the activities Boeije (2010) describes as *segmentation* and *reassembling*:

> Qualitative analysis is the segmenting of data into relevant categories and the naming of these categories with codes while simultaneously generating the categories from the data. In the reassembling phase the categories are related to one another to generate theoretical understanding of the social phenomenon under study in terms of the research question. (Boeije, 2010: 76)

In what follows, we will present the analysis of one of the written reflection log themes from the network meetings, and of one of the innovative sub-projects that took place in a 2nd grade classroom, and the teachers' reflections on making changes in the teaching of literacy.

Teachers' Reflections on Literacy Learning

One of the goals for the competence-raising project was to get teachers to reflect on how they could build good language learning environments in multicultural school, environments that could promote literacy learning and give varied opportunities to read, write and talk for pupils with different competences in Norwegian. In order to gain insight into the teachers' own practices and their thoughts about this, we challenged them at one network meeting (in January 2006) to reflect on what they thought were the best ways to stimulate the learning of Norwegian at school ('Hvordan tror du elevene lærer best norsk på skolen?'). Twenty-five network participants wrote their reflections logs. On average, the logs consist of 202 running words. The shortest is made up of 85 words and the longest of 367.

After working with the qualitative analysis activities of segmenting and reassembling, three main topics emerged as typical in the teacher reflections as good ways to promote language learning in school: talking, working on vocabulary and reading. Working with the data we also discovered another pattern; when the teachers reflected on different topics, they almost always commented on the best ways to organize the pupils in groups. We found that interesting because we had also observed in the innovation projects that the introduction of the principle of mainstreaming in combination with the more flexible way of grouping pupils in other forms than the traditional classes of 25–30[3] forced the teachers to spend more time and effort discussing how to organize the pupils than they traditionally had been doing. We will therefore comment upon both the topics mentioned by the teachers and on their reflections on how to group the pupils while working with the different topics.

It was an obvious common feature of the reflection logs that talk or oral conversation is designated as a key arena for language learning. Twenty-four of the 25 teachers mention conversation as vital for language learning. In the following, we present some examples of the ways the teachers formulate their reflections. All the logs were written in Norwegian. The extracts are translated by us. Each listed item represents translated quotations from one reflection log.

- The oral language develops in conversation/dialogue in interaction with others, children and adults. For a good development the activities must be teacher-directed – targeted. [It is] important to use different learning contexts. When learning about nature, you must go outside! [It is] important to make use of various activities – role play, practice dialogue, games – rhymes – riddles.
- Pupils must have the opportunity to use the language every day in school. The teacher must consider his/her own time of talking during the school day. She must also consider how the pupils are sitting in the classroom. Sitting in groups invites conversation. Pupils from minority language backgrounds should be allowed to sit with pupils who have progressed further in language development.
- Pupils develop their oral language in dialogue with other children in play and learning situations.

The teachers agree that pupils' opportunities to be active and to use language in interactions are of great importance. In school both peers and teachers are possible interlocutors, and we see from the quotes that both groups are mentioned. Peers as 'language role models' is a term used by many when they elaborate on how the interaction situations can be created:

- Norwegian and multilingual children in the same group. This will probably strengthen the Norwegian [pupils] by forcing them to focus

on the language they 'take for granted', while the multilingual [pupils] hear the Norwegian children's language and have them as role models.
• Exploit the opportunity for language models by mixing linguistic good/poor pupils.

The school as an arena for language learning offers possibilities of both planned and spontaneous conversations. The teachers mention play, games, drama, talk around themes from text books and other materials and talk about common experiences. The teachers express awareness of the importance of using both teacher-driven sequences and other situations that occur during the day to promote language learning. Most of them stress the importance of systematic language learning and the basic need of creating learning environments where the pupils feel safe and comfortable. In their reflections on the importance of conversation as a way to learn Norwegian, the teachers mention heterogeneous groups. The groups must be combined in such a way that those children who do not yet know much Norwegian will learn language in interaction with children who know the language better (e.g. the groups must be heterogeneous with respect to pupils' Norwegian language skills).

Vocabulary is mentioned as another area of special importance to multilingual pupils. Eighteen of the 25 network participants mention working with vocabulary in their reflection logs. To prepare the pupils for vocabulary that will turn up in their books, teachers seem to prefer more homogenous groups, for example to teach special courses for the second language users:

• Bilingual pupils should also come out of the classrooms and get the follow-up on words and concepts in advance of a topic that is to be taught at school.
• Preparation of complex issues. Prepare the pupils for difficult words and phrases in several subjects.
• Offer different courses according to demand. Be ahead in the learning of concepts.

Seventeen of the 25 teachers mention reading as the best way to learn Norwegian in school. In light of the political focus on reading in the schools in Oslo, it is rather surprising that not all the teachers underscore reading as a way of language learning. A general comment when the teachers reflect on reading is, however, their description of the clear relationship between linguistic competence and reading. 'The bottom line for good reading skills must be well-developed oral language,' one teacher writes in her log, adding: 'This means a necessary increase of investment in language training.' Focus on words and language awareness and analyses of linguistic forms are in addition mentioned by many also when they write about reading. Motivation, the development of reading pleasure and ensuring abundant supply of reading material and rich opportunities for varied reading are other issues the teachers are concerned with. Several stress that pupils often need help in choosing books:

- Pupils need guidance when they choose books for silent reading. When the pupils select a book on their own, they often choose too difficult books.
- The most important thing to do to promote reading enjoyment is getting reading material/books that fit the pupil's level.

Also when the teachers write about reading instruction, they focus on how the teaching should be organized. Here the need for more homogeneous groups and especially level-based groups are often mentioned as a response to the challenge of teaching reading in a linguistically diverse classroom.

- To divide the pupils into mastery groups is positive. Allowing pupils on the same level of reading to read in groups makes them motivated, and it becomes easier for the teacher to adapt the teaching.
- Dividing the pupils into level-based groups from time to time gives all the pupils an opportunity to have their say and get the feeling of being seen and heard and the feeling of mastering. It will lay the basis for good conversations.

The following excerpt from a teacher's reflection log illustrates how the different areas of talking, vocabulary learning and reading are related to each other:

- How do you think pupils learn Norwegian at school in the best way? Through discussions, training on words and concepts. The good conversation/dialogue on various topics is important. Talk about things that concern the pupil. Develop vocabulary and concepts. [...] Pupils who read a lot also have a well developed language. They evolve in line with the books they read. They increase their vocabulary and reading speed. By reading books they will have good experiences and 'hooks' to hang their knowledge on!

The analysis of the teachers' reflection logs shows that the teachers all express views that reveal a consciousness of the linguistic aspects of the challenges in diverse classrooms. They often refer to the basic skills of talking, reading and writing, and reflect in detail on how they can improve these skills among their pupils[4]. They emphasise how learners need to interact orally to learn the language of the subject areas, and advocate for level-based groups when it comes to reading. However, a view of literacy as integrated and embedded in social practices seem less protruding in the teachers' reflections.

Reading as Skill or as Social Practice: An Innovation in a 2nd Grade Classroom

One of the schools taking part in the action research was an inner-city primary school with about 40% minority pupils. During the research period, there were two classes in 2nd grade with about 20 pupils (seven years of age) in each of them. The teachers of the 2nd grade classes took part in the action research project throughout the whole school year, and the researcher visited them regularly, observed classroom practice and discussed issues of literacy learning with the teachers at the end of the school day and also at network meetings.

The main approach in literacy instruction in the 2nd grade classes was an example of literacy teaching practices being transferred around the world. One day a week, the two teachers organized a 'language workshop', with guided reading in level-based groups as an important principle. This was inspired by a literacy programme developed in New Zealand (Ministry of Education, NZ, 1997). As part of this programme, the pupils are divided into groups of four–six members according to their reading level and do activities at five different stations for about 13 minutes. At one of the stations, the teacher is occupied with guided reading. The core of this approach is the teacher's close observation and individual guidance of the readers. Due to restricted space in the classroom, the guided reading station in these 2nd grade classes is placed outside of the classroom. The rest of the children circulate between the different stations within the classroom and change stations when the teacher comes to pick out the next group for the guided reading sequence. It is important to note that although the teachers were inspired by an international approach toward literacy instruction, they had not had the opportunity to be informed theoretically about the original programme from New Zealand. They were to a large extent building on experiences from other teachers and with some guidance from the learning material that was used.

During the first phase of the action research, the preparation phase, the researcher made observations in the classrooms while the pupils were busy with the activities at the stations. We will focus on the reading station and the computer station and present some of our observations there.

At the reading station, the pupils were supposed to do free reading. There was a carpet on the floor in one corner of the classroom, with books in big boxes. The children picked a book of their own choice and read silently. During our observations, we noticed that some of the language minority children actually did not read. They just looked briefly into a book, and then went on to the next one. The reading was without any focus on the content of the book. And although the children were in a group, the activity was individualized. They did not talk together about what they were reading or the pictures in the books.

At the computer station, the children did pedagogical computer games which aimed at training them in phonological segmenting and phoneme–letter correspondences. One activity was to look at pictures and find the letter representing the first sound in the word. Again, we noticed that some of the language minority children had very little learning outcome of this activity. They just pressed the keys on the keyboard in a random way until a new picture turned up on the screen. One reason may be that they did not understand what they were supposed to do, or they did not know the names of the different objects that turned up on the screen.

The observations from the activities in the classroom reveal some problems that arise from a mainstreaming policy when it comes to literacy learning. Pupils of a linguistic minority background are subjected to the general approach of reading instruction, irrespective of their specific linguistic needs. In this case, the lack of language proficiency in Norwegian probably prevented the bilingual pupils to have any learning outcome of the activities at the free reading station and the computer station.

At the end of the school day, the researcher presented the observations to the two teachers, and we all took time to reflect on the implications of these findings. The teachers immediately expressed the usefulness of the observations: 'It is wonderful that you observe without interfering [in what the children are doing].' They realized that the observations made by the researcher yielded new information, as they in their roles as teachers never had time or opportunity to observe a whole sequence.

A topic that was highlighted as we discussed the observations in the classroom was reading and writing as social practices, reflecting the theoretical underpinning of the project. The children may be able to read – or decode – but apparently with little understanding and they were not able to use these skills in social situations since the activities at the language workshop in practice focused on skills and rituals and not on language in use. The observed situation in the classroom illustrated the necessity of broadening the perspective from reading as an autonomous skill to literacy as social practice (Barton, 2007; Street, 2008, 1984).

The teachers and the researcher decided to make some changes in the organization and the content of the language workshop, to make a shift from solitary reading to more communicative and interactive practices. The changes that we decided upon were as follows: to introduce conversation about the text or the pictures as part of the activity at the reading station, and to introduce writing at the computer station about the books the pupils just have been reading. One main objective was to put more emphasis and focus on language use. Furthermore, the changes tried to make the activities more cooperative – which is important in a classroom with linguistic diversity.

The teachers modelled the reading and talking activities for the children, being very explicit about the changes in the reading activities. Then the children were given books to read, and immediately afterwards they were to tell each other in pairs what they had been reading.

Table 9.1 shows an example from a conversation that took place when the pupils talked about the book they had chosen. Two boys with language minority background sit together. Damian has just read a book about animals and is about to tell his classmate Aden about it. Aden has not read this book, so he concentrates mostly on the pictures[5].

The boys are obviously inspired by the pictures in the book, which leads to a discussion about the names of the animals. It is also evident that solitary reading – as was the practice before the innovation – would not have given room for such a conversation. By talking about the text, the two boys are given a meaningful task that sets a goal for their reading, and they even solve their disagreements on the names of the animals by reading the text. This conversation also illustrates the mixture of written and spoken text which makes up a literacy event (Barton, 2007; Barton & Hamilton, 1998).

The innovation that was made in the organization and the content of the language workshop, show how minor changes can lead to more focus on the content of the book, more involvement and interaction, and more focus on the language, especially on vocabulary. It also can be seen as an example of the need to adapt the transition of pedagogical ideas to the actual context, as well as the need to ensure that the practitioners get insight into the theoretical basis for new activities.

In the retrospective interviews, the teachers mention how the engagement in action research has made them more conscious about their literacy practices in the classroom, and inspired them to make changes in the way they teach. A transcript from a classroom observation was an eye-opener for the teachers, when they saw in writing the pattern of interaction and turn-taking in the classroom. They realized that many language minority learners did not take part in the classroom conversation. Through this experience gained by the cooperation with

Table 9.1 Conversation between Damian and Aden

	Norwegian	English
Damian:	Det er en sommerfugl – og det er flaggermus	This is a butterfly – and this is a bat
Damian (reading):	Den gamle skilpadden – den jaktet på flu- insekter	The old turtle – it is hunting fly- insects
Aden:	Den der, den er sånn der, det ser ut som tusenbein	That one, it is like that, it looks like caterpillar
Damian (reading):	Og det er en mark. Den kryper opp av jorda	And this is a worm. It is crawling up from the soil
Aden:	Og det er en grevling. Det veit jeg	And that is a badger. I know that
Damian:	Og den spiser snegler og mark	And it eats snails and worms
Aden:	Æsj ja, ekkel	Uh yea, nasty
[...]	[...]	[...]
Aden:	Og det er en mus, det vet jeg	And that is a mouse, I know that
Damian:	Nei, det er hamster	No, it is hamster
Aden:	Neiiii	Nooo
Damian (reading):	Ha..am..ster	Ha..am..ster
Aden:	Å, det er den	Oh, it is

the researcher, they have become more aware of those pupils who are silent in the group, and on how to try to engage them more in classroom conversations.

The outcome of the action research approach is also clearly visible in a statement from one of the other teachers in the project, when she says that she had become more aware of the language dimension and the necessity to make things explicit for her pupils who were second language learners.

The personal and professional development was mentioned by the teachers as a very positive experience. They all appreciated getting the full attention from another person on their practice. They mention that normally there is not much interest in what they are doing in their classrooms. 'I got an extra pair of eyes in my classroom', one of the teachers said. This leads to more motivation: 'When you get positive feedback [...] you get motivated to go on with your work – and you feel you are getting somewhere'.

The retrospective interviews also revealed how action research promotes reflection. The following statement is quite representative for the dynamic interaction between the researchers and the teachers: 'You [the researcher] asked me questions, and I tried to think: Why did they [the pupils] behave like that?' Another teacher said that she had become more aware of what she did, and why she did it. One of the teachers was very explicit about the benefits of taking part in action research: 'A good thing is that you are forced to be more reflective of your own practice. That makes you become even more structured'.

Discussion

The global trends affecting teachers' practices both in Norway and in other countries in Western Europe cause a strong pressure on the everyday life of teachers and on teacher education (Darling-Hammond & Lieberman, 2012). The pressure of measurement through reading tests and the inherent competition among schools forced the school leaders and teachers we met to focus on improving the results on reading tests. Both the study of the teacher reflections and the innovation project from the 2nd grade showed that one way the schools responded to this new situation was to teach literacy in level-based groups. As we saw from the reflection logs, the teachers express an awareness of the challenges of the linguistic diverse classrooms and they are engaged in different ways to teach different skills, especially reading. More seldom, however, we met a broader view – seeing literacy as social practices.

The four teachers we worked together with in the innovation projects were eager to make changes in their teaching practices that could strengthen the literacy learning of all pupils in their new linguistically diverse classrooms. They had different approaches and answers to what they saw as adapted teaching for their pupils. The glimpse from one of the innovation projects that we have given in this chapter illustrates that reflections on what kind of reading and writing arise from different activities can lead to small changes that give richer opportunities for interaction and exchange of meaning in different literacy events. In one of the other projects, the teacher decided to explore different ways of teaching vocabulary as part of a newspaper project where the pupils read newspapers in different languages and wrote one themselves in Norwegian. There also was an innovation where the teacher decided to promote literacy by using drama, drawing and telling as a way of working with fairy tales and the last example was the common creation of a play language as an introduction to work on language awareness. Although their approaches were different, the four teachers reported that they found it inspiring to discuss their literacy teaching practices with the researchers adding research-based knowledge to their own teaching experiences.

Pedagogical ideas and literacy practices that are transferred between countries require informed adaptation and professional reflection. In our project, we saw how action research is useful to support teachers in their daily work with literacy learning under changing circumstances and how the dynamic interaction between teachers and researchers can promote reflections on teaching practices.

We look upon teacher reflection as an important way of adapting competence development and combining research-based and experience-based knowledge. In *Understanding Expertise in Teaching*, Amy Tsui (2003: 13) writes about the importance of reflections: 'To learn from experience requires that practitioners constantly reflect on their practices'. The action research approach we adopted sought different ways to fulfil this, and we met teachers who agreed upon the importance. One of them summed up her views in this way:

> Of course you develop as a teacher, but you don't develop without reflections. You have to want to develop. What really engages me is working with these low achieving students. I think at least I owe them excellent teaching.

Since language and subject learning in schools of today involve written texts in almost every subject area, the necessity of language support for second language learners must be strengthened with multiple ways to promote literacy learning. In Norway, there is a big shift in the ways teachers see research as a foundation for their practice. In 2008, a survey among Norwegian teachers told that 75% of the respondents thought it possible to be a good teacher without being interested in research relevant for their teaching subject (TNSGallup, 2008). In 2009, the largest teacher union, however, discussed this and decided to emphasize the need to combine experience-based and research-based knowledge in future professional development of teachers (Union of Education Norway, 2009).

To reach all Norwegian pupils with knowledge-based adapted teaching, we need a policy that strengthens the teaching profession in general, and especially regarding issues of literacy and cultural and linguistic diversity. The need to put stronger emphasis on multicultural and multilinguistic perspectives in teacher education and in the professional development of teachers is a clear advice from a recent OECD review on migrant education in Norway. Taguma *et al.* (2010: 8) state that 'schools need to be more responsive to linguistic and cultural diversity – improving the capacity of teachers and school leaders is the top priority'. In 2010 a new reform in Norwegian teacher education was introduced with intentions of meeting this challenge. The regulations also introduces an explicit focus on research-based teacher education, the purpose is 'to ensure that teacher education institutions offer integrated profession-oriented and research-based teacher education with high professional quality' and that the teacher education shall 'qualify for research-based practice' (Ministry of Education and Research, 2010).

The strength of action research approaches are their double objectives of contributing both to practice and to theoretical development. There is a strong need in Norwegian teacher education on developing knowledge about the heterogeneity of teaching literacy in multicultural schools. Action research offers a focus on specific contexts and situations. If the research reports are formed as thick descriptions, they can be important contributors to the needed knowledge base. Another advantage for teacher education is the focus on innovations and innovation processes. The description of such practices and the teachers' reflections on them might be an important way to stimulate the teacher candidates' development of their abilities to confront change. Hoffman and Pearson, writing about teacher education for the next millennium, stress the need for teacher educator researchers and teachers to 'become active participants in change'. They suggest that 'change, and rapid change, will characterize the next millennium' and quote Van Manen who in 1996 claimed that 'to be fit for teaching is to be able to handle change' (Hoffman & Pearson, 2000: 42).

Notes

(1) Erna Vibeke Gjernes was part of the research team the first year and collected data in two of the innovation projects.
(2) The innovation projects were carried out in two schools. Three other schools took part in the competence-raising and the network meetings.
(3) In 2003, the Norwegian Parliament gave the schools freedom to divide the pupils in groups of different sizes and different age levels. Normally, the children shall not be grouped according to competence, sex or ethnicity (The Education Act § 8-2, *www.lovdata.no*).
(4) The Norwegian language itself promotes a thinking of separate skills, as a Norwegian translation of 'literacy' only recently has been introduced in textbooks for teachers with the equivalent meaning as the English concept.
(5) The extract is transcribed from video recordings and translated to English by the authors. The names have been altered to preserve anonymity.

References

Barton, D. (2007) *Literacy: An Introduction to the Ecology of Written Language.* Malden, MA: Blackwell Pub.
Barton, D. and Hamilton, M. (1998) *Local Literacies: Reading and Writing in one Community.* London/New York: Routledge.
Blommaert, J. (2010) *The Sociolinguistics of Globalization.* New York: Cambridge University Press.
Boeije, H. (2010) *Analysis in Qualitative Research.* Los Angeles: Sage.
Danbolt, A.M.V. (2007) Fokus på innhold og samhandling. Om å gjøre endringer i andreklassingers språklæringsmiljø [Focus on content and interaction: On making changes in second graders' language environment]. *NORDAND* 2(2), 49–69.
Danbolt, A.M.V. and Kulbrandstad, L.I. (2008) *Klasseromskulturer for Språklæring. Didaktisk fornying i den flerkulturelle skolen* [Classroom Cultures for Language Learning: Didactic Development in the Multicultural School]. Valset: Oplandske Bokforlag.

Darling-Hammond, L. and Lieberman, A. (eds) (2012) *Teacher Education Around the World: Changing Policies and Practices.* London/New York: Routledge.

Elley, W.B. (1992) *How in the World do Students Read: IEA Study of Reading Literacy.* The Hague: The International Association for the Evaluation of Educational Achievement (IEA).

Heath, S.B. (1983) *Ways with Words: Language, Life, and Work in Communities and Classrooms.* Cambridge University Press.

Hoffman, J. and Pearson, P.D. (2000) Reading teacher education in the next millenium: What your grandmother's teacher didn't know that your granddaughter's teacher should. *Reading Research Quarterly* 35(1), 28–44.

Kulbrandstad, L.I. (2008) Å se språklæring som en aktiv prosess. En studie av systematisk ordforrådsundervisning i en flerkulturell elevgruppe [To see language learning as an active process: A study of systematic vocabulary teaching in a muliticultural group]. *NORDAND* 3(1), 55–79.

Kulbrandstad, L.I. (2010) Leseopplæring på ungdomstrinnet før og etter PISA 2000 [The teaching of reading in lower secondary school before and after PISA 2000]. In E. Elstad and K. Sivesind (eds) *PISA: Sannheten om skolen* [PISA: The Truth about the School?]. (pp. 176–198). Universitetsforlaget 2010.

Mejding, J. and Roe, A. (eds) (2006) *Northern Lights on PISA 2003: A Reflection from the Nordic Countries.* Copenhagen: Nordic Council of Ministers.

Ministry of Education and Research (2006) *Knowledge Promotion LK06: National Curriculum for Knowledge Promotion in Primary and Secondary Education and Training.* Oslo: Norwegian Directorate for Education and Training.

Ministry of Education and Research (2010). National Curriculum Regulations for Differentiated Primary and Lower Secondary Teacher Education Programmes for Years 1–7 and Years 5–10. Retrieved on the Internet 29 June 2010. http://www.regjeringen.no/en/dep/kd/dok/lover_regler/forskrifter/2010/Forskrift-om-rammeplan-for-grunnskolelarerutdanningene-for-17-trinn-og-510-trinn-.html?id=594357

Ministry of Education, New Zealand (1997) *Reading for Life: The Learner as Reader.* Wellington, NZ: Learning Media Limited.

Mohan, B., Leung, C. and Davison, C. (2001) *English as a Second Language in the Mainstream.* Harlow, England: Longman.

Municipality of Oslo (2004) *Handlingsprogram Lese-, skrive- og språkopplæring i Osloskolen 2004–2007 Språk for felles framtid* [Program for reading, writing and language development in the schools in Oslo 2004–2007: Language for a common future]. Oslo: The Municipality of Oslo.

OECD (2010) *What Makes a School Successful? Resources, Policies and Practices* (Vol. 4). Paris: OECD.

Postlethwaite, T.N. and Ross, K.N. (1992) *Effective Schools in Reading: Implication for Educational Planners – An Exploratory Study.* The Hague: The International Association for the Evaluation of Educational Achievement (IEA).

Street, B. (1984) *Literacy in Theory and Practice.* Cambridge: Cambridge University Press.

Street, B. (2000) Literacy events and literacy practices: Theory and Practice in the New Literacy Studies. In M. Martin-Jones and K. Jones (eds) *Multilingual Literacies.* Amsterdam: John Benjamins.

Street, B. (2008) New literacies, new times: Developments in literacy studies. In B. Street and N.H. Hornberger (eds) *Encyclopedia of Language and Education, Second Edition, Literacy* (Vol.2). New York: Springer.

Taguma, M., Shewbridge, C., Huttova, J. and Hoffman, N. (2010) *OECD Reviews of Migrant Education: Norway 2010*. OECD Publishing.

TNSGallup (2008) *Lærere og forskning. Resultater fra en undersøkelse blant lærere i grunn-og videregående skole* [Teachers and research: Results from a study among teachers in compulsory and upper secondary school]. TNSGallup: Oslo.

Tsui, A. (2003) *Understanding Expertise in Teaching: Case Studies of Second Language Teachers.* Cambridge: Cambridge University Press.

Union of Education Norway (2009) *Landsmøte 2009. Vedtak. sak 3.2. Morgendagens barnehage og skole.* [National Convention 2009. Descisions 3.2 Kindergardens and schools for the future], accessed 4 April 2010. http://www.utdanningsforbundet.no

Union of Education Norway (2011) *Lærerne mister troen på nasjonale prøver* [Teachers lose faith in national tests], accessed 10 June 2011. *http://www.utdanningsforbundet. no/Hovedmeny/Grunnskole/Fag-og-utdanning/Andre-artikler/Larerne-mister-troen-pa-nasjonale-prover/*

Zeichner, K. (2001) Educational action research. In P. Reason and H. Bradbury (eds) *Handbook of Action Research: Participative Inquiry and Practice* (pp. 273–283). London: Sage.

Zuber-Skerrit, O. (1996) Emancipatory action research for organisational change and management development. In O. Zuber-Skerrit (ed.) *New Directions in Action Research.* London: Famler Press.

10 Bilingual Teachers: Making a Difference?

Rita Hvistendahl

Bilingual Practices in Norwegian Schools

> *During my university studies I learned to reflect on my own, my pupils' and my peers' bilingual situation. I acquired a conceptual framework that helped me articulate the phenomena I encounter in my bilingual life. During my in-service training I met two recently arrived pupils who had great need of their teaching material and other messages being explained in their first language. My presence seemed to influence them very positively, and in a way improve their status in class.*
> (Author's translation from Norwegian)

The quote is by a teacher student who completed her teacher training programme for bilingual teacher students at the University of Oslo in 2006. It highlights how some of her students in lower secondary school, with whom she shares a first language, benefit from her bilingual competence in a class of recently arrived students from diverse linguistic backgrounds. She experiences being useful when she is able to support their literacy practices by switching between the dominant language Norwegian and Polish, which is the first language of some of her students. In this manner, she contributes to legitimizing these students' first language. Furthermore, during this 'translanguaging' (Creese & Blackledge, 2010; Dewilde, forthcoming; García, 2009), the teacher student becomes aware of the teaching potential of her bilingual competence. This chapter builds on this experience. It focuses on the ways bilingual student teachers understand and interpret biliteracy, how they struggle for a bilingual space in the Norwegian school and how they contribute to changing a predominantly monolingual literacy classroom practice to a multilingual one.

In Norwegian schools, non-European languages are held in low esteem, even when they are languages with which many students identify – 12% of the students in Norwegian schools and about one-third of the students in Oslo schools come from minority backgrounds (Statistics Norway, 2012). The traditional foreign languages such as French, Spanish and German have far more prestige, while English is a mandatory subject from the first year and can hardly be considered a foreign language any longer. Education in first languages other than Norwegian, as well as bilingual support, is therefore limited to recent arrivals and other students from language minorities with severely limited Norwegian skills. It is encouraged only for transitional purposes, that is until the student is proficient enough to learn the subject curriculum through Norwegian. Afterwards, any other education in the first language is mainly the responsibility of the parents. Consequently, the first languages of linguistic minorities have a quite limited role and function in the classroom. Bilingual teachers are first and foremost engaged to play a supportive role in curriculum learning and to assist in home/school links. This stands in contrast to classroom plurilingualism being officially celebrated as an important asset to enhancing competency in, and interest for, languages in general and the promotion of understanding and tolerance. However, as Jill Bourne (2001: 252) says, this does not necessarily challenge the accepted practice of teaching being primarily monolingual.

The present focus on the education of bilingual teachers in Norway is grounded in the idea that the teaching staff should be representative of the population at large, and that students from language minorities would benefit from having good role models (Norwegian Ministry of Education and Research, 2007). It is not justified in the need for multilingual competences or multilingual literacy in Norwegian schools. In line with an ecological perspective on language, this chapter argues that multilingualism will be a resource in teaching and learning if it is valued as such by the school and if the educational effort takes the diversity of languages and literacy practices that children and youth bring to school into account. With regard to its theoretical underpinning, this chapter is based on an ecological perspective on language and studies of the roles of bilingual teachers.

An Ecological Perspective on Language

An ecological perspective on multilingualism involves opening up space in the environment for as many languages as possible. Angela Creese and Adrian Blackledge (2010) use a language ecology perspective to describe the ideological, interrelational and interactional affordances of linguistically diverse classrooms. They define language ecology as diversity within specific sociopolitical settings in which the processes of language use create, and challenge particular hierarchies and hegemonies. Jim Cummins (2007) argues that the separateness of languages in the two-way bilingual immersion programmes of the United States builds on the assumptions that instruction should be carried out exclusively in the target language, and that translation between first and second language has no place in the teaching of language and literacy. An opposite example of language teaching and learning can be found in Chinese and Gujarati community language schools in the United Kingdom, where Creese and Blackledge (2010) describe a flexible bilingual approach to language teaching and learning. They argue for a departure from monolingual instructional approaches, and advocate teaching bilingual children by means of bilingual instructional strategies in which two or more languages are used alongside each other. Using the term translanguaging, they describe a flexible bilingual pedagogy including the use of translation across languages, the endorsement of simultaneous literacies and languages to keep the pedagogic task moving and the use of translanguaging for annotating texts. That latter is in order to provide greater access to the curriculum, and improved lesson outcomes. This is, according to Ofelia García (2009), a definition of translanguagings as multiple discursive practices in which bilinguals engage to make sense of their bilingual worlds. Translanguaging goes beyond code-switching, although it includes it as well as other kinds of bilingual use and bilingual contact. Indeed, García points out that the concept of translanguaging makes it obvious that there are no clear-cut boundaries between the languages of bilinguals. In this way, the term corresponds to a definition of multilingual competences as complementary language skills. However, carrying out instruction in two or more languages as well as translanguaging in class requires that multilingual competent teachers are given different roles in school. The different roles of bilingual teachers are identified in several studies which are presented in the next section.

The Roles of Bilingual Teachers

Bourne (2001: 262) identifies four different roles bilingual teachers have in British schools, and which correspond to findings in studies of bilingual teachers in Norwegian schools (Myklebust, 1993; Ryen et al., 2005). First, the studies all find that bilingual teachers act as role models for bilingual pupils, although this is considered a liability, not an asset if bilingual teachers have low status in school. Second, they are the class teachers' assistants with the main task of ensuring that the teaching proceeds without interruption due to language comprehension difficulties. Third, they assist class teachers in assessing bilingual pupils. Finally, bilingual teachers function as a link between home and school, a role in which they may experience conflicting expectations from the schools, children and communities. While performing these roles, bilingual teachers also take part in school literacy events and practices by acting as translators, mediators or facilitators. Joke Dewilde (2009) adds the role of collaborators to this picture, as the bilingual teachers often collaborate in one or other way, in particular with class teachers and subject matter teachers. Creese (2005) looks at the challenges bilingual teachers face in secondary schools and how they use their first languages to diversify mainstream classrooms. She observes that bilingual teachers are primarily focused on conveying subject content, and only secondarily on simplifying content so that students could learn English.

Alice Quicho and Francisco Rios (2000) highlight the societal functions of teachers from different ethnic minorities. In 'The Power of their Presence', they summarize the experiences of such teachers in teacher education and public schools. They argue that the presence of teachers from ethnic minorities in itself does not matter. What is important, however, is whether these teachers can help to change the structures of school and affect the people they work with. They also examine teacher education for ethnic minorities on the basis of a policy of equality and social justice in schools and in society at large. Although teachers from ethnic minorities may face many barriers on the road to recognition, many of these teachers are oriented towards reducing the systematic differences in school, working actively for reforms that can benefit students from ethnic minorities and developing a culturally more relevant educational content. While playing a vital role in the lives of pupils, influencing colleagues and initiating changes in school structures, they are at the same time contributing to a change in school practices with regard to students from linguistic minorities. The study presented in this chapter emerges from the teaching practices of teacher students taking part in a recruiting programme for bilingual teachers, and will be further elaborated in the next section.

Studying Bilingual Teacher Students' Practices

Among the limited number of bilingual teachers in Norwegian schools, only about a half are formally qualified teachers. Else Ryen *et al.* (2005) reports that out of six bilingual teachers in their study of the use of mother tongue education in six Norwegian primary schools, none formally qualified as teacher. Nevertheless, many had either a university or a university college degree from Norway or abroad, or many years of experience in language training. Due to the modest representation of bilingual teachers in schools, a recruiting programme at university and university college level with a scholarship for bilingual teachers was established in 2005. It was first and foremost based on a democratic ideal which emphasized that the teaching profession should reflect the population in general, and the teacher students in the present study were participants in this programme. This chapter emerges from a pilot project at the University of Oslo for the one-year teacher education course for bilingual minority language teachers, in which teaching of a first language other than Norwegian and supportive bilingual teaching were part of the study. Eight female students aged 25–45, most of them with an immigrant background, and with a bachelor or a master's degree from Norway or abroad in either languages, social or scientific studies, attended the university course. For these students, the course represented an opportunity to formally qualify as teachers in Norwegian school. It should be mentioned that some of these students were accepted on the basis of several years of practice as unqualified bilingual teachers. Some also had a foreign university education which was incompatible with Norwegian teacher education. The students were admitted on the basis of expertise in Persian, Somali, Turkish, Urdu, Italian, Polish, Bosnian, Serbian and Croatian languages as well as documented approval of their level of Norwegian skills, and they mastered a wide register of additional languages as well.

The teacher students wrote two theoretical and one practical assignment along with a reflective text for their portfolio assessment in the subjects of first language education and bilingual support. In their assignments, they discussed concepts of bilingualism and theories of bilingual teaching, and described literacy events and practices in which they took part during their teacher training. Their practical assignments and their reflective texts, each of 3–4 pages written in Norwegian, compose the data material of this chapter. In their assignments, the teacher students described and reflected on selected events and practices during their practical training, and in their reflective texts they commented on their own development during the 1-year university study. Consequently, the texts are qualitatively analysed as self-reports. As such they give insight into teacher practices towards students from linguistic minorities in Norwegian schools, but they are far from providing the full picture. All of the texts were written in Norwegian and translated into English by me. In line with Chapter 9 by Anne Marit Vesterås Danbolt and Lise Iversen Kulbrandstad, this chapter is based on analyses of teacher reflections, but in contrast to their analyses of reflections orally mediated in interviews with qualified teachers, my study analyses reflections in texts written by teacher students.

The analysis of the assignments is thematical and content based. The overall theme is bilingual teacher practices in school, and subthemes are the teacher students' ways of constructing a space for bilingual practices in school, and their handling of different roles as bilingual teachers. Although I was the manager of the practical pedagogical training of bilingual teachers at that time, and a teacher in the subject of bilingual support as well as in parts of the subject of first language education, I did not take active part in the in-service training in schools. Nor did I take part in the literacy events and practices which the teacher students describe and reflect upon in their assignments. Thus, the analysis is made with analytical distance to the practices being described. These practices are further elaborated in the next section.

The Teacher Students' Bilingual Practices

Despite most of the teacher students having grown up as bilinguals, they described the knowledge they acquired on bilingualism and bilingual teaching as entirely new to them. On the one hand, they evaluated the theoretical part of the practical pedagogical study as a necessary precondition for practical use, and as legitimizing the role of the bilingual teacher as well. 'After learning the concepts, I could categorize my school practice', one of the students wrote in her reflective text. Referring to first language education, another teacher student wrote that, at the end of the programme, she was able to give 'reasons why we must keep this subject in Norwegian schools and how important it is to work as a teacher of this subject'. On the other hand, some teacher students neither did evaluate their practical training as fully relevant because they were not given the opportunity to teach *about* their first language nor were they able to conduct teaching *in* their first language; even though the Education Act (Norwegian Ministry of Education, 1998) says that students with another first language than Norwegian or Sami have the right to an education in their first language as well as bilingual support on particular terms in a transitional period. Due to a strict interpretation of the Act by the school authorities of Oslo, only a few of the language minority students in primary and lower secondary schools receive such education.

Trying to make her practical training relevant to bilingual education, one of the Turkish speaking teacher students with Norwegian as her first language introduced bilingual support for the adult immigrant Turkish speaking women in her Norwegian language classes, reasoning that the first language was an important tool to empower the participants and teach them the significance of literacy skills. She focused particularly on explaining words and phrases in Turkish before she introduced the Norwegian equivalents, and she contrasted Turkish and Norwegian grammar to ease the language learning. Another teacher student, who taught Norwegian to newly arrived students in secondary school, initiated a school project in which the students from diverse language backgrounds during some of the lessons received bilingual support from teachers with relevant language competence. As teachers of Norwegian as an additional language, these two student teachers introduced bilingual teaching to their classes to support the language learning with the overall aim of empowering their students, either adolescents or adults.

Furthermore, during their practice period some of the bilingual teacher students, who had their practical training at the same secondary school, asked the school to change what the teacher students felt was discriminatory practice towards students from language minorities. Throughout their training period, all the teacher students expressed great empathy with their students and were concerned with making a difference in school, while considering themselves to be role models. In other words, they were trying to initiate transitional changes in school practices – either in primary or secondary school or in adult education – by giving bilingual support to the language minority students, with whom most of the teacher students shared languages as well as minority status. This stands in contrast to the teachers of Danish in adult second language teaching in Chapter 8 who were given authoritative power in the interpretation of Danish issues because of their superior command of the language as well as being Danish themselves. The teacher students in my study, however, had to obtain their authority as teachers from different national backgrounds with superior command of the languages which are not highly valued in school.

Constructing a Space for Bilingual Practices in School

During their in-service training period, most of the teacher students were mentored by bilingual teachers who had a university college education, but no formal teacher qualifications. This made those mentors particularly vulnerable when exposed to the students' criticism. For example, a student criticized bilingual teachers for giving inappropriate instruction to bilingual students in primary school, an incident which she explained as due to their lack of teacher qualifications. Furthermore, some of the teacher students who had their practical training at a lower secondary school, criticized the school for lack of professionalism due to the modest use of bilingual support, this because they were mentored by unqualified bilingual teachers. The teacher students argued that what was supposed to be bilingual support was in reality the teaching of bilingual students from diverse language backgrounds in Norwegian by a bilingual teacher in separate classes. 'Their interpretation of bilingual support is totally different from what we have learned from theory. The school has five teachers from multicultural backgrounds, but is unable to use them to improve the educational situation of the minority pupils', one of the teacher students claimed. This student conducted a survey among students from linguistic minorities in school about their use of native languages and their attitudes towards languages in school, and she presented the results at the school as well as in her practical assignment at the university. In her assignment she presented the bilingual literacies of the students and their attitudes to their first language in figures and diagrams, concluding that the responses first and foremost revealed the need both for greater bilingual support and for more positive attitudes towards bilingual education at the school where she practised. In this way, she acted as a kind of teacher researcher documenting students' practices and attitudes. In another practical assignment, she reported from in-service training at the same school:

> *[...] Moreover, I was told by my supervisor at school, who was also a bilingual teacher, that I had to use Norwegian only with my students because then they would feel secure. This pointed again to the school's negative attitude towards the mother tongue of the students (diversity is a problem), and that they must do precisely what others (majority language students) do, this means that homogeneity and similarity are favored. Nevertheless, I decided to try to give bilingual support to students who shared the same native language in class. I tried to use both the students' first language and Norwegian (shifting between the two languages). In the beginning of my practice the students were very reluctant to use their first language and reacted strongly against it. They felt ashamed to use their native language because it was a sign that the students were weak and unable to master the majority language in a proper manner. The students reflected exactly what the school's attitudes were towards their first language, and what the school expected of them. But after a few weeks, the situation changed. After I had worked with them for a few weeks, the students were able to understand that I knew my subject, and not only that, was able to convey the subject in both languages. [...] Then the students' attitudes towards their native language began to change. [...] I experienced something completely different from what I was told by my supervisor that I should do and not do. It is my impression that the school does not lack resources, but the right perspective, to consider minority students as a resource.*
(Author's translation from Norwegian)

The teaching in a separate homogeneous language group was organized by the teacher student herself on the approval of her supervisor at school. Previously, there had been no literacy practices involving both Norwegian and Urdu at school, although the supervisor was a bilingual teacher himself with Urdu as his first language. Due to the teacher student's commitment as well as to her language competences and teacher qualifications, biliteracy practices were encouraged in the subjects of math, social studies and natural sciences. In the excerpt from her practical assignment, she presents herself first and foremost as a subject teacher, not as a supportive bilingual teacher. This is in accordance with Creese's (2005) study of bilingual teachers in secondary classrooms using Turkish. These teachers were primarily focused on conveying the subject content and only secondarily on simplifying content so that the students could learn English. In this way, their practices differed from the practices of the teachers of English as an additional language.

When acting as a facilitator for bilingual subject teaching, the teacher student also created a space for the students' first language in school, which up to then had been non-existent. To do so the teacher student, on the one hand, negotiated with her supervisor, a bilingual teacher himself. On the other hand, she negotiated with the Urdu–Norwegian bilingual students to convince them of the value of bilingual teaching. In doing so, she used her language and teaching abilities as her best cards. In this way, both the students' first language and the teacher student's bilingual teaching conquered space and time at school – that is in the classroom as well as in lessons. That is to say, the multilingual practices expanded their domain in the period of the teacher student's practical training in this secondary school. However, although she claimed that her and the other teacher students' questions and discussions with the supervisors and the deputy head about bilingual teaching had affected the school, it is unknown to what extent these practices were continued after the teacher students' period of practice was finished.

Literacies are partially legitimated through the statuses and roles of people engaged in them, Tusting *et al.* (2000) argue. When the teacher students managed to change the school's standards for a group of bilingual students for a period, this most likely had to do with their status as university students in teacher education as well as their commitment to bilingual teaching. In this sense, the teacher students' presence at school proved powerful. Next we will turn to another aspect of the teacher students' bilingual practices, that is their role as literacy mediators.

Literacy mediators

The New Literacy Studies observed that a text and the literacy-related behaviour associated with it are always embedded in a social practice (Barton & Hamilton, 2000). The term practice is used in two ways. First, the term refers to observable details of literacy events and to those aspects of literacy which go beyond the text itself. Second, the term refers to culturally recognizable patterns of behaviour which include textual practices (Tusting *et al.*, 2000: 213). One of the teacher students in the group had practised as a bilingual teacher in a primary school that systematically facilitated bilingual support to bilingual pupils, either in separate or in inclusive classrooms. In her practical assignment, she tells about several literacy events during her teaching in which cultural patterns are recognizable and play an important part, and in which literacy is a key element.

There were two pupils who had never been to the movies before. They were very weak, both academically and linguistically. They held my hand to feel safe, especially because they did not speak Norwegian well. They came from a poor sociocultural family with little cultural capital. When they came into the movie theatre, they acted like they were in a completely different and unknown world. They were very excited. I sat in between them with one pupil on each side. 'I have never seen such a great TV,' said a boy as he jumped for joy. Another pupil asked curiously: 'How can the sound come from all directions, Ayesha, and do you have to pay for watching the TV?' When the lights were turned off, they were so frightened that they held my hands all the time! I was very surprised by this behaviour.
(Author's translation from Norwegian)

This story told by the teacher student clearly illustrates how fundamentally literacy, in this case multimodal literacy, is embedded in social practice. Going to the movies is usually categorized as a vernacular literacy practice. Nevertheless, watching movies belongs to the dominant literacy practice of school as well, and learning from movies, interpreting movies and even producing movies are part of the curriculum. However, whether watching movies belongs to the vernacular or dominant literacies is determined by the context in which the activity takes place, and by the persons participating in the activity. This means that going to the movies together with the teacher during school hours turned this into a literacy event in which dominant literacy was practised. The teacher student's surprise comes from the experience that two of her 10-year-old pupils from the same language background as hers neither had ever been to a cinema in their leisure time together with their parents nor had ever visited a movie theatre together with a teacher during their five years at school. This makes the teacher student's notion of watching movies somewhat ambiguous. In one sense, it is perceived as a dominant literacy, in another sense as a vernacular. This illustrates the fluid transition between practices belonging to the two domains, home and school, in which the teacher student's role then turned into that of a mediator. In her practical assignment, she reflects upon another event as 'strange'. This event took place in an inclusive classroom during a religious education lesson:

Another strange experience I had during my period of practice was during a religious education lesson. We were to go through the first chapter in the textbook, 'We in the world' for the 5th grade. The chapter was about Christianity and its history. We practised the text well because they were to take a test in this subject the next day. One student was very skeptical to this chapter. When she got the test the next day, she didn't write a single word. The class teacher asked her why she didn't write anything, but she was completely quiet. When I asked, she answered, 'We are Muslims, and how can we learn about Christianity and that Jesus was the son of God? Then I am not a Muslim anymore!' I talked to her and told her that what the book says is about Christianity, and if you read it, you do not become a Christian. I explained that I myself read about Christianity at school and about other world religions, but that does not mean I am not a Muslim anymore. She understood my point at last, and thought that if I as an adult Muslim bilingual teacher could do this, then it was probably safe for her, too. Such misunderstandings and poor knowledge among the parents often lead to such attitudes of the children. I talked to the parents and made them understand that this subject is not part of missionary effort at the school. It only provides knowledge. (Author's translation from Norwegian)

It should be mentioned that the curriculum for religious education at that time was criticized by several groups, religious as well as non-religious, and was later changed. In this case, however, the teacher student is obviously not affected by this discussion, but conveys the subject of religious education according to her mandate. While the class teacher fails in convincing the children to accept the curriculum, the bilingual teacher student succeeds, and even convinces the parents, due to her credibility as a Muslim herself and to her ability to communicate with the parents in their first language, Urdu. In this way, she bridges the gap between home and school and avoids a conflict of values from emerging. This is an example of what Bourne (2001) describes as the bilingual teacher's position in similar situations as being in a buffer zone between conflicting expectations. This does not, however, correspond to the teacher student's story. On the contrary, she considers herself as a professional representative of Norwegian schools. Nevertheless, she acts as a link between the student, home and school, and in this role she mediates the meaning of literacy practices as well. When the student interprets reading about other religions as a religious practice itself, the teacher student explains to her that reading about religions is something different from reading and practising religious texts. By using herself as an example, the teacher student tries to make the 10-year-old student understand and accept this distinction.

In addition to the teacher students' constructing a space for bilingual practices in school as well as acting as literacy mediators, the third aspect of their practices was their role as literacy facilitators, which will be elaborated in the next section.

Useful facilitators

One of the teacher students was in charge of a group of four students with family background from Pakistan, three boys and one girl, during a period of project work in secondary school. In her practical assignment, she tells about an episode taking place during this work:

The students had to work with a particular disaster. My job was to support them in their mother tongue during the project work. I experienced that the explanations, support and discussions in the first language improved the students' understanding. They were given different tasks to choose from. The students chose to make a presentation of the tsunami in South Asia in Christmas 2005. First, they chose a project manager, a boy. Gradually, they planned the project and divided the responsibilities between them. Everyone had to collect information from the internet, two boys had to write a storyline, a boy had to collect and choose important items from the information collected and the girl had to make a power-point presentation. They collected lots of information on the tsunami. From the beginning to the end of the project, I noticed a significant change in the girl's behaviour. She was very involved in the project, and she was the one who did most of the project work and commanded her group. (Author's translation of Norwegian)

The teacher student explains the improvement of the students' due to the use of bilingual support only. This claim, however, is not supported by detailed description of the bilingual teaching she conducted. Nor does the teacher student reflect on the gender differences of the group, or recognize her function as a possible female role model for the girl. She is focused on whether bilingual teaching was taking place or not. It is possible that she was immersed in the situation and had not obtained the necessary distance to consider the significance of the context of the literacy events in which she played an important part. Furthermore, it is likely that the presence of the bilingual female teacher student empowered the young girl, who was described as somewhat shy, to take command of a group with a majority of boys.

In contrast, another teacher student at the same secondary school describes in detail her supportive bilingual one-to-one-teaching of a Somali-speaking 14-year-old boy who had attended Norwegian school for one and a half years in a class for newcomers, and who previously had only had three years of schooling in Somalia:

The week before I started teaching him, Ali took a math test in which he made many mistakes. The mistakes were misunderstandings because he was not able to distinguish between how mathematical signs, particularly those for multiplication and division, are written in Norway and Somalia. My first impression then was that Ali had exactly the problems which the book Math's in a Language We Understand is about. I reviewed almost the complete test on the blackboard and explained to him the differences between the numeric symbols of counting in Somalia and in Norway. The language of teaching was Somali, but I had to teach him the mathematical notions in Norwegian as well. After the explanation and the teaching, he used mental arithmetic when he tried to solve the other tasks of the test. He wrote everything in his book.

This is the way I have taught during the rest of my period of training. In the natural sciences the lessons were almost alike, but this time we used more writing (both words and notions) in the mother tongue, and he had to try to read his book. One day, I wrote all the difficult words and notions in Somali and Norwegian on beforehand. (Author's translation from Norwegian)

This teacher student accounts carefully for her teaching and the bilingual literacy practices involved. First and foremost, she teaches the subjects in Somali, orally as well as in reading and writing. While contrasting the different systems of mathematical notions, she teaches in both Somali and Norwegian. The teacher student is scaffolding the student's learning by preparing writing books and writing translations of Somali and Norwegian words and subject expressions. On the one hand, she makes reading and writing in school more in tune with the student's everyday literacy experiences outside school. On the other hand, she focuses on subject teaching in a language the student understands to improve his subject achievements.

This teacher student's report expresses a wish to be of help for the students from linguistic minorities, a wish which is shared by all the other bilingual teacher students as well, whether related to changing monolingual practices in schools, impacting colleagues, facilitating bilingual support and bilingual subject teaching or act as literacy mediators and role models to the students. In this manner, they are legitimizing their presence as bilingual teachers in schools and arguing that their presence makes a difference. To what extent their biliteracy practices remained of secondary status in the school practices compared to the mainstream teaching will be further discussed in the last section.

Discussion

Literacy studies approach literacies as multiple, emergent and situated in particular social contexts (Ivanič *et al.*, 2009: 20). In this context, the reports from the bilingual teacher students' give a multi-faceted picture of reading and writing, for different purposes and according to different cultural values and practices. The focus is not so much on what is read and written, but in which language, by whom, why and under what conditions. Ivanič et al. (2009: 21) argue that literacy practices differ from one context to another, and purposes, values, knowledge, expectations and relations of power are embedded in them. The teacher students' practical assignments shed light upon different aspects of the bilingual space they created in school, and how this space varies between schools.

Creese (2005) argues that bilingual teachers choose to endorse dominant educational discourses and, in doing so, include bilingual children in the same activities as other non-bilingual children. The teacher student who brought her 10-year-old students to cinema for the first time and explained the importance of religious education in school to Muslim parents was acting as a literacy mediator, thereby bridging the gap between home and school with the overall aim of including her students in mainstream activities in school by the use of biliteracy practices. At her school both language homogeneous groups and teacher collaboration in inclusive classrooms were established practices. Consequently, her challenges of including the bilingual children were related to making them familiar with mainstream literacy and cultural practices by explaining the significance of these practices to her students and their parents.

In contrast, teacher students practicing in lower secondary schools either had to use their pedagogical creativity or to negotiate with their supervisors as well as their students to create a bilingual space in school. Although immigrant students start schooling in Norway at all levels, secondary schools are less familiar with bilingual educational practices. Employing bilingual teachers in schools does not guarantee for such practices unless they are encouraged by the municipalities, accepted as part of the schools' educational policy and supported by the school leadership. One of the teacher students succeeded in implementing a bilingual project involving other teachers in her classroom with recently arrived students, but this was time limited and depended on her enthusiasm. The three teacher students practising at the same lower secondary school struggled hard to obtain approval for bilingual subject teaching individually or in homogeneous language groups. This education took place outside the ordinary classrooms, but within school. Mostly, it remained secondary in the school practices compared to the mainstream teaching. The teacher students claimed that their initiatives contributed to changing the school's attitudes towards bilingual teaching and the use of the students' first languages in teaching and learning. However, it is not mentioned whether the teacher students' practices caused permanent changes in the teaching of bilingual students in this school. In contrast, the teacher student in adult language education transformed her teaching practices from monolingual to bilingual, in doing so drawing upon her bilingual teacher qualifications, and without having to negotiate her teaching. Either they had to convince supervisors, students or parents of the importance of their bilingual teaching or they acted as in-betweens negotiating their own practices using their multilingual competences as their primary assets. Furthermore, the teacher students were first and foremost concerned about the roles in which they were acting towards the students and their parents. The efforts they made for bilingual teaching in school were basically connected to their language competences and teacher qualifications. This argues for the importance of bilingual teacher education.

Creese (2005) argues that there is a need for a renewed debate on the understanding of bilingual teachers and community languages for teaching and learning in secondary classrooms. There is a great potential to develop bilingual pedagogies within the mainstream for subject knowledge teaching, and much greater thought is required on our understanding of linguistic diversity, she claims. The experiences of creating space for bilingual literacies in Oslo schools mediated through the teacher students' assignments support this argumentation.

References

Barton, D. and Hamilton, M. (2000) Literacy practices. In D. Hamilton, M. Hamilton and R. Ivanič (eds) *Situated Literacies: Reading and Writing in Context* (pp. 7–15). London/New York: Routledge.
Bourne, J. (2001) Doing what comes naturally: How the discourses and routines of teacher's practice constrain opportunities for bilingual support in UK primary schools. *Language and Education* 15 (4), 250–267.
Creese, A. (2005) *Teacher Collaboration and Talk in Multilingual Classrooms*. Clevedon: Multilingual Matters.
Creese, A. and Blackledge, A. (2010) Translanguaging in the bilingual classroom: A pedagogy for learning and teaching? *The Modern Language Journal* 94 (1), 103–115.
Cummins, J. (2007) Rethinking monolingual instructional strategies in multilingual classrooms. *Canadian Journal of Applied Linguistics (CJAL)/Revue Canadienne de Linguistique Appliquée (RCLA)* 10 (2), 221–240.
Dewilde, J. (2009) Teacher collaboration: A study of topics in planning sessions between a science and a bilingual teacher. In B-K. Ringen and O.K. Kjørven (eds), A. Gagné (hon. ed.) *Teacher Diversity in Diverse Schools: Challenges and Opportunities for Teacher Education* (pp. 267–283). Vallset: Oplandske Bokforlag.
Dewilde, J. (forthcoming) Ambulating Teachers – A case study of bilingual teachers and teacher collaboration. PhD-thesis. Faculty of Education. Oslo: University of Oslo.
García, O. (2009) *Bilingual Education in the 21st Century: A Global Perspective*. Oxford: Blackwell.
Ivanič, R., Edwards, R., Barton, D., Martin-Jones, M., Fowler, Z., Hughes, B., Mannion, G., Miller, K., Satchwell, C. and Smith, J. (2009) *Improving Learning in College: Rethinking Literacies Across the Curriculum*. London/New York: Routledge.

Myklebust, R. (1993) En analyse av den tokulturelle klassemodellen i Oslo: med vekt på den tospråklige undervisningen I matematikk og o-fag [An analysis of the bicultural class model in Oslo: with emphasis on bilingual education in mathematics and social and natural sciences]. *NOA – Norsk som andrespråk nr. 17.* Oslo: Institutt for lingvistiske fag, Universitetet i Oslo.

Norwegian Ministry of Education and Research (2007) *Equal Education in Practice! Strategy for Better Teaching and Greater Participation of Linguistic Minorities in Kindergartens, Schools and Education 2007–2009.* Revised edition February 2007.

Norwegian Ministry of Education (1998) Education Act.

Quicho, A. and Rios, F. (2000) The power of their presence: Minority group teachers and schooling. *Review of Educational Research Winter 2000* 70(4), 485–528.

Ryen, E., Wold, A.H. and de Wal Pastoor, L. (2005) "Det er egen tolkning, ikke direkte regler." Kasusstudier av minoritetsspråklige elevers morsmålsopplæring og bruk av morsmål ved tre grunnskoler ["It's my own interpretation, not spesific rules." Case studies of minority language students' mother tongue education and use of mother tongues at three primary schools]. *NOA – Norsk som andrespråk* 21(1–2), 39–66.

Statistics Norway (2012) Accessed 9 May 2012 and available online at http://www.ssb.no/emner/02/01/10/innvbef/.

Tusting, K., Ivanič, R. and Wilson, A. (2000) New literacy studies at the interchange. In D. Barton, M. Hamilton and R. Ivanič (eds) *Situated Literacies: Reading and Writing in Context* (pp. 210–218). London/New York: Routledge.

Afterword: On the Move[1] – Transitions in Literacy Research

David Barton

We are all on the move: everything is increasingly on the move and this has important implications for literacy learning and literacy research. There are different ways of visualizing this change. We can think of movement as being from one place to another, as a temporary interference of the stability of fixed places, going from home to school, going from one country to another or switching from one language to another. This stable paradigm has been the way of visualizing language and literacy practices over recent decades, as with all other social phenomena. However, there is a growing alternative: we can turn all this upside down and see the movement, the mobilities, as the default, where change is the normal state of being, rather than the exception. Different things then become foregrounded and highlighted and a new view of literacy develops.

Literacy Practices in Transition: Perspectives from the Nordic Countries explores situated examples of this change in perspective, which is all brought together in the book by the concept of *transition*. This works very well and enables quite different topics to be brought together and juxtaposed. Starting with education, transition has been an important way of discussing children moving first into schools, then from junior to secondary schools and finally on to work or colleges. This can be broken down into year groups where each year of 'moving up' involves a transition, so for much of the time students are in transition. In these transitions, students tend to move from the safe and familiar to somewhere which is unfamiliar and which is seen as more complex and demanding. Some students are hesitant about such a move, others are waiting for it and looking forward to change. As this book emphasizes, literacy is central to these transitions. The new situations students are moving into often make new literacy demands and they are participating in unfamiliar literacy practices. If there is preparation, literacies can aid such transitions, or they can impede and disrupt change. So, for example in England the transition from primary to secondary school has often been the place where pupils, especially boys, falter in their reading and writing as they move from often a smaller, familiar, more stable environment with just one teacher, to a more demanding unfamiliar place. What worked and was acceptable in one environment is now not adequate and needs to be superseded.

These transitions continue throughout education, where what was adequate is no longer sufficient. So even at a postgraduate master's level (as in Chapter 7), students have to learn new ways of reading and writing. What was acceptable for undergraduate assignments is now called into question and is not good enough for graduate level work. Then this continues for doctoral students, where their work can be criticized as being at master's level. Within schools and universities, different subjects make different literacy demands (Chapters 7 and 6) and students can have to juggle with these on a daily basis as they move from class to class.

People constantly move between different domains of life and the contrasts between home and school, between in and out of the classroom has always been a key concern of literacy studies research going back, of course, to Heath's early work (1983) and returned to more recently (Heath, 2012). In going in and out of education, children are also often going in and out of languages (Chapter 4). Sometimes, the languages – and cultures – are left at the school gates. At other times, languages are turned into valuable educational resources (Chapters 3, 5, 9 and 10). Pupils and teachers' supermobility is realized as super-diversity. The movements of migration of people across countries (Chapters 1 and 2) is another transition which impacts on classrooms, where it can be treated either as a threat or as a valuable resource.

The day-to-day practices of classrooms are framed more broadly by policies and the transition of policy to practice, and of practice to policy, is of increasing interest (Chapters 3 and 8). This broader framework is important as people explore the global context of local, situated activities. This comes from a realization that seemingly local changes are part of global patterning. Global changes in technologies affect the details of local practices bringing shifts in the relations between modalities which are touched upon in several chapters (including chapters 3 and 6).

There are many actors in this book. There are students of all ages up to adulthood in many different settings, alongside teachers in different roles. Different identities are drawn attention to and the complexity of concepts like migrant are apparent when migrant doctors (Chapter 1) are discussed next to unaccompanied refugee children (Chapter 2), a juxtaposition which also moves across the domains of workplace and education. With a common focus on literacy practices such juxtapositions are revealing and we can see how people's agency is central and how learning is located in their acting within the framing of their past histories, their current practices and their imagined futures (as explored in Barton *et al.*, 2007). People's lives today are lived in transition.

Concentrating on the transitions rather than on the fixity draws attention to the boundaries between activities and to what goes on at the margins. These edges are not neat, narrow impermeable lines, and should probably not even be thought of as edges. Rather, they are spaces which people inhabit, spaces where change takes place. Practices, including literacy practices, do not move or transfer between domains in any straightforward way. Rather, people draw on different aspects of literacy practices in a complex way as they move across contexts (as in Ivanič *et al.*, 2009). Re-contextualization is no straightforward matter.

Literacy Practices in Transition demonstrates the wide range of areas within and beyond education where literacy studies provide an insightful framing. Detailed work in specific areas, such as academic writing, second language literacy and classroom literacy has been carried out. While the studies in this book are specific situated examples from the Nordic countries, they are also contributions to global discussions. What holds these different studies together is the approach of seeing language and literacy as a social practice. What is also striking in the book is how this literacy studies approach fits so easily and valuably alongside other 'middle-level' sociocultural areas of work which are looking in detail at people's changing language practices. They are all looking in slightly different ways with different emphases and foci, but the different approaches work together well. Examples in the book include how literacy studies is drawn upon alongside narrative analysis, discourse analysis and policy analysis. Particular studies place it next to multimodality, multilingualism research and situated learning. Concepts of performance and theories of identity also fit in well. The field of literacy studies is in transition as people here and elsewhere are working across framings. A broad coherent sociocultural theory of language is being articulated. Finally, this is appropriate for a time of great fluidity and uncertainty and, as the reference to transition cities in the Preface makes it clear, this is a positive message that literacy research and practice can impact on contemporary social action.

Notes

(1) *On The Move* was an innovative BBC television series in the 1970s, drawing attention to issues of adult literacy in Britain. It involved a van driver who could not read addresses for deliveries and who was persuaded to go to adult literacy classes. Several literacy campaigns have come and gone since then.

References

Barton, D., Ivanič, R., Appleby, Y., Hodge R. and Tusting K. (2007) *Literacy, Lives and Learning*. London: Routledge.

Heath, S.B. (1983) *Ways with Words: Language, Life and Work in Communities and Classrooms*. Cambridge: Cambridge University Press.

Heath, S.B. (2012) *Words at Work and Play: Three Decades in Family and Community Life*. Cambridge: Cambridge University Press.

Ivanič, R., Edwards, R., Barton, D., Martin-Jones, M., Fowler, Z., Hughes, B., Mannion, G., Miller, K., Satchwell, C. and Smith, J. (2009) *Improving Learning in College: Rethinking Literacies Across the Curriculum*. London: Routledge.

For Product Safety Concerns and Information please contact our EU Authorised Representative:

Easy Access System Europe

Mustamäe tee 50

10621 Tallinn

Estonia

gpsr.requests@easproject.com

www.ingramcontent.com/pod-product-compliance
Lightning Source LLC
Chambersburg PA
CBHW070558300426
44113CB00010B/1308